OXFORD STUDIES IN DEMOCRATIZATION

Series editor: Laurence Whitehead

....

CITIZENSHIP RIGHTS AND
SOCIAL MOVEMENTS

OXFORD STUDIES IN DEMOCRATIZATION

Series editor: Laurence Whitehead

. . . .

Oxford Studies in Democratization is a series for scholars
and students of comparative politics and related disciplines.
Volumes will concentrate on the comparative study of the
democratization processes that accompanied the decline and
termination of the cold war. The geographical focus of the
series will primarily be Latin America, the Caribbean,
Southern and Eastern Europe, and relevant
experiences in Africa and Asia.

OTHER BOOKS IN THE SERIES

The New Politics of Inequality in Latin America:
Rethinking Participation and Representation
Douglas A. Chalmers, Carlos M. Vilas,
Katherine Roberts Hite,
Scott B. Martin, Kerianne Piester,
and Monique Segarra

Human Rights and Democratization in Latin America:
Uruguay and Chile
Alexandra Barahona de Brito

Regimes, Politics, and Markets:
Democratization and Economic Change in Southern and
Eastern Europe
José María Maravall

Democracy Between Consolidation and
Crisis in Southern Europe
Leonardo Morlino

The Bases of Party Competition in Eastern Europe:
Social and Ideological Cleavages in Post Communist States
Geoffrey Evans and Stephen Whitefield

The International Dimensions of Democratization:
Europe and the Americas
Laurence Whitehead

Citizenship Rights and Social Movements

A Comparative and Statistical Analysis

....

JOE FOWERAKER

and

TODD LANDMAN

OXFORD UNIVERSITY PRESS
1997

Oxford University Press, Great Clarendon Street, Oxford OX2 6DP
Oxford New York
Athens Auckland Bangkok Bogota Bombay
Buenos Aires Calcutta Cape Town Dar es Salaam
Delhi Florence Hong Kong Istanbul Karachi
Kuala Lumpur Madras Madrid Melbourne
Mexico City Nairobi Paris Singapore
Taipei Tokyo Toronto
and associated companies in
Berlin Ibadan

Oxford is a trade mark of Oxford University Press

Published in the United States
by Oxford University Press Inc., New York

British Library Cataloguing in Publication Data
Data available

Library of Congress Cataloging in Publication Data
Foweraker, Joe.
Citizenship rights and social movements : a comparative and
statistical analysis / Joe Foweraker and Todd Landman.
(Oxford studies in democratization)
Includes bibliographical references and index.
1. Civil rights—Case studies. 2. Human rights—Case studies.
3. Democracy—Case studies. 4. Social movements—Case studies.
I. Landman, Todd. II. Title. III. Series.
JC571.F637 1997 322.4'4'098—dc21 96–52314

ISBN 0–19–829225–2

1 3 5 7 9 10 8 6 4 2

Typeset by Graphicraft Typesetters Ltd, Hong Kong
Printed in Great Britain
on acid-free paper by
Biddles Ltd, Guildford and King's Lynn

....
Acknowledgements
....

I WISH to thank the friends and colleagues who have helped to make this book. Rob Stones and Bryan Turner guided and encouraged my early reading and thinking about citizenship. Sid Tarrow sharpened my sense of social movements through his own research and writing, and offered advice on the research itself. Ivor Crewe reviewed and improved the first draft of the research proposal. David Sanders, Eric Tanenbaum, and Hugh Ward all participated in shaping the research design and the statistical analysis.

I also wish to acknowledge the support of the University of Essex and of the Economic and Social Research Council (ESRC). The prototype of the University's Research Promotion Fund bought out part of my teaching in 1991–2 to release time for studying citizenship; and a subsequent year of study leave in 1994–5 was spent writing the first draft of the book. A research award from the ESRC paid for a year of full-time research in 1993–4 for both myself and a research officer.

A particular word of thanks is due to my research officer and co-author, Todd Landman. Since joining the project in October 1993, Todd has worked with unstinting energy and enthusiasm. Consequently, we were able to carry the research forward together, and collaborate closely in presenting the results. For me, it has been challenging and enjoyable work.

Finally, I wish to add a special 'thank you' to Clare Dekker, who has accompanied every step of this intellectual journey, and who never fails to bring good cheer.

Joe Foweraker

Great Bentley, July 1996

I WOULD like to thank colleagues, friends, and family, who in their own way, all contributed to this book. In the Department of Government at the University of Essex, Hugh Ward, David Sanders, David McKay, Eric Tanenbaum, Neil Robinson, and Charlie Malcolm-Brown offered methodological advice, substantive critique, and a stimulating intellectual environment in which to work. I would also like to thank the University of Essex for its financial support and academic opportunities over the last three years.

Thanks to Clare Dekker, Dave Smith, Leigh Amos, Malcolm Latchman, and Rachel Webster, whose selfless hospitality, support, and good humour accompanied the writing process. In the United States, I send a long-distance thanks to my eldest brother and sister-in-law, Drew and Kate Landman, whose unflagging good will and generosity are deeply appreciated. I extend my gratitude to Hank Landman for his eternal scepticism and biting wit. Warm thanks to Vincent McGuire, Susan Clarke, Gary Gaile, Matt and Margret Greene, Brad and Lee Anne Rosenstein, and Cynthia and Jack Zubritsky. In the United Kingdom, I thank Patricia and Antony Warren, and Catherine and Keith Law, who have shown tremendous warmth, friendship, and hospitality.

I would like to thank my mentor and co-author, Joe Foweraker, without whom none of this would have been possible. From the early conversations in Boulder to the last revisions at Essex, Joe has provided guidance and vision, and has afforded me sufficient intellectual latitude to bring this book to fruition. The last three years have been a time of unparalleled learning and growth.

I send special thanks to Laura Landman whose personal and professional triumphs, intellectual curiosity, good grace, and unwavering support of my endeavours is a constant source of strength. To Miriam, my companion and fiancé, thanks will never express the depth of my happiness in being with you nor the extent of my gratitude for your support. Finally, I wish to dedicate my portion of the book to my father Dirk Landman, whose honesty, integrity, and clear analytical thinking will never be forgotten.

Todd Landman

Dedham, July 1996

....
Contents
....

List of Figures

List of Tables

Abbreviations

AI-5	Fifth Institutional Act (Brazil)
BLUE	Best Linear Unbiased Estimates
CNI	National Intelligence Centre (Chile)
CNPA	National 'Plan de Ayala' Coordinating Committee (Mexico)
CNS	National Sindical Coordinating Committee (Chile)
CONAMUP	National Coordinating Committee of the Urban Popular Movement (Mexico)
CTM	Confederation of Mexican Workers
CUD	Coordinating Committee for Earthquake Victims (Mexico)
DINA	National Intelligence Directorate (Chile)
ETA	*Euzkadi Ta Askatasuna*, Basque Nationalist Organization (Spain)
FDN	National Democratic Front (Mexico)
FSTSE	Federation of Public Service Workers' Unions (Mexico)
ICCPR	International Covenant on Civil and Political Rights
ICESCR	International Covenant on Economic, Social, and Cultural Rights
ILO	International Labour Organization
LOPPE	Law on Political Organizations and Electoral Processes (Mexico)
MDB	Brazilian Democratic Movement
MDP	Popular Democratic Movement (Chile)
MDSD	Most Different Systems Design
MITS	Multiple Interrupted Time-Series
MSSD	Most Similar Systems Design
MUPs	Urban Popular Movements (Mexico)
OEPs	Popular Economic Organizations (Chile)
OLS	Ordinary Least Squares
PCM	Mexican Communist Party
PDM	Mexican Democratic Party
PRD	Party of the Democratic Revolution (Mexico)

PRI	Institutional Revolutionary Party (Mexico)
PST	Socialist Workers Party (Mexico)
QCA	Qualitative Comparative Analysis
SNI	National Information Service (Brazil)
SUTERM	Sole Union of Electrical Workers of the Mexican Republic
2SLS	Two-Staged Least Squares
UNDP	United Nations Development Programme

Variables Used in the Statistical Analysis

Arat	Arat's score of democraticness
BANKSLII	Banks legal-institutional index
CL	civil liberties
CRI	combined rights index
DEFEXP	low defence expenditure
DEMRAT	ratio of political and civil demands to material and economic demands
DUFFMC	Duff and McCamant repression index
ECON	economic crisis
ENER	peak energy consumption
FJII	Fitzgibbon-Johnson image index
GAP	residuals from regressing rights-in-practice (CRI) on rights-in-principle (IPI)
Humana	Humana's human rights index
HFI	human freedom index
INFL	high inflation
IPI	institutional procedural index
PL	political liberties
POLD	political demands
SMA	social movement activity
SR	strike rate
SV	strike volume

Introduction

Citizenship Rights and Social Movements

Objectives and Scope

The principal focus of this enquiry is the relationship between the individual rights of citizenship and social movement activity. Its main aim is to discover the mutual influence of citizenship rights and social movements over and through time. Its specific objective is to measure this influence and compare it across cultures. Its method requires the construction of a parsimonious model that can sustain systematic research and support substantive interpretation. Its primary achievement is the construction of a consistently comparative argument that is modulated by the results of the statistical analysis.

Beyond the specific aims of the enquiry, it addresses two large social scientific literatures which do not usually 'talk to each other'. There is a large literature on social movements, which tends to divide between high-flown theorizing and specific case studies. There is also a large literature on individual rights, which tends to be confined either to political philosophy or to specialized but non-theoretical studies of human rights. But there are relatively few comparative studies of either social movements or rights, and, to the best of our knowledge, no such study of the relationship between them over time. A systematic and comparative study of this relationship may therefore add a new dimension to both literatures.

The enquiry reaches beyond the confines of welfare capitalism, or the liberal democratic polities associated with developed capitalist countries, to political cultures where the integrity and freedom of the individual is still a primary political concern, and where the individual rights of citizenship are far from being secure. *It is our contention that the relationship between social movements and individual rights can best be explored in the political context of these modern authoritarian regimes.* Certainly the choice of such regimes influences the construction of citizenship rights as an object of comparative research. Broadly speaking, citizenship is disaggregated into three discrete research objects which are, first, the dissemination of the normative attributes of citizenship into the constitutions of different regimes; second, the degree to which the practices and policies of these regimes approximate or conform to these prescriptions; and, third, the processes of political organization, mobilization, and struggle which aim to make the practices so conform, or promote this as a contingent result through pressing their demands in terms of *rights*. In sum, citizenship is a process which may be approached through the three perspectives of (constitutional) *forms*, (political) *practices*, and (social movement) *struggles*.

Methods and Design

Since the primary research objective is to achieve measurable comparisons of both rights provisions and social movement activity over time, the enquiry sets out to construct time-series data sets that can support indices of the three main objects of citizenship research (forms, practices, and struggles) during periods of authoritarian rule and through moments of democratic transition. In short, the primary data was used to construct three main indices, namely, a legal-institutional index that describes *rights-in-principle*, or the presence of constitutionally or legally prescribed rights; a *rights-in-practice* index, that describes the degrees to which the real rights enjoyed by different populations at different times fall short of or exceed these formal rights;[1] and a social movement measure (or measures) that shows the incidence and extent of social movement activity over time. In this way the indices facilitate and condense the description of the evolution and fluctuation of rights provision and social movement activity in each case. Subsequently, the indices enter the statistical description and analysis of the relationship between rights and movements; while the statistical analysis itself promotes more qualitative comparisons which remain sensitive to the political and cultural specificities of the different cases.

The tasks of designing the research and making the argument met with recurrent methodological challenges. These challenges arose at each stage of the enquiry, including those of the collection, synthesis, and analysis of the data. The methods employed in the construction of the databases and in the measurement of the

---

[1] A further index designed to monitor the variable 'gap' between the rhetoric and the reality of citizenship rights was calculated as the residuals that result from regressing the rights-in-practice index onto the rights-in-principle index, using ordinary least squares (OLS).

main variables are described in Chapter 3, while the statistical techniques, and their subsequent applications and modifications, are explained in Chapters 6 and 7. But questions of method also surface in Chapters 2, 4, and 5, and there is a continual effort to make the methods explicit throughout the argument. This certainly serves the proper social scientific purpose of enabling the independent replication and testing of results, and may also encourage the reproduction of the research methods in different contexts. But the broader, and more self-conscious intention is to make the argument simultaneously substantive and methodological, and so provide a 'primer' for a new style of comparative work. The success of this enterprise you must judge for yourselves.

The methodological choices which inform the enquiry inevitably tend to privilege some analytical paths, just as they exclude others. Not surprisingly, therefore, this study cannot do everything! Thus, it cannot provide a comprehensive approach to the question of social movement strategy, nor can it pretend to reveal the changing 'political opportunity structures' which may catalyse successful collective action (Tarrow 1994*b*). This order of analysis has been carried out elsewhere (Foweraker 1989, 1993). But the consistent focus on the relationship between individual rights and social movements brings its own rewards. By concentrating on one key aspect of strategy, which is the presentation of demands in the language of rights, the enquiry provides hard measures of at least one aspect of social movement 'success', which is the impact on rights provision (cf. Chapters 2 and 8).[2] Conversely, by isolating one enduring aspect of the 'political opportunity structure' faced by social movements (McAdam, McCarthy, and Zald 1996), which is the provision of rights (whether rights-in-principle or rights-in-practice), it is able to measure social movement responses to changes in this provision.[3]

[2] Studies of social movement impact tend to adopt a narrative, single-case approach. There are exceptions which attempt a comparative or statistical enquiry, including: Gamson (1975), Welch (1975), and Piven and Cloward (1977) on North American movements; and Tarrow (1989), Jenkins and Klandermans (1995), and Kriesi et al. (1995) on European movements. This study is both comparative and statistical, and moves beyond the North American and European contexts.

[3] There is a further respect in which the enquiry may elucidate the idea of a 'political opportunity structure'. The literature remains ambiguous about the quality of this structure, and fails to resolve whether its existence is 'objective' or primarily 'subjective', insofar as opportunities must be perceived before they can influence collective action (e.g. Melucci 1988). By measuring the 'gap' between rights-in-principle and rights-in-practice, and by tracing the influence of this gap on social mobilization, the enquiry provides some empirical evidence for evaluating the impact of this 'perception' on social mobilization.

The Cases Described

The enquiry aspires to make a general argument about citizenship and social movements, but it draws on evidence from just four contemporary cases, namely Brazil, Chile, Mexico, and Spain. The number of cases was constrained by resource limitations and the difficulties of data collection and data synthesis. The choice of cases was determined by the research design, in two main ways. First, the enquiry seeks to compare similar variations in individual rights and social movement activity across similar cases (characterized in Chapter 3 as the 'mirror-image' of the 'most similar systems design' or MSSD). All the cases show strong similarities in their periods of authoritarian rule, forms of regime, relationships between regime and individual, variations in the gap between rhetoric and reality of citizenship rights, and waves of social movement activity (cf. Chapters 1 and 2). Second, the enquiry aims not only to measure variations in the relationship, but explain them, and so the positivist thrust of the research needs to be complemented by a more contextually sensitive commentary. In short, there was prior research knowledge of each case (including field research experience), and this fostered a fuller dialogue between statistical measures and political culture. This hermeneutic reading is important to the presentation of the data in Chapters 4 and 5, but gives way to a more exclusively statistical analysis in Chapters 6 and 7.

Brazil

A military coup on 1 April 1964 installed an authoritarian regime that would last until 1985, with vestiges remaining until 1989. The new regime adhered to a Doctrine of National Security and Development (Stepan 1971) which combined theories of war and internal subversion with a vision of Brazil's role as a world power (Alves 1985: 8). Through a series of decree-laws, Institutional Acts, and Constitutions, the military first set up a two-party version of the 'bureaucratic-authoritarian' state (O'Donnell 1973; Collier 1979), and then presided over a gradual return to democracy. The regime faced a series of challenges from political parties and professional groups, and from grass-roots movements and new labour organizations. Consequently, these twenty-five years of military rule were characterized by successive cycles of repression and liberalization (Alves 1985: 256).

These cycles responded to distinct waves of opposition from

students and labour in 1967–8; from the formal opposition party, the Brazilian Democratic Movement or MDB, in the early 1970s and after (Kinzo 1988); and from professional groups, grass-roots movements (Alves 1984; Mainwaring 1987, 1989), women's movements (S. E. Alvarez 1990), and the new union movement (Alves 1985; Keck 1992) in the late 1970s and early 1980s, culminating in the campaign for direct elections of 1984. Once the moment of democratic transition had been reached in 1985, political parties assumed the main role in negotiating a return to formal democracy, and social movements tended to lose political impetus. The exception was the labour movement.

The combination of cycles of repression with waves of protest suggests a dialectical relationship between state and opposition in military Brazil (Alves 1985). The repressive apparatuses of the national security state and popular collective action define the two poles of this relationship. In her distinctive account, Alves demonstrates the interaction between repression, liberalization, and opposition struggles. Both regime rules and regime behaviour prove sensitive to popular protest of different kinds. In the same spirit, our study sets out to examine the relationship between the individual rights of citizenship (as described in Chapter 1) and social movement activity. Furthermore, by providing clear measures of year-by-year changes in both rights provision and movement activity, it aims to achieve a fuller description of the cycles of repression and liberalization (Chapter 4), and of the waves of opposition (Chapter 5).

Chile

Despite initial support from moderate sectors of civil society, the military coup of 11 September 1973 brought in a harshly repressive regime. Over the following months power was consolidated in the hands of the dictator, General Pinochet, and repression was centralized in the National Intelligence Directorate or DINA (renamed the National Intelligence Centre, CNI, in 1977, largely for cosmetic purposes). The dictator sought to provide a quasi-legal foundation for the regime through decree-laws, the Constitutional Acts of 1976, the 1978 Plebiscite, the 1980 Constitution and Plebiscite, and the 1988 Plebiscite, in which he lost the legal means of remaining in power for a further eight years. Through three main cycles of repression in 1973–4, 1974–7, and 1977–88 the regime set out to eliminate any opposition from political parties, labour unions, or other social movements (Oxhorn 1995: 65–8). The democratic transition was announced by the legalization of political parties and the extension of the suffrage in 1987 (Oxhorn 1995), and proceeded rapidly through the 1988 Plebiscite and the 1989 national elections.

Despite the repression, various forms of grass-roots opposition began to appear in the mid-1970s, reaching a peak in the early 1980s, and subsiding during and after the democratic transition. The first sign of opposition came from the Catholic Church in the mid-1970s, to be followed by labour unrest from 1979 to 1982, and mass mobilization in 1983 and 1984 by unions (Angell 1991), popular movements on the urban periphery (Oxhorn 1995), women's groups (C. Schneider 1992), and clandestine political parties (Garretón 1989*b*). The pattern of opposition changed after the state of siege of late 1984 and early 1985, which convinced the more moderate organizations to pursue their opposition according to the regime's own rules (Angell 1991; Oxhorn 1994, 1995). These moderate elements formed the National Accord for the Transition to Democracy in 1985, the Command for the No in 1988, and the Command of the Parties for Democracy in 1989, to contest the dictatorship in the electoral arena (Angell 1991: 374–9). Only the most radical parties and some urban popular movements maintained a more confrontational stance, led by the Democratic Popular Movement or MDP. Hence the democratic transition is described as elite-dominated and classified as a 'transition by agreements' (Oxhorn 1995).

There can be no surprise that the relationship between regime and opposition in Chile has been described differently to that in Brazil. In contrast to Brazil's dialectical relationship, it appears that the institutional and personal power of Chile's dictator was able to control the pace and timing of political change, from the promulgation of the 1980 Constitution, through the 1988 Plebiscite and 1989 elections. But a revisionist view defends the impact of popular protest on the democratic transition (Oxhorn 1995), and it remains true that the 1988 Plebiscite did not give the dictator the result he wanted. In this study, the use of time-series data tends to show that there is much more interaction between regime and opposition in Chile than previously allowed. In particular, the popular protests of 1983–4 emerge as a turning point in the political history of the regime. Pinochet was not permissive, but he was not entirely unresponsive.

Mexico

This one-party dominant political system was originally founded on the 'triple incorporation' of labour, peasants, and the popular sectors in the decades following the Revolution of 1910–17

(Cornelius and Craig 1991; Hellman 1983). Over time, the formal legal-institutional framework of the 1917 Constitution has been superseded by informal and metaconstitutional powers vested in the Presidency (Garrido 1989). The carefully nurtured image of a modernizing and benevolent regime was dispelled by the 1968 student uprising and the massacre in Tlatelolco Square in Mexico City. Since that time the regime has been characterized as achieving an 'incomplete liberalization' (Cornelius and Craig 1991; Loaeza 1994; Whitehead 1994*b*), and as remaining on an uncertain middle ground, somewhere between authoritarian and democratic.

For many years the party-of-government, the Institutional Revolutionary Party or PRI, achieved legitimate rule through symbolic appeal to the Revolution, regular elections, and its success in achieving national conciliation and socio-economic modernization (Whitehead 1994*b*: 328). More recently, the regime has been weakened by economic crises and growing social inequality, and challenged by newly independent labour organizations, the rise of social movements, and increasing electoral opposition (Loaeza 1994: 114). With co-optation made more difficult, repression became more widespread, and by the early 1990s the country lagged behind many of its neighbours in Latin America according to standard democratic measures. The contemporary period has been one of 'increasing popular combativeness against a progressively less legitimate government' (Foweraker 1993: 2).

The regime response to the challenges is best described as a mixture of intransigence and change. On the one hand, there have been no fundamental constitutional changes and the dominant party has clung grimly onto central government. On the other, there have been recurrent electoral reforms, leading to an increasing number of opposition victories in local and regional elections. But increasing electoral contestation has often been accompanied by increased repression, so that there is a growing gap between formal liberalization and informal practice, between a tolerance of political freedoms and attacks on civil liberties (Foweraker 1996). The evidence assembled in this study suggests that this has complicated but not constricted the close and continuing interaction between regime behaviour and popular protest.

Spain

The Franco regime was born of military victory in the Spanish Civil War of 1936–9. In the following decades Franco created a 'stabilized authoritarian regime' (Carr and Fusi 1979: 48) characterized more by passive mass acceptance than by popular support (Linz 1964). The constitutional order was constructed by a series of Organic Laws, but political power was maintained by the careful manipulation of the 'institutionalized families' of the military, Church and Falange, and of the 'political families' of the Franco loyalists, monarchists, and technocrats (Carr and Fusi 1979: 31–5). Traditional labour organizations were suppressed, and class conflict outlawed, in the interests of social peace, which was to be reproduced through the corporatist controls and intermediation of the Vertical Syndicate (Maravall 1978).

In the first decades of the regime close authoritarian political controls were matched by an autarkic economic policy favouring the landed oligarchy and domestic finance capital. Inflation was kept low, but growth was sluggish. However growth sharply accelerated after a policy switch in the late 1950s opened up the economy and welcomed foreign capital. The rapid increases in industrialization and urbanization favoured the emergence and spread of clandestine labour organizations, such as the Workers' Commissions, and led to more strikes (Carr and Fusi 1979: 15). The new pressures acting on the regime are explained by the institutional strains induced by rapid industrial growth (Maravall 1978), and by the growing organizational strength and strategic innovation of the oppositional working-class movement (Foweraker 1989). Consequently, fissures began to appear in the political carapace of Francoism.

Despite the accounts of popular mobilization by students (Maravall 1978), the labour movement (Foweraker 1989), and urban social movements (Castells 1983), most explanations of the democratic transition in Spain focus on the political accommodation between regime moderates and the growing political opposition at home and abroad (Preston 1986), and on the democratic openings created by elite interaction between 'continuists' and 'rupturists' (Colomer 1991). In sum, like transition studies everywhere, they can be criticized for overemphasizing 'elite interaction and formal rule making in the process of regime change, while neglecting "bottom-up", civil society-based, and participatory aspects of democratization' (Whitehead 1994b: 333). Yet the statistical analysis of time-series data in this study clearly reveals the critical importance of popular mobilization to the moment of democratic transition in Spain.

The Cases Compared

All these regimes are strongly authoritarian in the straightforward sense that government insists on social discipline and tight

political control at the expense of political freedom and the individual rights of citizenship. As a corollary, political power tends to
be highly centralized, and mainly vested in the government executive. Yet, they all have more or less elaborate legal-institutional
frameworks, and all exhibit greater or lesser degrees of political
liberalization over time. In all cases rights-in-practice may exceed
or fall short of rights-in-principle, and all prove more or less sensitive to the fluctuations in social movement activity. In terms of
the citizenship process (cf. Chapter 1) they demonstrate similar
variations and similar outcomes.

But if the cases are similar they are also different enough to
make comparison interesting. Two (Brazil, Chile) are examples of
military-authoritarian regime, and two (Mexico, Spain) of civilian
authoritarian regime. Two (Chile, Spain) have personal dictator-
ships, and two (Brazil, Mexico) have highly institutional government. The latter have regular or frequent elections, the former do
not. Two (Chile, Spain) experience 'rapid' transitions to democratic rule, and two (Brazil, Mexico) more protracted or incomplete
transitions. Perhaps most significantly, given the importance of
the labour movement to social movement activity overall across
the cases (Chapters 2, 5, and passim), the four cases span the
spectrum of corporatist control and intermediation, from the universal and uniform system of Franco's Spain, through the comprehensive but variegated state-chartered corporations of Mexico and
the mixed, uneven, and unwieldly model of Brazil, to the complete
absence of such intervention in Chile. These differences tend to be
reflected in the statistical findings.

The comparative method seeks to discover the similarities and
differences across cases that can support general statements, and
construct argument accordingly. The single-case study, in contrast,
assumes that its *sui generis* qualities are more interesting or more
important, or are simply intractable to comparative analysis. These
analytical tensions are never easy to resolve. In many purportedly
comparative studies of the processes of liberalization, democratic
transition and consolidation, for instance, the emphasis remains
on the single case, with several such cases loosely organized within
a general framework (cf. O'Donnell and Schmitter 1986; Higley
and Gunther 1992; Przeworski 1986, 1991; Diamond, Linz, and
Lipset 1989). Consequently, the typologies derived from these studies often have as many categories as cases, on the explicit assumption that such processes are 'not measurable according to a common
scale for all cases' (O'Donnell and Schmitter 1986: 9).

In this study we set out to compare equally complex political processes by constructing common scales in the form of standard indicators. In other words, the measures of social movement activity and rights provision are *commensurate* across cases and over time. By adopting this approach the study inevitably loses the kind of contextual information and commentary that is the stuff of single-case studies, and of some of the more loosely 'comparative' work. But, as Chapters 4 and 5 demonstrate, the standard indicators can achieve their own order of description, which is rich in a sense of historical process; and they can support tightly controlled comparisons which focus attention on specific aspects and moments of this process. The comparisons can suggest where to look and what to look for, in these cases and beyond.

Nonetheless, it may be objected that the methodological result is neither beast nor fowl. On the one hand, the standard indicators restrict the focus and range of the study. On the other, they do not provide truly 'objective' measures that can underpin formal analysis. We would not wish to quarrel on either count. In the classical comparative tradition, the study fixes on one central theme (the relationship between the individual rights of citizenship and social movement activity) and sticks with it throughout. In the positivist spirit, it seeks to do so by providing clear, numerical and commensurate indicators. But there is no illusion that these are hard numbers. On the contrary, the majority of the measures depend, more or less directly, on a contextually sensitive reading of political case histories, and are therefore imbued with different styles of analytical judgement.[4] The result is neither 'thick description' (Geertz 1983) nor numerically laden 'large-N cross-national comparisons' (Przeworski and Teune 1970), but something in-between.

The Shape of the Argument

Although the enquiry is contemporary in context and empirical in its objectives and delivery, it is rooted in history and framed by theory. The opening chapters explore the characteristic connections observed between individual rights and social movements in theory and (modern) history, and begin to draw out the general

---

[4] A more polemical riposte might also claim that there are no hard numbers in social science, even in the dismal science. If this claim is valid, there is little reason for the sectarian divisions in empirical social science. The cultural sensitivity of qualitative enquiry and the methodological machismo of numbers may find common ground. It is certainly our hope that this study may find some favour with both the numerate and the literate.

propositions that are tested in the case-specific analysis. (These propositions are summarized in the first half of Chapter 8.) Chapter 1 looks at the complexities and contradictions of citizenship rights, as well as their relation to histories of social struggle, and explicates their normative content. It also seeks to defend the exclusive focus on the civil and political rights of citizenship. Chapter 2 explores the mutualities of the relationship between rights and movements, suggesting that rights empower movements just as movements vindicate and occasionally achieve rights. Citizenship is then 'operationalized' as an object of research in the ways already suggested. Furthermore both chapters explain the relevance of the general propositions to the particular cases under study.

The overall shape of the argument is simple. Chapters 1 and 2 set the scene in the ways described. Chapter 3 explains the methods of data collection and presentation. Chapter 4 describes and measures the variation in citizenship rights over time, both within and across cases; and Chapter 5 does the same for social movement activity and the composition of social movement demands. Chapter 6 proceeds to examine the relationship between rights and movements over time, using correlation and autoregression to compare and contrast the relationship across cases; while Chapter 7 reveals how the relationship develops through time, using multiple interrupted time-series analysis (MITS) and Boolean algebra to search out the key moments and crucial conditions that do most to configure it, and to calculate the likelihood that the mutual impact of rights and movements will occur at all. Overall, this mix of methods produces robust results which are mutually reinforcing (a happy outcome that could not have been predicted). Finally, Chapter 8 summarizes the results of the statistical enquiry, and integrates them into a comparative argument, before bringing that argument to bear on the current debates over democratic transition and democratic consolidation. The results of the enquiry are seen to offer significant new insights into contemporary struggles for democracy.

A recent essay on state organization in Latin America in this century notes the 'insecurity and unpredictability' of individual rights, and the consequence that 'citizenship is a promise that must be repeatedly renegotiated' (Whitehead 1994*a*: 87). The newly constitutional regimes of the 1980s tended to reaffirm the 'individualistic ethic of citizenship' (Whitehead 1994*a*: 86–7), but this advance remained fragile and subject to reversal. The essay concludes by calling for more study of 'the intermittent, fragmentary, and unequal appearance—and disappearance—of citizenship rights' (Whitehead 1994*a*: 84). This enquiry takes one step in this direction by focusing on the popular and political dynamics of these appearances and disappearances; and the inclusion of Franco's Spain is one small indication that recent struggles for citizenship rights have extended far beyond Latin America, and now represent a global phenomenon. The analytical lessons of the enquiry may therefore be relevant to a wide range of citizenship struggles in very different political cultures.

Citizenship, Collective Action, and the State

Popular Struggles for Citizenship: The View from Below

There is a remarkable degree of academic consensus about the genesis of citizenship.[1] Its main premiss is that citizenship must be understood in terms of rights. Its main conclusion is that rights are won through social struggle by subordinate groups. It is by struggling to 'improve their lot' (Giddens 1982: 171) and being 'willing to fight' (Tarrow 1990: 103) that these groups come to 'demand and obtain citizen rights' (Clarke 1993: 19). Even if this struggle involves 'apparently trivial, ineffectual, or self-serving actions', it can have an eventual impact on the great issues of 'political right and obligation' (Tilly, Tilly, and Tilly 1975: 299). But, these rights are not granted easily or willingly. On the contrary, the historical record suggests that 'collective violence' is often required to 'overcome the resistance of the government' (Tilly, Tilly, and Tilly 1975: 184). It is not political protest by single individuals but the 'collective struggles of the dispossessed' that have won the 'rights of citizens' (Bowles and Gintis 1987: p. x). Almost paradoxically, the essentially *individual* rights of citizenship can only be achieved through different forms of *collective* struggle.

Traditionally, these collective struggles have been understood to express class conflict, and especially the rise of the working class. The English school of social history (Dobb 1963; Hill 1958; Thompson 1974; Hobsbawm 1968; Hilton 1976) has shown that

[1] The consensus encompasses historians (Thompson 1974; Hobsbawm 1968, 1977), historical sociologists (Moore 1973; Kimmel 1990; Smith 1991), political sociologists (Therborn 1976, 1977), sociologists (Turner 1986; Barbalet 1988), political theorists (Held 1989; Giddens 1982, 1985; Young 1987, 1989; Clarke 1993), and political economists (Bowles and Gintis 1987).

poor and working people began early to speak the language of
rights, and successfully defended the freedom of association as
part of the lexicon of rights. Historians have also demonstrated
beyond much doubt that, across nineteenth- and early twentieth-
century Europe, the biggest working-class struggles were spurred
by the prospect of electoral reform. Recent scholarship confirms
that the emergence of citizenship rights has been closely tied to
the success of the working-class movement (Rueschemeyer, Stephens, and Stephens 1992). Even without an emphasis on class
struggle itself, citizenship rights may still be seen as the mediated
outcome of the tensions between the inequality of class society and
the equality principle of liberal society (Marshall 1963; Barbalet
1988: 30).

The working-class movement is just one of many social movements to emerge in the modern period. Insofar as these movements
struggle to defend or expand social inclusion and participation
they are 'inevitably about the rights of citizenship' (Turner 1986:
92). In other words, citizenship is the result of 'the way in which
different groups, classes and movements have struggled to gain
degrees of autonomy and control over their lives in the face of
various forms of stratification, hierarchy and political oppression'
(Held 1989: 199). Even though different movements clearly have different objectives (Held 1991*a*: 20), their struggles usually converge
on equal rights, or 'full citizenship status under the equal protection of the law' (Young 1989: 250). The *general* rights of citizenship
are the historical result of *specific* struggles over rights to 'freedom
of speech, expression, belief, information, as well as the freedom of
association on which trade-union rights depend, and freedom for
women in relation to marriage and property' (Held 1991*a*: 20).

In this way citizenship is seen to be won by social struggles
'from below'. This picture is both simple and comforting. It implies
that citizenship rights will everywhere always expand and deepen,
and that the poor and oppressed will eventually be able to redress
the injustices they suffer. But the record reveals that 'struggle
may also lead to repression rather than increased rights' (Barbalet
1988: 108), and that rights may have little or nothing to do with
social struggles. It is difficult for subordinate groups to wrest the
initiative from dominant classes which, together with the state,
are able to decide the timing and form of the delivery of rights
(Therborn 1977; Barbalet 1988: 34); and the working-class movement, in particular, has rarely been able to win rights on its own,
but has had to wait for political allies, splits in ruling-class coalitions (Rueschemeyer, Stephens, and Stephens 1992), or incursions

by conquering foreign armies (Therborn 1977). It is also argued that in recent decades the state is the main source of rights, supplanting the variable success of social movements in winning rights during the nineteenth and early twentieth centuries (Boli-Bennett 1981).

State Control of Citizenship: The View from Above

Citizenship rights are meant to protect the citizen against the arbitrary exercise of state power (Barbalet 1988: 18). But, irrespective of the force or scope of the popular struggle for these rights, it is self-evident that 'it is the state which ultimately grants them' (Barbalet 1988: 110). In short, citizenship both depends upon and is threatened by the state, because what the state gives it can also take away. If the state can protect legal equality, which underpins one kind of 'sameness', it can also suppress pluralism and attack difference; if it can enhance citizenship rights, it can also control access to those rights and restrict political membership. For this reason, a main premiss of this study is that the core civil and legal-political rights of citizenship can never be negotiable parts of its definition.

Although rights are usually understood to protect the individual against the state, the accumulation of such rights can also strengthen the state by creating a greater 'regulation and institutionalization of social life' (Bellamy 1993: 69). Since these rights tend to draw individuals into the arena of state regulation, the spread of rights tends to accompany broader constitutional statements of 'both citizen duties and state authority' (Boli-Bennett 1981: 173–4).[2] Insofar as the reason of state may require that citizens act as 'more or less passive bearers of rights', there is always a danger of surrendering the 'life of the citizen . . . for the life of

---

[2] Citizenship is ambiguous insofar as citizenship rights empower both individuals and the state; and the discourse of rights (the liberal ideology of citizenship) is also ambiguous insofar as it addresses both the haves and the have-nots. Civil citizenship guarantees equality before the law at the same time as it reinforces property rights (Barbalet 1988: 44), so introducing a 'tension between property rights and personal rights' (Bowles and Gintis 1987: 28). In Marshall's optimistic view, the extension of civil and political rights gradually enabled the propertyless to challenge class privilege and the power of capital (Marshall 1965). Insofar as they do so, citizenship and social class come to represent 'opposing principles'. But property rights remain an integral and sacrosanct component of the individual rights of citizenship (Bowles and Gintis 1987: 175).

the subject' (Clarke 1993: 11–14). Consequently, citizenship must be an active condition of struggling to make rights real (Phillips 1991: 77).

Consider the citizen in her/his first modern manifestation as the *citoyen/ne* of the French Revolutionary regime. The legal and political forms of the regime were not traditional or rational, in Weberian terms, but charismatic: the regime made up the rules as it went along. This was starkly demonstrated during the Reign of Terror, which took place despite the Declaration of the Rights of Man and of the Citizen; and it soon became clear that such declarations were meaningless without the rule of law. It was the National Convention itself which created a separate judiciary for political offences in the Revolutionary Tribunal, and then continued to meddle with its procedures and composition. In these circumstances citizenship cannot be defined by normative expectations, but can only be imagined as a struggle which either achieves rights against the state or extends the protections and guarantees of the state—in a game which is sometimes expanding-sum, sometimes zero-sum.

This example indicates that it is important to separate the general contradictions of citizenship from the particular problems it may encounter under specific forms of regime. In general, civil and political rights developed through a process of compromise between state and citizen, so that the limits imposed on state action were only won by conceding power and authority to the state and recognizing the legitimacy of state legal jurisdiction. Since the state is the only agency to which the citizen can turn when rights are violated, the state must have the authority to act as guarantor (Boli-Bennett 1981). But particular political regimes are more or less conducive to the exercise of citizenship, and some are frankly hostile. And wherever the quintessentially liberal separation between state and civil society fails, civil and political rights tend to be suffocated, all claims by the state itself notwithstanding. For this reason Mann's attempt to defend Fascism as enshrining a certain form of citizenship remains incoherent (Mann 1987). A mere admixture of a bastard civil citizenship with social welfarism simply does not qualify. To repeat our premiss, any defence of citizenship which excludes its core rights under the rule of law must remain spurious.

These observations apply directly to this enquiry into citizenship struggles in four countries where authoritarian and sometimes military governments have resorted to repression and political violence in order to crush dissent and enforce political loyalty or

cultural and ideological homogeneity. As suggested in the Introduction, their histories demonstrate that, even where the state
was not openly at war with its own people, the rule of law was far
from complete. Their laws and constitutions accorded broad discretionary powers to the executive, under different kinds of 'emergency' clauses, to declare a state-of-seige and suspend civil and
political rights, sometimes indefinitely (Loveman 1994). Even rights
that are considered inalienable, such as habeas corpus, were in
fact conditional (since what the state decreed it could also revoke);
and even the violation and torture of the human person, which
was never legal, was legitimized by the higher reasons of the state
and its defence.

The lessons are clear. Whether the context is the French Revolutionary state, the Fascist state, or the contemporary authoritarian
state, citizenship invokes rights but is conformed by power. Citizenship is therefore a political process, and its constitutional and
procedural codes are constantly changing and contested, negotiated
and interpreted. The outcomes depend on the balance of political
force in civil society, and the degree of separation between that
society and the state. Hence, civil and political rights may enjoy
an 'autonomous' legal status, but they are simultaneously the formal expression of political struggles, and sometimes provide the
legal and institutional terms of these struggles themselves. Political claims to citizenship are only effective if agreed as reasonable
and legitimate, but, since agreement is hard to get, citizenship
rights can sometimes only be attained through struggle (Barbalet
1988: 16).

These assertions bring the argument full circle, but they neither
demonstrate nor explain the relationship between social movements
and the individual rights of citizenship. There have been many
attempts to characterize the connections between them, by focusing,
variously, on the context, catalysts, and constraints of collective
action,[3] both in relation to the development of capitalism and the
emergence of modern civil society and in relation to the growth of
the modern state and the process of nation-building. This chapter
will review the main explanatory themes, and so prepare the ground
for the subsequent empirical enquiry. But, although shifts in social

---

[3] This continues to provide a fairly precise focus that still falls a long way short
of a fully fledged theory of citizenship. This focus responds to the salutory warning
that 'the scope of a "theory of citizenship" is potentially limitless—almost every
problem in political philosophy involves relations among citizens or between citizens and the state' (Kymlicka and Norman 1994: 353).

structure and the formation of the national state system (Tilly 1990) are certainly relevant to the enquiry, historical conditions are not the same as historical results. No explication of the relationship can exclude the 'independent' influence of new forms of collective action and an emerging discourse of rights (which are examined in Chapter 2). This is not ultimately a story of social structures and states, but of strategic collective action and the power of ideas.

Capitalism, Civil Society, and Citizenship

It has been argued forcibly that citizenship can only be understood as the historical result of the rise of capitalism (Habermas 1973), and, in particular, of the separation of the political from the economic in capitalism, which created a special realm 'for the realization of political rights and freedoms' (Held 1989: 205 *après* Poulantzas 1973*a*: part III). But it is not the 'individuated individuals' (K. Marx 1976) created by changing social relations of production that mattered to the first manifestation of modern citizenship so much as the 'possessive individuals' (Macpherson 1972) who appear in the market place. Philosophically, their self-concious appearance had to await the Cartesian revolution, and the new theories that imagined the individual as possessing its own body, and, by extension its own property (Locke 1975). Economically, their appearance was catalysed by the price revolution of the sixteenth century, and the growth of commercial transactions and credit mechanisms (P. Anderson 1974). With increasing trade and the growth of commercial (in contrast to landed) property came insecurity, and the need for a new kind of political authority which could protect property rights, guarantee commercial contracts and govern the operation of the market.[4] These rights and guarantees

---

[4] Even if civil law and property rights were sufficient to secure contracts in the market place, a recurrent recourse to law would certainly impair the price mechanism. Hence, civil citizenship also required civility if the 'invisible hand' of the market place were to work at all well. Civility in this sense is the original ideology of citizenship, and a primary if restricted form of social solidarity. Civility meant honest trade and proper commercial practice. This is why rationality in Locke is linked not only to property but also to civility: Locke believed he could recognize a civil gentleman even if he met him in a forest (that is, outside of his natural habitat of the market place). But the civility of capitalist civil society is not ultimately a civility of equality, and the majority remain 'trapped in one or

can now be seen to compose what Marshall (1963) called *civil* citizenship, which is contemporary citizenship's historical core.[5]

Civil citizenship was rooted in the market place and the protection of private property, but it did begin to create rights not only through but also against the state. Although social contract theory is often understood as a liberal theory of the origins and underpinnings of the state, it is clear in both Hobbes and Locke that the real contract is never with the sovereign, but merely between the individuals in market society (Macpherson 1972). The contract can then be read as a metaphor and epitome of the political conditions of market reciprocity. Nonetheless, it is clearly important that the new form of citizenship placed legal limits on the state's prerogatives over persons and property. The growth of a capitalist civil society may not have determined the dissemination of modern and liberal ideas of individual rights, but it certainly provided propitious conditions for it.

The significance of these observations for a comparative approach to citizenship is that such civil societies developed very unevenly because of the 'combined and uneven' development of capitalism itself (Lenin 1967). Individual rights could only take root where civil society provided the proper conditions, but civil society could only grow where labour was unfettered and the social division of labour could increase in exponential fashion. Reflexive patterns of economic growth on the capitalist periphery produced variable effects. In those societies where extant forms of political domination were strong enough to immobilize labour on the land, civil society remained constrained and burgherdom stunted by the restrictive power of landowning elites. The spread of direct labour control in *latifundia* in many countries of Latin America and during Engels's

---

another subordinate relationship, where the "civility" they learned was deferential rather than independent and active' (Walzer 1989). Analogous points emerge from the later discussion of the discourse of rights.

[5] It was precisely the market basis of this original form of citizenship that Marx objected to so strongly in *The Jewish Question*. He refused to characterize these market-based rights as citizenship rights because they were 'quite simply the rights of the member of civil society ie of egoistic man, of man separated from other men and the community' (K. Marx 1981: 229). These rights added up to nothing more than property rights and the right to self-interest: 'egoistic man is the passive and merely given result of the society which has been dissolved [into] . . . civil society, the world of needs, of labour, of private interests and civil law' (K. Marx 1981: 233–4). Against this it can be argued that the civil freedoms of civil society are ultimately indispensable to political rights, since only when the individual is recognized as an autonomous agent does it make sense to regard that individual as politically responsible (Clarke 1993).

'second serfdom' in Eastern Europe crippled their nascent civil societies.[6] Hence, with the benefit of hindsight, it was possible to argue that the rise and extension of citizenship rights demanded the elimination of the peasantry which fed the 'huge reservoir of conservative and reactionary forces' (Moore 1973: 30). In Moore's argument such forces influenced the composition of dominant class coalitions and the forms of regime they supported. In analogous fashion, Gramsci distinguished the plastic civil societies and relatively secure regimes of the west from the more autocratic and brittle political forms found in Russia (Gramsci 1973).[7]

Civil Society, the Public Sphere, and Political Associations

If market relations and an increasing functional division of labour create the conditions for the growth of civil society they do not describe it. For a narrowly economic definition of civil society will entail an impoverished and passive definition of citizenship (K. Marx 1981). A more active definition first requires a sense of civil society as a public sphere where citizens may meet in mutual recognition, and so make plural society possible. Possibly this sphere was engendered in the civic arenas and corporate bodies which were the heirs to the mediaeval guilds and estates (Habermas 1989); but, contemporarily, it contains all the institutions, practices, and conventions which create and reproduce the cultural heritage that Marshall (1963) understood as sustaining citizenship. On the one hand, the public sphere fosters a public which knows the rights and responsibilities which create community. On the other, it promotes pluralism by providing a forum for intra-ruling class competition, and even, as Marshall suggested, for institutionalizing the clash of class interests and projects in capitalist society. More generally, activities within this sphere tend to generate a cultural consensus around the differences that the culture can contain, so promoting a civil definition of membership.

---

[6] Where no such secure pattern of political control existed, or where the frontier could subvert attempts to impose one (as in North America and Australia), civil society could grow apace in the economic and political space created by a relatively homogeneous capitalist environment.

[7] This highly condensed argument is just a first sketch of some of the historical conditions that may influence the development of citizenship, and must not imply a simple determination of citizenship at the level of international political economy. A fuller exposition of the argument, and a range of illustrations, can be found in Foweraker (1981: chapter 9).

The second sense of civil society that is important to citizenship is the Hegelian one of the autonomous institutions that mediate the relationship between individual and state, and judge state action in a rational and moral manner. For present purposes this meso-institutional level is also taken to contain the political associations so dear to de Tocqueville, and so close to the heart of Dahl's theory of polyarchy (Dahl 1971). Durkheim insisted that such associations are 'essential if the state is not to oppress the individual' (Turner 1992), and this is because these associations are essential to the defence of rights (Bellamy 1993: 70). Dahl took up the point and demonstrated that rights were better assured by associationalism than by legal guarantees, since it is only by forming and supporting active associations like political parties and trade unions that citizens can protect and extend their rights. In this way the political associations of civil society act to 'operationalize' the legal content of citizenship, so specifying one aspect of social movement activity and the struggle for rights.[8]

In construing the political character of civil society, it is plausible that the public sphere and political associationalism combine in the construction of a public domain that is separate from privately organized economic activity (Giddens 1985). Accounts of the development of the liberal discourse of rights often assume that it begins with civil equality and civil liberties (the negative liberties of laissez-faire economics) before promoting the more positive liberties of freedom of association and political participation. More recent theories suggest, on the contrary, that civil and political rights develop in tandem, and that 'civil rights thus have been, from the very early phases of capitalist development, bound up with the very definition of what counts as "political"' (Giddens 1985: 207). Hence the public domain itself cannot be construed as entirely separate from the state, for liberal discourse has to be rooted in an institutional framework of rights that is adjudicated by 'an "impersonal" structure of public power' (G. Andrews 1991: 24).

The double dimension of the public domain is reflected in Dahl's sense of citizenship as combining the two dimensions of *participation* and (sufficient organizational resources and rights to achieve) *public contestation* (Dahl 1971). A singular emphasis on participation links citizenship struggles to the growth of urban society and the process of modernization writ large (Turner 1986). This study,

---

[8] Under the authoritarian regimes of this study, where civil society is constricted and trade unions and political parties suppressed or carefully controlled, social movements can take a leading political role in the struggle for individual rights.

on the contrary, sees both dimensions expressed in the political activity of social movements in civil society, and so gives them equal weight. In the context of modern authoritarian regimes, it is our judgement that citizenship rights are as crucial to contestation as to participation, and that most political struggles have to do with defending or vindicating the viability of these rights in more or less adverse legal and institutional contexts. The specific role of social movements in this regard is examined in detail in the following chapter.

The State, Nation-Building, and Citizenship

The commonality of citizenship is clearly an artifice insofar as it makes formally equal individuals who are in fact very different from one another. But the artifice serves to create the conditions for new forms of political rule, since the egalitarian content of citizenship underpins the political mechanisms that constitute the political subjects of capitalist civil society. Equality before the law, universal suffrage (one person, one vote), universal education and equality of opportunity all contribute to create the 'individuated individuals' (K. Marx 1976) who claim the rights of equal citizenship (Poulantzas 1973*a*: part III).[9] It can be argued that, over time, they not only construct new forms, but a new mode of political rule that is potentially hegemonic (Gramsci 1973).

It is this modern state that must entrench citizenship rights legally by framing and supporting the legal system which protects these rights and punishes infractions. Rights rooted in national legal codes could free citizens from a cluster of feudal, communal, and guild tyrannies (Durkheim 1960); and once state procedures are themselves made normative, with constitutions that shape the profile of public power and chart the principles of legitimate government, then citizenship may actually empower individual citizens and widen their degrees of freedom. In this positive view citizenship combines an awareness of membership in a bounded political community and a shared conception of justice.[10] It becomes

---

[9] Marx's strictures on the true content of civil citizenship are matched by equally scathing comments on the political construction of the new subjects of civil society: 'in the state on the other hand, where he is considered to be a species-being, (man) is the imaginary member of a fictitious sovereignty, he is divested of his real individual life and filled with an unreal universality' (K. Marx 1981: 220).

[10] In large degree this depended on the formation of a national state system, since it is the political boundaries of national states that are essential to the

a 'common status with respect to the regulation of society' (Clarke 1993: 4).

But citizenship also served the purposes of the state. The costs of enforcing political and military obligations, in particular, were greatly reduced by the extension of individual rights, and the increasing administrative power of the state (and especially its capacity for surveillance) came to depend less on the use of force and more on cooperative forms of political control (Giddens 1985). At the same time citizenship proved to be an effective means of 'securing national identity' (Bowles and Gintis 1987: 38), and of creating the 'new principle of collectivity' (Pérez-Díaz 1992: 15) that is nationalism.[11] Thus, citizenship rights served to mediate not just new forms of political rule but the process of state construction itself.

Yet citizenship rights were not simply conceded. On the contrary, the 'states were becoming cages, trapping their subjects within the bars' (Mann 1993*a*: 117). Consequently, 'the nationalizing state' became a 'target for claims', and created new 'opportunities for collective action' (Tarrow 1995: 10). In particular, the rise of social movements in the late eighteenth and early nineteenth centuries responded directly to the process of state construction by developing new 'repertoires of contention' (Tilly 1978). Previous political struggles had been predominantly local, specific, corporate, and communal. The new struggles took advantage of the 'unified political space' (Tarrow 1993*a*: 84) created by the state to press

achievement of identity as nationhood, and therefore to the construction of citizenship (Tilly 1990). These boundaries enabled new forms of calculation and the creation of statistics, and so underpinned the management of scarce resources, distributive justice, principles of inclusion and exclusion, and, crucially, the ability to enforce citizenship rights and prevent predators from diminishing those rights.

[11] In other words, if national boundaries served the imperatives of resource extraction, the waging of war, and the process of state construction, they were also imagined in the way political community is imagined, through common language, nostalgic and utopian myths, cultural legacies, and the civic culture itself (B. Anderson 1983). With the development of the technology of the imagination (printing press, communication networks and pedagogical techniques), citizenship could be constructed as the political and cultural product of a new social order as citizens became 'members of a common society' (Barbalet 1988: 1). As a corollary, the rights that inform citizenship are not simply or wholly a result of struggle but also a mark and acceptance of membership. The historical result is that the political and cultural elements of citizenship become inextricably intertwined, so increasing the specificity of citizenship (within national boundaries) and the variety of possible citizenships. This point is important to later discussion of the normative and descriptive contents of citizenship.

more general claims for political rights. The struggle for the freedoms of speech and association, as well as for the rights to vote, hold office, and initiate legislation, broke communal loyalties and built the new forms of collective action that were social movements.

Thus there is a historical coincidence between the increase in state administrative power and political control, and the popular empowerment implicit in the expansion of citizenship rights. A similar coincidence occurs in the construction of modern forms of the authoritarian state in Spain and Latin America, which mimicks the process of state-building in Europe. Social movements arose within a more differentiated civil society and began to contest the 'bars' of state incursion and control; while state attempts to quash dissent 'called forth a new form of politics' (Tilly 1990), and especially new kinds of contestation. In particular, the recent pretensions of authoritarian governments to deny civil and political rights made these rights central to contemporary social movement activity, with the state becoming both target and terrain of this activity. These analogies will take on resonance as the argument advances.

The Discourse of Rights and the Rule of Law

Participation in a capitalist market place had strongly egalitarian implications for feudal societies or societies with strong feudal residues, and civil citizenship provided a radical critique of the institutionalized inequalities of the *anciens régimes* during the rise of the national state. It was in this context that citizenship took on an explicitly normative character, as the legal codes and statutes that had buttressed these inequalities were assailed by moral philosophy and normative political theory. In place of privilege the critique asserted that each member of society was entitled to the same rights and freedoms as every other member. Citizen equalled citizen. In addition to the freedoms of speech, thought, and association that characterized 'civility', citizenship now came to include equality before the law and rights of participation in political decision-making.

This egalitarian ethos gained currency as the political project of an ascending class of merchants and industrial capitalists. But the outcome of the project far surpassed the self-interested radicalism of the bourgeoisie. For this was the moment when citizenship became irreversibly fused with liberalism, in the sense of a liberal view of government and of its main task of promoting and defending the rule of law as essential to effective equality. Indeed, it was precisely the location of the notion of equality within a legal framework that put the whole question of citizenship *rights* on the historical agenda and at the heart of political discourse. The discourse of rights gave added impetus both to the political associationalism of civil society and to national state formation (an assertion which can be confirmed in virtually any account of the French Revolution).

However, this normative moment in citizenship history took a long time to work itself out. On the one hand, the first forms of legal citizenship were often elitist in constitution and restricted in scope (even, or especially in the United States). On the other, citizens may enjoy equality before the law, but the law 'is silent on their ability to use it' (Bendix 1964). Consequently, subsequent generations saw continual popular struggles to extend the forms of citizenship, or make them politically effective. In particular, social movements like the labour movement began to state their demands in terms of rights, or to claim rights they had never enjoyed on a national scale. In this way, as suggested above, citizenship was slowly operationalized through political associationalism, organizational pluralism and social struggle. In this optimistic view citizenship rights become ever more universal, despite the many defeats and reversals.

Just as social movements fight for rights, so the discourse of rights serves 'as a source of bonding and a framework for the expression of group demands' (Bowles and Gintis 1987: 170). In this respect the discourse is simply a 'set of tools' used to 'forge the unities' required for social struggle (Bowles and Gintis 1987: 153). Like a set of tools, rights discourse can be picked up and applied to new contexts without great difficulty. Its core content has proved easy both to assimilate and to disseminate across widely different cultures. It can therefore serve the strategic purposes of different groups and movements in different places and times, since strategic economy favours the adoption and adaption of a rights discourse that appears universally effective. In this sense it is the perfect example of a 'master frame' (Snow et al. 1986; Snow and Benford 1992) that gives political and ideological coherence to a broad range of (sometimes very specific) social struggles.[12]

---

[12] In Chapter 5 we show how the discourse of rights gradually penetrates the demands profile of social movements across our four case studies. In this way the discourse informs and shapes the character of collective action. But it is the political and institutional context of this action, and the strategic use of the discourse, that will determine its political impact (Tarrow 1994*b*: chapter 7).

Far from being incompatible with market outcomes, the civil and political rights which compose this discourse 'provided the foundation of equality on which the (modern) structure of inequality could be built' (Held 1989: 87). In short, the discourse is indeed about rights, not goods, and therefore has only limited distributive implications. It was this that made it such a powerful political instrument. Nonetheless, once it was apparent that legal equality did not prevent and might even deepen social inequality, the combination of the two tended to spawn social disruption and broaden the base of political struggle.[13] These were matters either for the police or for social policy; but over the long term the state tended to respond with a range of measures designed to assuage the inequalities of market outcomes and provide basic social security for the mass of the population. These measures correspond to the era of what Marshall called social citizenship, comprised of so-called social rights. Whatever the virtues of these rights (and there are many), they do not qualify as integral to the discourse of rights, and therefore cannot serve the purposes of a comparative study of citizenship.

Core Rights versus Social Rights

In contemporary political theory, citizenship is 'defined almost entirely in terms of the possession of rights' (Kymlicka and Norman 1994: 354). In legal practice it is often seen as the 'rights to have rights'.[14] These citizenship rights comprise the civil rights necessary to individual freedom and the political rights of participation in the exercise of political rule. Civil rights are associated most directly with the rule of law and the system of courts, political rights with parliamentary institutions of different kinds. Contemporarily, both civil and political rights are widely recognized and disseminated across nearly all countries of the world.[15]

[13] The combination provoked Marx to criticize citizenship as expressive of nothing more than bourgeois individualism, and led Durkheim to argue (in a more modern and sociological vein) that there are no individuals outside of social relationships.

[14] From US Supreme Court, *Trop* v. *Dulles*, 356 US 86, at 102 (1958).

[15] Basic civil and political rights are enumerated by the Universal Declaration of Human Rights, the International Covenant on Civil and Political Rights (ICCPR), and the International Covenant on Economic, Social and Cultural Rights (ICESCR). The Universal Declaration was adopted by the UN General Assembly in 1948, and

Both civil and political rights represent universal claims which are amenable to formal expression in the rule of law and in the equality of political opportunity. Social rights, on the other hand, are substantive and must therefore be limited in their scope and delivery. Since social rights are fiscally constricted and require distributional decisions they are best described not as equal and universal rights but as 'conditional opportunities' (Barbalet 1988: 67). These opportunities have mainly been available in the advanced capitalist countries which can afford a full package of educational and welfare policies, but even here they are subject to strong fluctuations (Esping-Anderson 1989).[16] The massive disparities of wealth and income in the international political economy mean that, unlike civil and political rights, social rights have never been broadly disseminated across the globe.

Although vested in individuals, civil and political rights are a 'form of power' which are used to create 'movements of every kind' (Marshall 1965: 142). By defending freedom of thought, speech, assembly and association, they allow 'citizens to organize in defense of their own interests and identities' (Fox 1994: 152). In other words, they define 'freedoms the state cannot invade' (Barbalet 1988: 21) and so are rights *against* the state. Social rights, on the contrary, are claims to benefits guaranteed *by* the state and provided by the administrative apparatus *of* the state (Macpherson 1966). Consequently, social rights can reduce citizens to passivity and lead to the 'clientelization of the citizen's role' (Habermas 1989). In short, on both ontological and political grounds, civil political and social rights are quite different from one another.

Social rights play a special role in political systems characterized by pervasive forms of clientelistic control, such as those in this study. The particularistic lines of subordination and control which define these systems operate through a selective delivery or denial

the approval of the ICCPR and the ICESCR gave the Declaration the force of international law. As of January 1989, 92 states had ratified the ICESCR, 87 the ICCPR, 94 the Convention on the Elimination of All Forms of Discrimination against Women, and 28 the ILO conventions. In addition, there are customary laws that states consider binding even if they are not embodied in formal statutes, and many provisions of the Universal Declaration have the force of customary law even for states, like the United States, which are not signatories to the conventions (Nagengast, Stavenhagen, and Kearney 1992).

[16] It is even mooted that Marshall's theory of social citizenship (Marshall 1963) corresponded to a unique post-war period of intensive welfarism, which was itself a response, first, to the global conflict between liberal and Fascist regimes, and, second, to the Cold War.

of benefits and favours. These lines of protection and allegiance come to structure the relationship between the individual and the state, so blurring the division between the public and private domains, and limiting equal access to and application of the law (Pérez-Díaz 1991: 31–4; Panizza 1993: 209).[17] The rule of law is therefore eroded both by the elite manipulation typical of patrimonialism (Paoli 1992: 153), and by the particular controls of clientelism, which prove inimical to the universal claims of civil and political rights (Fox 1994: 153).[18] Through its implicit rejection of these rights, clientelism acts as a system of political exclusion and retards the development of citizenship.

In political systems that are both clientelist and authoritarian the 'frame of meaning' which is civil rights takes on a double significance, and suggests two motives for citizenship struggles. First, as suggested above, the explicit denial of basic rights and freedoms by repressive governments reinforces the importance of these rights and creates a new agenda for political activism. It is the regime itself that provides the axis, and often creates the context for the struggle for rights. Second, the claims for universal rights (equality before the law, equality of political opportunity) create a direct challenge to the particularism of clientelistic controls (Foweraker 1993: chapter 10).[19] In sum, insofar as social movements are able to press for civil and political rights, they both seek to defend

[17] Panizza is commenting on the 'ambiguous nature of traditional liberalism' in Latin America (Panizza 1993: 209), and goes on to argue that the dominant ideologies of the continent (Catholicism, nationalism, corporatism, populism, and socialism) all have a holistic view of society that stands in opposition to the individualism of liberalism. Each of these ideologies expressed a grand narrative that attributed a central role to collective rather than individual actors, to the nation, people, or working class rather than the citizen; and each of them failed to express rights as rights of individuals irrespective of belief, ethnicity, sex, race, and language. These latter arguments are less convincing, perhaps, but do not detract from Panizza's main point.

[18] The communitarian position on rights is vitiated by clientelism. The communitarians argue that citizenship is about both individual rights and membership of a political community; and that social rights are a means to membership and therefore necessary to the exercise of civil and political rights. In short, the individual rights of citizenship require an effective public domain, and social rights provide the conditions of entry into that domain (Phillips 1991; Held 1989). But the social rights implicit in clientelism tend to deny such entry, and to impair the exercise of civil and political rights.

[19] This is one possible result rather than an iron law. In some circumstances social movements may simply seek to reconfigure clientelist controls in their own favour and so reproduce the pattern of patronage politics.

fundamental liberties and come to contest the culturally specific delivery of social rights.[20]

Normative versus Descriptive Accounts of Citizenship

Citizenship has a normative content, but most descriptions of this content are cross-cut with historical references because the norms have been established by a process of historical accretion. An ideal-typing of historical developments is often used to supply meta-phors for these norms (much in the way we have done here). The problem with this approach is that there are different genealogies of citizenship, or different pathways to its achievement. These will vary according to national political culture, the process of state-formation, and the balance of political force between those strug-gling for citizenship rights, on the one hand, and the dominant classes on the other. For these reasons Bendix suggested that 'for each nation state and for each set of institutions we (should) pin-point chronologies of the public measures taken and trace the sequ-ences of pressure and counterpressures, bargains and manoeuvres, behind each extension of rights beyond the strata of the tradition-ally privileged' (Bendix 1964: 79). The present enquiry sets out to provide a systematic response to Bendix's brief, through a compar-ative analysis of these sequences in its four case studies.

Citizenship struggles are not only struggles against the state but also struggles between contending forces within society. One of the key determinants of the different genealogies is 'dominant

[20] This empirical critique of the clientelist delivery of social rights is not equi-valent to a philosophical defence of liberalism. In the liberal view, civil and polit-ical rights are sufficient to equip each individual to compete in the social market place. Furthermore, since there can never be any consensus on social rights, there will never be a principled way of deciding the distribution of those rights. In the literature the debate between communitarian and liberal positions is usually resolved in one of two ways: either analytically, by demonstrating, for example, that liberal arguments assume communitarian positions insofar as rights emerge as secondary principles which are always derived from *a priori* ideas of the 'good' (Bellamy 1993: 53); or practically, by demonstrating that in real life no state apparatus or set of government policies will ever reflect a uniquely liberal or communitarian *Weltanshauung*, no more than they will enshrine uniquely negat-ive or positive rights. In this study, in contrast, the debate is resolved differently by explicating the dynamic relationship between the claims for the two types of rights (social versus civil and political) as it emerges from the struggle for citizen-ship. This point is developed in the following chapter where citizenship is not finally defined as a static set of rights but as a process.

class requirements for security' (Barbalet 1988: 43), and the achievement of this security through specific combinations of 'dominant economic class and the political and military rulers' (Mann 1987). In the European context these translated into the variable success of different *anciens régimes* in managing the demands of both the bourgeoisie and the proletariat in the wake of the Industrial Revolution. Their tactics are strongly reminiscent of the manipulatory politics of the authoritarian regimes in this study, and included both the denial of citizenship rights to large groups of the bourgeoisie, working class or peasantry (in any combination), and the granting of illusory rights that were vitiated by fraud and by arbitary and sudden (re)definitions of status.

Thus there are two distinct conceptual and historical approaches to citizenship. The first is characterized by the claim that citizenship has a normative legal and political content that is universal, without denying that this content was born of specific historical traditions and experiences that are condensed in the Enlightenment and the progress of modernism.[21] The second describes citizenship as the complex result of specific societies in specific moments, and, by extension, as the practical experience of particular peoples, or, more narrowly, as the specific status of individuals in relation to particular forms of political regime. The difficulty of reconciling these approaches is illustrated by citizenship rights. Normatively, these rights are recognized as universal and as having equal validity across time and culture. Descriptively, rights cannot be understood in this abstract fashion, but only in relation to a common culture which is achieved and expressed through the public sphere of a particular political community.[22] Without such a culture people cannot share the meanings that make rights apparent. Moreover, rights themselves are the result of a particular history, particular memories, and a particular tradition of rhetoric; while legal traditions compose incompatible histories that may imagine and deliver rights in very different ways.

Contemporarily there are good analytical reasons for (re)affirming the normative content of citizenship and rejecting the stronger forms of cultural relativism. Contemporary developments have

---

[21] Clearly the idea and practice of citizenship per se has a much longer pedigree, but the claim to a normative content corresponds to the modern form which develops with the transition to capitalism and with the making of the contemporary world system.

[22] It was Marshall who made the decisive advance in this regard by arguing that citizenship must be understood in relation to the institutional context in which rights are expressed (Marshall 1965).

created a (near) universal acceptance of the normative content of citizenship, and have endowed it with a concrete and constitutional presence in distinct political cultures. At the same time there are good methodological reasons for recognizing the different genealogies of citizenship, but for refusing the task of explicating them. This task would entail detailed enquiry into the ways in which the different constitutive elements combine and re-combine in history to produce the different genealogies, a task that is complicated by the amorphous nature of the elements[23] and the complexities of their combinations in different historical circumstances and national contexts. Lost in the trees, we would miss the significant opportunity for comparative citizenship research created by the spread of formal citizenship rights and the widespread social movement activity that aims to vindicate those rights and make them real.

Rights-in-Principle versus Rights-in-Practice

In recent decades the normative approach to citizenship rights has been mirrored in the analogous and equally normative development of a theory of human rights. Human rights are not citizenship rights, since there is a clear distinction between 'membership of a national political community' and 'the development of international law which subjects individuals, non-governmental organizations and governments to a new system of regulation' (Held 1989: 202).[24] Unlike citizenship rights, which must be expressed in nationally specific laws, human rights 'offer a meta-political moral framework for politics' containing criteria of what is just and what is not (Bellamy 1993: 46). Nonetheless, the rise of human rights doctrine has heightened recognition of the normative content of citizenship itself, and reinforces the consensus on the core cluster

[23] By way of illustration these elements might include the social structure and especially the balance between a free labour market and other forms of production that immobilize labour; state formation and especially the degrees of direct rule and of territorially homogeneous bureaucratic procedures for taxation and conscription; characteristic forms of political mediation and the constitution of political subjects; national political culture as it is configured by and expressed through ruling class strategies and the relationship between ruling classes and the state; popular political organization, strategy, and struggle; the balance between practices and discourses that promote citizenship as participation or that constitute citizenship rights as a means of promoting and protecting public contestation, and so on and so forth.

[24] To be a citizen of the world is to adopt a certain style, not to enjoy a certain status.

of civil and political rights, or the core set of modern citizenship components which effectively establish its presence or absence. Almost without exception, the rights which win such widespread recognition are civil, juridical, and political rights, and not social or community rights.

The global reach of this core set of rights is such that there now exist very few political regimes that remain uninfluenced by it. In other words, however diverse the genealogies, there has been a convergence of regimes towards a commensurable set of citizenship components and attributes. This is the force of the United Nations' International Bill of Human Rights, or the American Declaration of the Rights and Duties of Man.[25] These international treaties have accelerated the spread of formal rights, so that the normative content of citizenship is now embodied in the legal and constitutional forms of different political regimes across the globe, achieving a remarkable degree of cross-cultural consistency in a relatively short span of time. Yet it is readily admitted that the simple spread of such forms may leave political and juridical practices unchanged, with some regimes paying lip-service to the forms for the purposes of legitimation, or for the sake of international recognition, aid, or investment.[26] As a consequence, 'to unpack the domain of rights is to unpack both the rights citizens formally enjoy and the conditions under which citizens' rights are actually realized or enacted' (Held 1989: 201).

Most political constitutions of Latin America have guaranteed the basic bundle of citizenship rights since Independence, but there exists 'an appreciable gap between protection on paper and enforcement in practice' (Panizza 1993: 209). This gap was thrown into high relief by the military authoritarian regimes of the 1970s and 1980s and the widespread denial of these basic rights. The strategic requirements of the political opposition, and a reassessment by the Left of the value of formal rights and liberal democracy, sharpened the salience of the discourse of rights, and especially

---

[25] The American Declaration was adopted by the 9th International Conference of American States in Bogotá, Colombia, in 1948, which also saw the birth of the Organization of American States. The Declaration was the first instrument of its kind to be approved.

[26] There is every reason to believe that civil and political rights advance faster precisely because they have achieved a merely formal presence; whereas social rights have real and immediate distributive implications, and will remain imperceptible without the corresponding commitments to welfare provision and educational opportunity. But this formal presence is important, if only because it can act as a beacon for protest and a guide to political struggle (as we argue in Chapter 2).

human rights. Yet, despite the many recent transitions to democracy across the continent, rights violations continue, often unabated.[27] Indeed, the return of political rights sometimes seems to multiply the violations of civil rights. Thus the key variable is not the confection of the political regime but the rule of law, both 'what the law *says*, that is its substance, and the extent to which that law is *implemented*' (Anglade 1994: 240). The failure of the rule of law leaves a yawning gap between the formal legal structure and the real reach of the law, between rights-in-principle and rights-in-practice, and this gap (we will argue in Chapter 2) is of fundamental importance to the relationship between citizenship rights and social movements.

This gap only matters if citizenship is understood to have a normative content with cross-cultural validity. Yet this has been denied on the grounds that constitutional rights in Latin America are simply 'future goals for society to achieve' (Wiarda 1982: 34). In this view the imposition of 'world culture' offends the distinctive cultural traditions of Latin America, and leads to an unjust criticism of the gap: 'what is a violation of human rights in one cultural context may not be in another' (Wiarda 1982: 51). There is therefore little point in judging such violations 'by our own criteria of democracy and human rights' (Wiarda 1982: 49).[28] But, as this conclusion reveals, such an extreme form of cultural relativism represents an abdication of judgement that will inevitably vitiate any attempt at comparative enquiry.[29]

[27] 'There are hundreds of disappearances and extra-judicial executions every year; death squads, including both uniformed and off-duty members of the security forces, the army and the paramilitary groups, target peasants, trade union leaders, human rights workers, lawyers, academics and minor delinquents (including children). Those responsible are usually known but the authorities do little to bring them to justice' (Anglade 1994: 239).

[28] Wiarda sees Fitzgibbon and Johnson's definitions and measures of democracy and rights in Latin America (see Chapter 3) as 'a peculiarly North American set of expectations and practices inapplicable in culture-areas other than our own' (Wiarda 1982: 33). In his view, 'what such indices purport to measure—democracy—is not being measured at all. Instead, what is actually measured is the presence or absence of North American institutional molds in Latin America' (Wiarda 1982: 41).

[29] It is also a relativism that is founded more on assertion than evidence. As Schmitter observes, 'not only has this notion of a more "authentic" African, Asian ("Confucian"), Latin American ("Iberian") or just plain non-Western democracy repeatedly been used as a cover-up for autocratic practices, but it has rarely been accompanied by any evidence that citizens in the specific society in question actually possessed the distinctive values or political cultures that would require them to hold their rulers accountable in some different fashion' (Schmitter 1993: 14).

Designing Comparative Research

These strictures on more extreme forms of cultural relativism do not mean that political context and culture can simply be ignored when designing comparative citizenship research. Whether the focus is citizenship rights, social movement activity, or the relationship between them, it must take 'particular political institutions and cultural traditions' into account (Tarrow 1989: 4). Hence, the question of commensurability (Feyerabend 1975) remains central to the definition of the field of comparative enquiry. This problem is common to all comparative research, since 'it is hard to find a mind or method capable of dealing both with the richness of the individual case and with the common properties of many cases' (Tilly, Tilly, and Tilly 1975: 14). The Tillys suggest that 'comparative history offers a way forward', while Rustow opts for an 'intermediate course' between the 'inclusion of all relevant cases' and 'concentration on a single country' (Rustow 1970: 349).

The problem of commensurability becomes acute where the object of study, citizenship, is itself contested by normative and descriptive approaches. For this reason the enquiry opts for a 'comparative history' of a few cases which are selected for their political similarities (see Introduction). All four cases exhibit long periods of authoritarian rule under similar forms of political regime. They all describe a similar profile in the legal and political relationship between regime and individual, and reveal a visible if variable gap between rights-in-principle and rights-in-practice.[30] They all experience recurrent waves of social movement activity which, to a greater or lesser degree and more or less directly, come to claim or contest citizenship rights. And in all the cases the political regimes undergo slow and halting processes of political liberalization. In sum, in methodological terms, the cases were selected according to the 'mirror-image' of the 'the most similar systems design' (MSSD), which is suitable for studying 'similarities . . . in similar cases' (Faure 1994: 317).

---

[30] The comparability of rights-in-principle, or of the constitutional and legal forms themselves, was also important. In many modern constitutions 'rights are increasingly defined as alienable, or subject to restriction by the state, rather than as inalienable, or inherent in the individual without restriction' (Boli-Bennett 1981: 174), and this was certainly true of the constitutional configurations of Franco's Spain, military Brazil, Pinochet's Chile, and, in lesser degree, the PRI's Mexico. Moreover, these are all highly legalist political cultures, as illustrated in Boli-Bennett's cross-national statistical survey, where Latin America scored highest on both the Citizen Rights and the Citizen Duties Indices (Boli-Bennett 1981: 182).

The cases were selected to create an effective laboratory for the comparative study of the relationship between citizenship rights and social movements. They all exemplify authoritarian regimes where the practical denial of these rights was deep and durable. But it is worth insisting that what is at issue is rights and the rule of law, and not democracy or democratic transitions. It is the rule of law and not democracy that protects citizenship rights, even if democracy may contribute to protect the rule of law by making government accountable.[31] But in Latin America it appears that democratic government is not always accountable. On the one hand, competitive elections may not take government through the 'democratic threshold' (Fox 1994: 181) because 'elections are not necessarily free, and representation is not necessarily genuine' (Sartori 1987: 31). On the other, the separation of powers proves ineffective because of 'delegative democracy' (O'Donnell 1992) and the lack of executive accountability to Congress or the judiciary. Consequently, it cannot be assumed that democratic transition assures 'fundamental rights' (Fox 1994: 151) and equality before the law (Moisés 1993). The point is not that democratic transitions from authoritarian rule necessarily diminish citizenship rights, but that the outcome is indeterminate where formal democratic arrangements cannot provide sufficient support for the rule of law.[32]

---

[31] In the United States it was the impeachment trial of Supreme Court justice Samuel Chase in 1805, and the treason trial of former vice-president Aaron Burr in 1807, which confirmed the independence of the federal judiciary and the autonomy of the juridical process. It is the combination of the institutional independence of the judiciary with equality before the law that creates the political conditions for the expansion of citizenship rights.

[32] Three different, but not incompatible, explanations have been advanced for this state of affairs. First, there is the territorial and functional breakdown of government authority under the impact of economic crisis and social decay. The symptoms are crime, illegal police activity, torture and illegal executions, the negation of minority rights, the impunity of the drug trade, the abandonment of children, and the disappearance of any defensible 'public space' (O'Donnell 1993). Second, there is the emergence of a culture of 'paralegality' which blurs the division between the legal and the illegal by creating a permissable illegality which is simultaneously illegal but accepted and unpunished. Some see this culture as a legacy of the 'anti-subversive' operations of the military-authoritarian regimes (Panizza 1993). Third, there is a more general argument that the democratic transitions are 'combined and uneven', leading to a 'composite of "partial regimes"' (Schmitter 1992) that are unintegrated, variegated and often set against each other. In addition it is probable that the political culture of the administrative apparatus of the state retains authoritarian traits, and that the essential liberal separation of state and civil society is difficult to achieve or maintain without a vigilant associationalism throughout that society (Munck 1993: 494). Consequently, and similarly to other major transitional moments in citizenship history, like the

If commensurability may be increased both by controlling for context (mirror-image of MSSD), it may also be deepened by controlling for content through the provision of a parsimonious definition of a core set of citizenship rights. This core set includes both the individual legal rights of civil citizenship and the participatory rights of political citizenship (D. King 1987). The civil rights assure liberty of the person, freedom of speech, thought, and association, and the due process of equality before the law; while, in the formulation of Article 21 of the International Bill of Human Rights, political rights assure both suffrage and equality of political opportunity. This definition of citizenship is normative in the sense that these citizenship rights derive from 'normative statements of democracy (for evaluating procedures) and justice (for evaluating outcomes)' (Kymlicka and Norman 1994: 368). In our view this core set of rights represents the non-negotiable and irreducible content of the modern form of citizenship.

There appears to be a close correspondence between this core set of citizenship rights and the liberal defence of citizenship as composed of 'negative rights'.[33] Certainly, as argued above, this definition of citizenship excludes the social rights associated with state welfarism. But it is worth repeating that the exclusion is made not for philosophical or political but for methodological reasons. Social rights mitigate economic uncertainty and market outcomes, and so may be construed as modern means of social cohesion, which seek social consensus and bind anomic and fragmented capitalist society to itself. As such, social rights entail a fundamental reconstruction

---

expansion of electoral participation in the years after World War I, there is both more democracy and more repression, more rights and less rights (or more formal rights and less capacity to exercise those rights).

[33] For the liberals, citizenship is about legal rights which allow the pursuit of individual purposes which do not harm others. Its ethic is composed of rules which secure the principle of equality, and the purpose of government is to provide the legal framework for these rules. Moreover, citizenship equality is inevitably a legal and political status and not a social or economic one because there is and can be no consensus which might allow political rather than market processes to allocate citizenship rewards. In other words, since there is no shared morality of social justice, government cannot be expected to secure such justice. Similarly, just as the liberal framework takes account of normative dissensus, so it promotes pluralism by providing the preconditions for autonomous choices, and the conditions for dialogue between different views. Thus, it may be said that the liberal argument does require a common adherence to notions of mutual tolerance, but, beyond this, liberals do not think it politically viable to pursue any vision of 'the good society'. Indeed, liberals believe that the promotion of such a vision by government initiative will not develop citizenship but damage it.

of the core set of citizenship rights, so restricting the possible scope of comparative citizenship research by constricting commensurablity.

Last but not least, the argument will seek to ensure commensurability through taking care to specify the possible range of contemporary connections between collective action and citizenship rights. This is the task of the next chapter, and it begins with the assumption that social movements cannot be explained without an assessment of the rights which may act to capacitate or empower them, just as rights cannot be understood without an appreciation of the concerns and struggles which give rise to them or which vindicate them. The question of commensurability remains central simply because the point of the enquiry is to provide the conceptual underpinnings of *measurable* comparisons. In the past, it is now evident, the analysis of the relationship between social movements and citizenship was pursued in a broadly philosophical and sometimes speculative vein, cross-cut by historical reference. The present objective is to take the historical arguments into the context of the contemporary struggles for citizenship rights under authoritarian regimes, and provide measures of the mutual influence of citizenship rights and social movements both through time and across cultures. The aim is to improve our understanding of the relationship between the two both in the past and in the present.

Individual Rights, Social Movements, and Waves of Protest

Universal Rights and Particular Restrictions

Citizenship as a universal status implies that all citizens must be the same and equally capable of knowing and acting on the common good. The history of citizenship shows that this principle of commonality has also served as a principle of exclusion (Young 1989), and the 'Western' variant of this history can be described as a gradual extension of civil and political rights from 'white property-owning Protestant men . . . to women, the working class, Jews and Catholics, blacks, and other previously excluded groups' (Kymlicka and Norman 1994: 354). In short, alongside the expansion of the rights of citizenship there was also an expansion of the class of citizens, as new categories of persons came to qualify for citizenship (Barbalet 1988: 29). Consequently, the advance of citizenship in terms of the rights enjoyed by the population of any political community can clearly be measured along two axes: first it can be measured in depth, to see what civil and political rights have been legally and constitutionally encoded; and second it can be measured in breadth, to gauge the extension of these rights to the different groups, sectors, classes, and regions of the community. It will be clear that either or both axes may contribute to create the gap between rights-in-principle and rights-in-practice (see Chapter 1).

In Latin America and Spain many groups were traditionally excluded from the rights of citizenship. The extremes of social inequality tended to deny these rights to the poor and deprived. The sharp division between city and countryside tended to do the same to country-dwellers, 'since they have almost always faced indifference, if not prejudice, from a now predominantly urban society which has historically treated rural workers as non-citizens' (Navarro 1994: 150). And greater or lesser degrees of institutionalized racism also excluded most indigenous groups at most times.[1] Moreover, the highly variegated pattern of political power-holding has also excluded certain regions and sectors from the political community, and it is this form of exclusion that is central to the recent critiques of citizenship in these countries.

There is a growing awareness that national regimes are compromised by territorial fiefs or 'sultanates' that contain particular, patrimonial, and 'private circuits of power' (O'Donnell 1993: 130). These 'redoubts of persistent authoritarian clientelism can coexist with new enclaves of pluralist tolerance' and so create 'subnational regimes' (Fox 1994: 157). In Brazil these fiefs imbue the political system with a high degree of 'territorial and functional heterogeneity' (O'Donnell 1993: 129), while in Mexico 'official respect for human rights varies directly by the victim's race and region' (Fox 1994: 157 n.18).[2] In other words, there are many regions where the law's writ does not run, and where citizenship cannot be upheld by the rule of law. In particular, although political rights may spread to these regions through real or bastard forms of electoral politics, civil rights remain precarious and under constant attack. This 'chaotic mosaic' of rights (Jelin 1993) creates conditions of 'low intensity citizenship' (O'Donnell 1993: 130) where rights-in-practice fall far short of rights-in-principle.

Consequently, as argued in Chapter 1, this study sees citizenship as a matter of rights and the rule of law first, and democracy second. Contemporary democratic transitions tend to lead to political systems that are 'part authoritarian and part free' (Pye 1990: 13), that is to 'hybrid political regimes' (Moisés 1993: 14) which are 'not yet theorized' (O'Donnell 1993). The academic response is to call for more subtle typologies to capture the strange mixture of authoritarian and democratic attributes of this 'schizophrenic state' (O'Donnell 1993). But the combination of clientelistic forms of electoral politics with the partial and variegated presence of citizenship rights is nothing new, and would effectively describe many of the pre-1930 oligarchic regimes of Latin America, as well as Republican Spain; while the search for 'finer shades of typologies' (Pye

---

[1] Since 1917 Mexico has had the most advanced Constitution in the continent, in citizenship terms, and state agencies and programmes have consistently sought to integrate its indigenous groups into the national political culture. Even here, however, it was only in 1992 that the Mexican Senate finally approved a constitutional amendment recognizing indigenous rights.

[2] Thus, citizens' groups from the north are treated quite differently by officialdom than groups 'from the much poorer, largely indigenous southern areas' (Fox 1994: 157).

1990: 13) will only create arcane debates that mix and confuse normative and descriptive accounts of democracy (Sartori 1987). For these reasons, this study suggests a different strategy that shifts the focus away from regime definition, and towards the real depth and breadth of citizenship rights in the political community; away from the commanding heights of the state, and towards the real political experience of social actors on the ground.[3]

Universal Rights and Specific Struggles

The historical attraction of individual rights is that they are universal, insofar as they can apply to all individuals equally. But they tend to emerge from struggles that are specific and circumscribed, insofar as they may involve culturally, sectorally, regionally, or ethnically specific actors. Once organized in social movements, these actors may make idiosyncratic and restricted demands. They may use idioms that are not easily assimilable to citizenship codes. They may be embroiled in power relations which are particularistic and patrimonial. And, above all, they may aspire to rights, such as professional rights or corporate rights, which are not universal, and which may or may not serve as a proxy for citizenship rights.

There is more than one way of posing this problem. First, there is the tension, already signalled, between group or sectional interests and the general interest. Social movement theorists make much of group or movement identity, which tends to be seen as a good thing (Foweraker 1995: chapter 2). But how can the specific demands that derive from specific identities be reconciled with the universal concerns of citizenship? Does politics begin with the group or the wider community (Phillips 1991: 82)? Second, there is the (closely related) tension between the heterogeneity of social movements based on group identities of gender, race, community, or workplace, and the homogeneity of citizenship. For citizenship is

[3] In this perspective citizenship is viewed as a process which is captured through time-series data on both rights and associational activity of different kinds. In this respect it differs from Gasiorowski's pooled cross-sectional analysis of discrete moments of regime change (from democratic to non- or semi-democratic and vice versa) which 'necessarily focuses on broad, systematic causal processes that hold across time and space rather than more idiosyncratic causal processes that hold only at certain times or in certain countries or regions' (Gasiorowski 1995: 893–4). Yet we believe that our more contextually sensitive measures can also achieve systematic and comparative analysis (see Chapter 3).

not only understood as rights that should be extended to everyone, regardless of who or what they are (so abstracting from the specificities of identity), but also as a status that is common rather than differentiated, and universal insofar as it represents a rule of law that applies to everyone in the same way (so possibly suppressing the specificities of identity) (Young 1989: 250). Finally, there is another tension (analogous rather than related) between the (struggle for) autonomy of social movements and the heteronomy of citizenship, which is defined and upheld by the state (see Chapter 1).

These theoretical debates themselves reflect political agendas. On one side, it is argued that universal rights cannot correct historical wrongs, so special rights are also required. If society is socially differentiated, then citizenship should be so as well (Young 1989: 251–3).[4] On the other, the zero-sum view retorts that claims to special rights can only succeed 'at the cost of driving out all rival assertions' (Bellamy 1993: 63). The former view appears to provide a warrant for social movement activity, but only by sacrificing its contribution to universal and equal rights. The latter seems to deny that such activity can make citizenship more inclusive (Bellamy 1993: 60), and to reject social movement theory as a 'vanguard theory of the active and intense small group' (Sartori 1987: 114). In our opinion neither argument is convincing on its own terms, but, more importantly, they both repose in the political luxury of plural society and liberal democratic government. In the very different authoritarian political contexts of the countries in this study, it is difficult to argue that social movements diminish or damage citizenship rights.

There is little doubt that in all these countries the majority of social movements are initially motivated by immediate, concrete, and material demands of an economic, corporate, or communal kind. But these social and economic demands usually precede and are transformed into claims for civil and political rights (Foweraker 1989, 1993, 1995; Foweraker and Craig 1990). Since the initial social demands can rarely be satisfied in their entirety, and are often restricted, repressed, reversed, or delayed, they frequently generate further demands which have to do with the civil and political

---

[4] In our view any notion of differentiated citizenship is fraught with difficulty, since the organization of political rule on the basis of rights or claims that derive from group membership is sharply distinct from a concept of government based on citizenship. Most critically, the notion violates the principle of equality because granting rights to some but not others on the basis of group membership will set up a hierarchy of rights where some are more equal than others.

conditions for putting demands and making claims; and these demands are more directly legal and political in content. In different language, struggles over the control and distribution of material and communal resources finally come to 'challenge the *legitimacy* of the dominant system's decisions over this material control and distribution' (Paoli 1992: 145). Thus, in authoritarian conditions, specific struggles and universal rights are linked through the citizenship process, since the spotty presence of social demands catalyses the struggle for these rights. This conclusion is confirmed by the Latin American literature that until the 1980s, broadly speaking, tended to focus on the material struggles that reflected the popular demands of peasants, workers, women, and poor urban residents; but that later reflected the progressive shift to claims for basic civil and political rights (Jelin 1993). The demand-making of social movements was increasingly directed to the core set of citizenship rights.[5]

In all these countries the most salient of these movements was the labour movement, which also tended to take the lead in the struggle for citizenship rights (see Chapter 5). This appears counter-intuitive to those who argue that the labour movement fought primarily for special or 'economic-corporate' prerogatives (Gramsci 1973), and so tended to trade civil and political rights for social rights (Malloy 1987: 254). But the conundrum is again resolved through a sense of historical process. In both modern Spain and Latin America the labour movement was often the first to win rights, in the sense that citizenship rights were 'limited to those rights represented by their place in the productive process, recognized by law' (dos Santos 1979). But the 'regulated citizenship' achieved through the struggle for 'economic rights' (Held 1989)[6] provided a political platform for subsequent demands for civil and political rights, and eventually made the labour movement into

---

[5] This proposition is demonstrated in Chapter 5.

[6] 'Economic rights' are those rights won by the labour movement in the workplace, and, in Held's view, they must be distinguished from civil, political, and social rights. At first sight they are equivalent to Marshall's 'industrial rights'. But Marshall saw these rights as civil rights, since they strengthen the hand of the workers in the market place. However, Marshall also recognized that the collective use of civil rights by trade unions to make claims on employers was anomalous, since civil rights 'were in origin intensely individual' (Marshall 1963: 93). It will be apparent that these debates turn on the relationship between the individual rights of citizenship and collective action: individual civil rights may empower social movements, just as collective action can win individual rights. The precise relationship between them will depend on the historical, political, and institutional context.

the vanguard of the citizenship struggle.[7] The movement's demands expanded as it wrestled with the 'official institutions and codified organizational structures built to limit its actions' (Paoli 1992: 144–6), a process which accelerated under the authoritarian regimes.

The Impact of Rights on Social Movements

Citizenship defines membership of a political community, and so invites the excluded to struggle for inclusion; and an awareness of citizenship rights can provide both a measure of exclusion and a promise of new capacities. Anyone with a sense of rights will treat their infringement as 'a uniquely serious matter' (Barbalet 1988: 17), but 'rights are much more significant for those without social and political power than they are for the powerful' (Barbalet 1988: 18). The historical record shows that the 'obverse of integration' in the political community 'is not disintegration nor even conflict but movement' (Barbalet 1988: 97); and the Latin American reality demonstrates that, although it is difficult for the disadvantaged to exercise individual rights in their daily lives, there has been a long history of social movements that seek to vindicate and expand such rights. This confirms the 'central role of the notion of rights in shaping new forms of thought and action' (Paoli 1992: 145), which in contemporary Latin America includes the rise of urban social movements, the women's movements, and the black movement, not to mention the 'truly civil war around a right to land which may be ruled by peasants' and rural workers' conceptions' (Paoli 1992: 147).

In this interpretation rights assume a 'symbolic power', especially once they become the 'current language of political debate' (Paoli 1992: 147). In Latin America this process was accelerated by the military and authoritarian regimes of the 1970s and 1980s, since the paradoxical result of their oppressive policies was that the 'popular classes' began to appropriate the discourse of human rights, making them 'into synonyms of the overall rights of the marginalized majorities' (Faria 1989: 95). In other words, the

---

[7] Once again these assertions are grounded in past programmes of empirical research in Brazil, Spain, and Mexico (Foweraker 1981, 1989, 1993). The case of Chile during the Pinochet period may be different. On the one hand, the labour movement was heavily repressed, with its organizations smashed and its leaders exiled or executed. On the other, Chilean civil society in the pre-Pinochet years had already developed a fairly broad-based culture of rights, and this cultural memory remained available to the struggle against the dictatorship.

emergence of a discourse of rights acts as an 'associational idiom' (Tarrow 1993*a*) that both stimulates social movement activity and inspires it with a more proactive character.[8] Evidence for this is found both in the dissemination of rights demands across social movements and in the shift of the political centre of gravity of specific movements towards a rights discourse and rights demands (see Chapter 5).[9] At the same time the discourse of rights plays a key role in translating the specific (communal, sectoral, or class) demands of particular movements into a common language, and in facilitating the construction of political alliances and movement networks. In this way the lack of resources available to social movements can be overcome by the 'synthesizing force' (Bowles and Gintis 1987: 155) of political discourse, which brings together 'coalitions of people with overlapping claims, sometimes purposefully constructed, but often contingent' (Tarrow 1995: 10).[10]

The Impact of Social Movements on Rights

However important the discourse of rights, symbols alone do not have the power to instigate collective action. The discourse of rights

[8] Tarrow reports Sewell's argument that the French Revolution created a new 'associational idiom around the idea of a state based on natural right and contract, an idiom that extended to the ways people conceived of association in civil society', so that 'rather than mounting *reactive* and *competitive* challenges based on corporatism, the French increasingly made *proactive* challenges through the associational vocabulary that was a heritage of their Revolution' (Tarrow 1993*a*: 73). Tarrow disagrees that this associational idiom on its own can explain these changes; but, in the contemporary realities of Spain and Latin America, we think that this idiom—the discourse of rights—influences both the incidence and the form of social movement activity (see Chapter 6).

[9] Once again, it is the overt suppression of rights by authoritarian regimes, whether in Spain or Latin America, that contributes to raise the profile of rights and makes them so central to social movement activity. In Tarrow's account of social protest in the Italy of the late 1960s and early 1970s demands that could be characterized as specific rights demands only accounted for 3.5 per cent of total demands (Tarrow 1989: 124).

[10] As already suggested, therefore, the discourse of rights acts as a 'master frame' for social movement activity in the contemporary period. In the civil rights movement in the United States the core notion of 'equality of opportunity' acted as an effective bridge (based on traditional North American political rhetoric) between the movement's main internal constituency, the southern black middle class, and the white liberal 'conscience constituents' whose support was necessary to bolster it from the outside (Tarrow 1994*b*: chapter 7). The discourse of human rights acted as an analogous bridge between the movements of the urban poor and the urban middle classes in the Latin America of the 1970s and 1980s.

has no independent capacity for action, and cannot simply 'shower meanings on the society below' (Tarrow 1994*b*: chapter 7). On the contrary, this discourse can only be effective when attached to social actors and organizations. Social movements, for their part, do not merely perceive or receive rights as symbols, but are active in discovering, shaping, and disseminating these rights. On the one hand, social movements often emerge from contexts where rights are not apparent or are plainly denied, and it is through the process of organization and demand-making that a knowledge of rights arises. In this way movements are deeply involved in naming and interpreting grievances, and connecting them to other grievances within a common 'rights frame' (Snow and Benford 1992). As suggested above, their original demands may be transformed in the process. On the other, social movements are both schools for understanding rights and vehicles for disseminating ideas and perceptions of rights. Participants learn their rights lessons through the rigours of organization and the debates over strategy, so learning the language of rights 'through collective action itself' (Tarrow 1990: 21). Thus the rise of the movements slowly spreads this language 'throughout society' (Paoli 1992: 144). In political contexts where individual rights are restricted, social movements may be defined as associations that can make plausible claims to make a perceptible impact on the exercise or extension of such rights.

In the early life of modern social movements, at the end of the eighteenth century, they drew on two kinds of resource, print and association. The slow creation of a public sphere meant that the emergent commercial press could make potential activists aware of one another and conscious of their common grievances (B. Anderson 1983; Tarrow 1995). But contemporarily the efficacy of the print or electronic media in disseminating demands may be severely curtailed by state censorship, and by the repressive response of authoritarian governments; and in societies where the public sphere has been suppressed by violence or segmented by clientelist controls, whatever knowledge of rights may subsist is 'left to survive in isolated, silent and therefore inoffensive niches' (Sartori 1987: 101). In these circumstances social movements can play a vital role in diffusing social struggles and spreading a statement of (sometimes specific) demands in terms of common rights. Yet, far from being an automatic outcome of mobilization, this process depends on active leadership and an equally active creation of rights claims. By speaking the language of rights to both people and state, these leaders define and delimit a field of political action, which is then expanded by the iteration and reiteration of rights in assemblies, meetings, marches, and demonstrations, as well as in petitions and broadsheets. Thus, the discourse of rights cannot simply be read like a 'text' that is independent of social struggle (Tarrow 1994*b*: chapter 7): it only has meaning in the social movements that articulate it and make it politically potent.

Implicit here is an idea of individuals who constitute themselves as citizens of the political community by organizing in social movements to press their claims in terms of rights. This interpretation of social movement activity derives from the 'constitutive character of action', or 'the notion of becoming-by-acting' which 'asserts that individuals constitute themselves in important part through their joint projects' (Bowles and Gintis 1987: 151–2).[11] This does not deny that common life circumstances, and especially the shared experience of oppression and manipulation, may provide a basis of social solidarity; but it does mean that such shared experience is not a sufficient basis for collective action, and that the processes of communication, organization, and strategic choice are essential to the shaping of social movement activity. These are the lessons of ground-level studies of grass-roots movements in Spain (Foweraker 1989) and Latin America (Foweraker 1993, 1995); and this self-constitution of citizens indicates that, at least in the adverse conditions created by authoritarian regimes, citizenship is an active principle of political contestation and participation.

The Mutuality of Social Movements and Citizenship Rights

Citizens constitute themselves because 'rights are created through being exercised, and . . . it is the exercise of rights which generates the capacities associated with them' (Barbalet 1988: 16). For rights to be exercised there must be association, since the civility or 'civicness' (Putnam 1994) that supports a sense of rights 'can only be learned in the associational networks of civil society' (Walzer 1992: 104). The association implicit in social movements derives in some

---

[11] In a fuller statement, Bowles and Gintis 'argue that an adequate conception of action must be based on the notion that people produce themselves and others through their actions. According to this conception, action is neither instrumental towards the satisfaction of given wants nor expressive of objective interests, but it is an aspect of the very generation of wants and specification of objective interests. Individuals and groups, accordingly, act not merely to *get* but to *become*. The politics of becoming, we believe, provides a central corrective to both the normative and the explanatory dimensions of traditional political theory' (Bowles and Gintis 1987: 161).

degree from the shared experience of community, work, gender, and sheer physical survival (and hence from a sense of mutual obligations), but also depends on organization, leadership, and a knowledge of the strategic terrain of struggle. Insofar as the movements are motivated by a struggle for rights, a sense or perception of rights can only come through the struggle itself. Indeed, 'if they have a "culture" it is not the culture of association in general that animates them but the culture of struggle' (Tarrow 1993*a*: 75). Hence, it is not just a question of vision,[12] but of engagement (in the French sense). It is through struggling for rights that rights are defined and known; and since social movements change direction and orientation over time, so the meaning of rights changes (Held 1989: 200).

One example of this is the way that women's rights have emerged from the struggles of urban social movements in Latin America, even in the absence of women's movements or of a self-conscious women's agenda (Foweraker 1995: chapter 2). It is the fact of women-getting-organized that redefines the dividing lines between public and private and so sharpens perceptions of women's rights. Similar processes occur in other areas of social, community, and working life, so that the language of rights becomes a way of demanding an active role in 'democratic decision-making' and active participation in 'workplaces, communities, groups and self-defined public spaces' (Paoli 1992: 153). It is therefore the combination of social movement and a discourse of rights, and their imbrication in communal 'demands for justice' (Paoli 1992: 148), that vindicates and creates a public domain. In the perspective of a social struggle for justice, movements and rights do not merely coexist or cohabit in this domain, they make each other, and so may be understood to be mutually constitutive.[13] Put differently, 'while social movements may advance the development of citizenship, citizenship rights facilitate the emergence of social movements' (Barbalet 1988: 97).[14]

[12] Messianic movements may be thought to have too much vision, and an immature sense of organizational, logistical, and strategic constraints.
[13] The rights of modern citizenship may encourage those struggling for a justice that is defined in their own terms and on their own ground but is denied by existing patterns of social and political power. But an understanding or knowledge of such rights will inevitably arise out of the struggle itself, so the relationship between the two will be both complex and reciprocal. More than cohabitation, therefore, it is a marriage.
[14] This relationship is complex both for intrinsic reasons and because it is mediated by other actors in civil society, especially elite actors, and by state structure and form of regime. It is also a relationship that is not configured by a constant

Modular Forms of Movement and a Common Language of Rights

The rise of the modern social movement has mainly been interpreted in terms of changing forms of collective action (see Chapter 1). It is suggested that collective action that was communal, corporate, and primarily reactive changed to action that was associational and proactive; or that collective action that was local and sponsored changed to action that was national and autonomous. Most influentially, it is argued that the specificities of local and regional forms were filtered into a defined 'repertoire of contention' that underpinned the modern movement, sharpened its strategic response to its political and institutional environment, and prepared it for sustained campaigns of collective action (Tilly 1978, 1979, 1984). But Tarrow has objected, correctly, that 'some of the most spectacular modern movements combine corporate and communal identities with proactive claims, whereas reactive and competitive claims are typical defensive reactions of such modern secondary associations as trade unions and trade associations' (Tarrow 1993*a*: 74). Collective action did indeed increase in scope and change in style but its repertoire was not so much fixed as 'modular', meaning 'first, that its forms were relatively few and were very flexible; second, that they were distinct from the identity of those who used them and those they were aimed at; and third, that they could be adopted by different groups in a variety of settings and serve as a common denominator for different groups acting together or in series' (Tarrow 1993*a*: 77).

The newly modular form of collective action had a clear strategic value in 'facilitating the formation of coalitions across localities and around general claims among people who hardly knew each other' (Tarrow 1993*a*: 81). In large part these modular forms arose during the period of state-formation in the nineteenth century, and the state helped to shape them by 'standardizing the procedures for citizens to use in their relations with the authorities' and 'providing cues for broad mobilization and frameworks in which challenging groups could compare their situations . . . and make alliances with those with similar or parallel grievances' (Tarrow 1993*a*:

---

flow of mutual influence but by the halting step-by-step process of history, with its pauses, deviations, and contingent outcomes. But each period of struggle can leave 'a residue of policy and cultural change, of new social actors within the political community, and of new forms of collective action that have been forced into the routine repertoire of participation' (Tarrow 1990: 5).

83). Furthermore, long cycles of protest refined the modularity of the repertoire (Tarrow 1993*b*: 284), which then served to underpin 'the national cycles of protest of the next century' (Tarrow 1993*a*: 85).

Tarrow's rather triumphalist view of the rise of the modern social movement, in relation to the rather benign role of the state, can be usefully compared to Tilly's more sober account of the relationship between citizens and the state in the nineteenth century (Tilly 1990). Instead of the impetus of newly modular forms of action, these citizens must use the 'weapons of the weak' (Scott 1985) to resist more or less doggedly state attempts to extract resources and wage war. This broadly Weberian perspective betrays a certain pessimism about the growth of legal-rational and bureaucratic authority, with citizenship imagined as a modulated form of subjection (cf. Foucault 1977*a*). Only in the later stages of the 'nationalization' and specialization of the state does popular collective action itself become more nationalized and autonomous. To the degree that the state begins to influence more directly the lives of workers, peasants, and ordinary people, then they begin to band together to make claims on the state and defend their rights. But even this relatively optimistic conclusion may depend on a selective reading of national histories. The majority accounts argue that it was the early bourgeois revolutions of the eighteenth to mid-nineteenth centuries which promoted liberal rule and strengthened legal citizenship, while later revolutions, designed to push through capitalist industrialization from above, were far less favourable to civil and political freedoms (Kimmel 1990, *après* Moore 1973).[15]

Nonetheless, modularity is a key concept for understanding the diffusion of social movement activity in the context of contemporary authoritarian regimes, and in our comparative cases in particular (so long as it is tempered by a little Tillyesque pessimism). Moreover, the shaping of modular forms by the modern state-in-formation

[15] In illustration, Mommsen agrees that the state passed through a liberal and emancipatory phase in the early and middle nineteenth century as it mustered force to combat and remove the die-hard elements of the old regime; but in the latter part of the century (especially in Italy and Germany) the dominant classes used state power to reinforce the political and cultural homogeneity of the nation as a means of projecting political strength externally. The integralist view of the national state and the growth of intolerant nationalisms were intensified by the politics of high imperialism. Citizenship then took on the negative connotations of forcible conformity, and aggression against ethnic, religious, and social minorities, ending in the anti-Semitism of National Socialism and the holocaust (Mommsen 1990).

provides significant analogies for the rise of contemporary movements within institutions chartered by these regimes, or on a legal and institutional terrain configured by them (Foweraker 1995: chapter 3). But it is surprising that Tarrow explicitly rejects any linkage between modular movements and 'a new cultural vocabulary' (Tarrow 1993*a*: 78),[16] especially since he emphasizes that the newly modular forms created 'a key role for movement entrepreneurs whose speciality was diffusing word of new claims and designing ways of making them' (Tarrow 1993*a*: 78). In our view, on the contrary, these modular forms emerge in tandem with the new discourse of rights that frames social movement struggles for citizenship. Just as collective action becomes more modular and anchored in new networks of relationships, so collective aspirations and demands come to be expressed in a newly common language of rights; and just as modular forms facilitate the diffusion of the language, so the language catalyses the spread and increases the scope of citizenship struggles. In all of our cases it is the combination of new forms of movement with a new language of rights that reinforces claims to autonomy in the context of clientelism and co-optation, and sustains mobilization against demobilizing authoritarian regimes.

Social Movements and Waves of Protest

At first it appears that the political and cultural specificity of social movements will make them difficult to compare cross-nationally. This perception is reinforced by the theoretical literature's obsessive enquiry into the identity of social movements (Foweraker 1995: chapter 2). But there is nothing essential about social movement identity. On the contrary, in behavioural terms it is clear that identity is a dependent variable, which depends, at least in part, on prior organization, leadership, and strategic decision-making (even if it is finally achieved, if ever, in relation to multiple others) (Foweraker 1993: chapter 12). In other words, identity has to do with nothing more than maintaining a degree of organizational cohesion and

---

[16] In an earlier publication Tarrow had suggested that cycles of protest were capable of opening up a new 'universe of discourse' and of 'permitting once unacceptable claims to be made and even sometimes accepted' (Tarrow 1990: 49); and in his most recent book he suggests that the rights frame of the civil rights movement in the United States 'was expanded and became a collective action frame of the movement only when it was combined with an innovative action repertoire'— which included non-violent direct action (Tarrow 1994*b*: chapter 7).

loyalty in specific circumstances and at specific moments, and so is both dependent and conjunctural. Movements are therefore highly precarious constructs which are composed of different groups with widely different beliefs and different strategies for action, and these groups coalesce around salient issues and demands (Kriesi 1988).

To compare social movements therefore is not to compare social movement identity but social movement activity. Social movements mobilize in order to press demands or protest against social conditions, government policy, political repression, and so forth. Protest is 'the use of disruptive collective action aimed at institutions, elites, authorities, or other groups, on behalf of the collective goals of the actors or of those they claim to represent' (Tarrow 1989: 8); and the incidence of protest 'is the major indicator of the level of mobilization to the population and the elite' (Tarrow 1989: 9). Consequently social movement activity can be studied in terms of the incidence of protest, the number of people protesting, the kinds of people protesting, and the reasons for the protest. The incidence of protest means the amount of protest over time; the people protesting can be categorized according to social sector, occupation or gender (as in rural, urban, workers, students, women, popular sectors); and the reasons for protest can be known from the principal demands of the movement (Foweraker 1993: chapter 12). The specific weight of the labour movement in most contemporary protest makes it important to distinguish strike from non-strike movement activity, and it is sometimes possible and perhaps even desirable to distinguish violent from non-violent protest.[17] Specific movements may then be discerned 'from the clustering of protest events around similar social actors, common grievances, and characteristic forms of action' (Tarrow 1989: 364).

Social movements are specialists in demand-making, and so it is crucial to establish the nature of their demands. Demands at least have the virtue of being explicit, but since they are conditioned by organization, leadership, knowledge of the legal and institutional context, and an appreciation of the balance of force, they cannot always be taken at face value. This caveat applies a fortiori to movements that emerge under authoritarian regimes. In liberal democratic contexts movements may challenge interest groups, trade

[17] The record of violent protest 'depends largely on officially collected data, a source that suffers from the state's obsessive interest in violence and subversion' (Tarrow 1990: 27). Tarrow also follows Gamson in suggesting that the correlation between violent protest and collective action is both low and unpredictable (Gamson 1975: 74), but this finding may be specific to the history of the United States.

unions, political parties, and other actors in civil society to take up their demands. But in authoritarian polities demands will almost inevitably be addressed to the regime and may imply an antagonistic and dangerous relationship with the state. For this reason demand-making in these polities will inevitably come to focus on rights (including the right to make demands), and especially civil and political rights (Foweraker 1995: chapter 3).[18] In other words, whether the demands are reactive or proactive, expressive or instrumental, material or political, they will tend sooner or later to take the form of rights demands; and so it is important both to distinguish such demands and trace their evolution over time (as we do in Chapter 5). Ceteris paribus, the balance of demand-making by social movements in authoritarian polities should shift progressively towards rights demands as mobilization increases and protest intensifies.

The development of social movement activity is clearly critical to its analysis, for only 'by relating protest events to one another over space and time' is it possible to discover their 'underlying dynamic' (Tarrow 1989: 29). For Tarrow this dynamic regularly describes the 'cycle of protest' which serves as a 'guiding beacon' of his research (Tarrow 1989: 29). Protest comes to compose such a cycle 'when it is diffused to several sectors of the population, is highly organized, and is widely used as an instrument to put forward demands' (Tarrow 1989: 15). This initial account of the cycle is general enough to apply to very different political contexts, but its expanded definition finally restricts its possible range of application. For the 'parabola of mass mobilization' (Tarrow 1989: 10) is shaped not only by the development of movement organizations but by the responses of 'traditional associations' like 'parties and interest groups' (Tarrow 1989: 18). This appears to locate the cycle of protest squarely in liberal democratic polities with developed and relatively untrammeled civil societies.

This account of the protest cycle reposes on historical evidence that clusterings of collective action tend to coincide with increases in political activity in general (Snyder and Tilly 1972; Tilly, Tilly, and Tilly 1975; Tilly 1984); and Tarrow's Italian cycle demonstrates that 'just as confrontational and violent forms of collective action rose during the period, so did routine and conventional

---

[18] In authoritarian polities this is as true of the labour movement as it is of any other social movement. But Tarrow argues that working-class mobilization through strike action in Italy was intended to defend the workers' own material interests and nothing more, and this conclusion holds throughout the period of his study (Tarrow 1989).

ones' (Tarrow 1993*b*: 290). Tarrow explains the expanding phase of the cycle as one of competition for mass support between social movements and traditional associations, and the declining phase as one of absorption of mass pressure by traditional organizations and traditional ways of doing politics.[19] As a corollary, it is suggested that the broadest protests occur at the peak of the cycle, when demands are universalized, whereas the beginning and end points of the cycle are dominated by specific demands from narrow constituencies. Cycles occur, therefore, 'not when a few people are willing to take extraordinary risks for extreme goals, but when the costs of collective action are so low and incentives so great that even individuals or groups that would normally not engage in protest feel encouraged to do so' (Tarrow 1989: 8).

This expanded definition of the protest cycle cannot describe social movement activity under authoritarian regimes. But some critical insights can certainly be salvaged and applied to our cases. First, there is no doubt that this activity rises and falls in a discernible rhythm. There is no compelling evidence to suggest that the rhythm is cyclical, but there are waves and troughs of social mobilization through time.[20] It is plausible that the waves occur when 'conflicts arising in one part of society are quickly diffused to others' (Tarrow 1989: 15); and it makes sense to suppose that waves subside because of repression, the satisfaction of demands,

---

[19] 'A protest cycle begins with conventional patterns of conflict within existing organizations and institutions. As it gathers strength, new actors use expressive and confrontational forms of action, demonstrating to others less daring than themselves that the system is vulnerable to disruption and that they have grievances in common. This expands the range of contention to new sectors and institutions, but without the confrontation or the excitement of the "early risers". Confrontation gives way to deliberate violence only towards the end of the cycle, as mobilization declines, repression increases, people defect to interest groups and institutions, and extremists are left to compete for support from a shrinking social base' (Tarrow 1989: 8). But Tarrow is clear that it is the intensive peak of mobilization that 'provides the models of disruption, the personnel, the issues, and the interpretative frames of meaning for an increase in conventional protest within the polity' (Tarrow 1989: 14).

[20] More recently Tarrow has commented that 'the peaks that leave indelible impressions in public consciousness are really only the high ground of broader swells of mobilization that rise and fall from the doldrums of compliance to waves of mobilization more gradually than popular memory recognizes' (Tarrow 1993*b*: 288). These 'protest waves do not have a regular frequency or extend uniformly to entire populations' but they are characterized by 'heightened conflict, broad sectoral and geographic extension, the appearance of new SMOs (social movement organizations) and the empowerment of old ones, the creation of new "master frames" of meaning, and the invention of new forms of collective action' (Tarrow 1993*b*: 284).

or the sheer exhaustion of the mobilized. It is equally plausible to suggest that such waves 'mobilize the organized but also organize the unmobilized' (Tarrow 1990: 47). Second, it is likely that the broadest protests will indeed occur at the height of the wave, where (according to our analysis of the discourse of rights) specific demands will be increasingly couched in terms of rights. It is also possible that social movement activity responds to perceptions of the gap between rights-in-principle and rights-in-practice, and that the waves represent significant thresholds in the struggle for citizenship rights.[21] Finally, Tarrow's comments on the institutional or conventional settings where cycles begin (Tarrow 1989: 13) resonate in the authoritarian context, since the most important labour movements to contest the regime and press for citizenship rights in Spain, Brazil, and Mexico arose within the state-chartered union corporations of the regime itself (Foweraker 1989, 1993). But, whereas in the liberal democratic context trade unions count as 'traditional associations', in our cases the opposition labour movements take the lead in mounting social movement activity (Rueschemeyer, Stephens, and Stephens 1992).

Legal Forms, Political Practices, and Social Movement Struggles

The closely symbiotic relationship between social movement activity and citizenship rights suggests that, in the contemporary context, citizenship describes a process of putting the prescribed content into its ubiquitous legal and political forms. In this perspective social movement struggles aspire to close the gap between the rhetoric and the reality of citizenship, between rights-in-principle and rights-in-practice, by pressing political regimes to conform more closely to state laws and constitutions. In nearly every case this is a process that begins when social movement demands begin to be stated in terms of rights. Thus, contemporary citizenship may be

---

[21] Even where the waves are not successful in winning demands, they may leave organizational or cultural residues that may feed subsequent swells of activity (Fox 1994: 161). This process of sedimentation is especially important in segmented societies with clientelistic patterns of power relations. In these societies social movement activity may continue to occur alongside reactive and inchoate protests, and therefore the waves of mobilization 'leave large pockets of citizens uninvolved, produce conflicts between groups of mobilized citizens, and usually awaken a backlash against disorder' (Tarrow 1990: 44). Tarrow's description is evocative even if it is designed for a different context.

constructed as an object of comparative research by disaggregating it into three discrete research areas. First, there is the spread of the normative attributes of citizenship into the laws, constitutions, and institutional procedures of different regimes, where formally inscribed national rights may be compared to the core set of citizenship rights. Second, there is the degree to which the practices and policies of the regimes approximate or conform to these formal codes. Third, there is the social movement activity that seeks to make these practices so conform, or promotes such conformity as a contingent result of pressing their demands in terms of rights. In short, contemporary citizenship may be studied in its three main dimensions of *forms*, *practices*, and *struggles*.

Disaggregating citizenship in this way does not resolve the problem of commensurability (see Chapter 1), but it does clarify it. The normative content of citizenship will have influenced the encoded rights and norms of different regimes in different ways and in different degrees, but it is possible to compare the presence of these formal codes to the established core set of citizenship rights as this presence varies over time. On the other hand, the degree of fit or the gap between formal codes and regime practices will always be nationally specific, but the variation in that gap over time may itself be compared cross-nationally. Finally, insofar as social movement struggles respond to either rights-in-principle, rights-in-practice, or the gap between the two, they are responding to nationally inscribed legal and constitutional forms, except where they invoke rights that may not be so inscribed, such as ethnic rights or rights of self-determination.

The gap between rhetoric and reality, between principle and practice, varies over time both because regime practices vary and because the formal codes themselves are continually contested, negotiated, interpreted, and changed; and just as social movement activity can impinge on regime practice, so can it contribute to reconfigure laws and constitutions. For the laws, constitutions, institutional procedures and political norms do not merely provide a static statement of rights, but also contribute to construct the strategic terrain of social movement activity; and since this terrain defines the terms of representation, terms of legal immunity, and terms of political engagement with the state—in sum, the rules of political struggle—it is actively contested by both social movements and state agencies and actors. Hence the contest may enhance or restrict the right to contestation, and the struggle for rights may strengthen or injure the right to have rights. In these circumstances, and in this perspective, the legal forms can never guarantee the conferment or protection of citizenship which must be seen, on the contrary, as an active process of vindication and achievement.

In this connection it is clear that the relationship between social movement struggles and citizenship rights will always be mediated both by state actors and the state apparatus (Davis 1988). In the social movement perspective, therefore, these struggles will always involve a strategic appreciation of the political conditions of struggle, or of what the theory often calls the 'political opportunity structure' (e.g. Kitschelt 1986; Brockett 1991). In any one moment these conditions may include, variously, possible political alliances, political party programmes (where parties exist), the effects of political discourse, divisions or 'openings' within the legal-bureaucratic apparatus of the state, and the presence of 'elite reformers' (Tarrow 1993*b*) or the emergence of elite 'reform coalitions' (Tilly 1984).[22] Consequently, since the outcome of citizenship struggles will always depend in some degree on the political context and the political conjuncture, their analysis will always require an element of 'structurally disciplined' hermeneutic enquiry (Stones 1991). But if the enquiry stops there, the study of citizenship is condemned to the incommensurable contexts defined by national political cultures, and so cannot be constructed as an object of comparative research.

For this reason this study sets out to achieve measurable comparisons of citizenship, understood both as a relationship between social movements and citizenship rights and as a process which discovers and disseminates these rights through social struggle. The purpose of disaggregating contemporary citizenship into the discrete research areas of forms, practices, and struggles is to construct proxy objects of research which are susceptible to measurement, and so to promote these measurable comparisons. The advantage of constructing citizenship as a relationship is to bring together those things that are usually kept apart. On the one hand, there is now a surfeit of social movement theory, but a dearth of enquiry into the political impact and outcomes of social movement activity.[23] On the other, there are philosophically versed discussions of political rights (often tied to different forms of democratic theory)

---

[22] Recent research suggests that the 'political opportunity structure' should also focus on political constraints, and so include measures of political repressiveness (McAdam, McCarthy, and Zald 1996).

[23] The exceptions to prove this rule in the North American and European literature include Gamson (1975), Welch (1975), Piven and Cloward (1977), Goldstone (1980), Jenkins and Klandermans (1995), and Kriesi, Koopmans, Dyvendak, and Giugni (1995). For our cases they include Foweraker and Craig (1990), Foweraker (1989, 1993, 1995), and Oxhorn (1995).

which are either divorced from any sense of political context or suffer from different degrees of ethnocentrism. The advantage of constructing citizenship as a process is that it reveals the dynamic nature of this relationship and encourages measurement of the variation in the proxy objects of citizenship research over time.

Contemporary 'truths' about citizenship, or about the relationship between collective action and citizenship rights, tend to be rooted in archetypal historical contexts, such as the French Revolution or 1848, which are understood as shaping the contours of citizenship in the modern era. However compelling the historical evidence which supports these truths, it is difficult to gauge their relevance to contemporary citizenship as it has evolved and is experienced outside of the original boundaries of the Enlightenment project. In the contemporary context, enquiries into collective action and citizenship are mainly confined to historical sociology and political theory, and their empirical base is at best a qualitative comparative history. As a result most statements about the political impact of social movements are 'primarily descriptive or taxonomic' (G. T. Marx and Wood 1975). In contrast to the methods of history, historical sociology, and political theory, this study is a first attempt to operationalize citizenship as an object of contemporary, comparative, and quantitative enquiry. Like any first attempt, it faces considerable methodological challenges, and these are recounted in the next chapter. Our strategy is to hold fast to the primary purpose of our enquiry and marry it, as best we can, to what can be measured.[24]

---

[24] Tilly, Tilly, and Tilly deliver a *culpa nostra* that nicely captures our sense of this first attempt: 'that there are errors in our numbers we are sure. That they are open to disproof we take to be a virtue. That our procedures could be improved we have no doubt; we hope that someone else will soon take up the task. In the meantime, we want to make it clear that we did not adopt our particular methods and our particular sources because they were quick, easy and cheap. They were none of these. We adopted them because they were the best we could manage' (Tilly, Tilly and Tilly 1975: 16).

3

Methods and Sources

Chapters 1 and 2 outlined the main theoretical debates about citizenship, social movements, and the relationship between them, in the past and in the present. Citizenship is understood to consist primarily of civil and political rights, as expressed in rights-in-principle, rights-in-practice, and the gap between them. Social movements arise from different forms of popular organization, including labour organization. The task of this chapter is to operationalize these different aspects of citizenship and social movements in order to examine the questions posed in the first two chapters. It is divided into two parts. First, it gives a brief overview of the main issues in comparative methodology and outlines the research strategy used in this study. Second, it proceeds to show how the three aspects of citizenship and the two types of social movement activity are measured.

Comparative Method

The goal of comparative method is to develop general political and sociological rules by comparing across countries. The real world of politics cannot be subjected to experimental control, and comparison acts as a substitute for experimentation. Whether the focus is on political institutions, political culture, political processes, social classes, or the 'functional equivalences' among various countries, two main comparative methods tend to be employed: large cross-national studies with few variables and many cases, or small-N comparisons with many variables and few cases.[1] According to J. S. Mill (1843/1970), these methods rely upon two techniques of comparative analysis: the method of agreement and the method of

[1] For a review of the issues and strategies of comparative politics, see Dogan and Pelassy (1990).

difference. The method of agreement requires cases in which a similar outcome is present. The method of difference requires cases where that outcome is either present or not.[2] The method of agreement leads to what Faure (1994) calls the 'most different systems design' (MDSD), where the outcome of different cases is the same. Alternatively, the method of difference leads to what he calls the 'most similar systems design' (MSSD), where the outcome of similar cases is different (See Chapter 1).

For cross-national studies, variance across many cases promotes theory generation. For small-N comparisons, variation over time provides explanation. The continuum along which these research strategies lie is divided between what Ragin (1994: 300) calls 'variable-oriented' and 'case-oriented'. The former are considered to be extensive and the latter intensive. Variable-oriented studies posit 'general dimensions of macrosocial variation' (Ragin 1994: 300). To falsify hypotheses and generate theory, the method aims to raise the number of cases (N) through a variety of strategies (Przeworski and Teune 1970): the use of history to provide more instances of the political phenomena under enquiry; the isolation of the variation within a case; a focus on one region of the world, or the reduction of the specificity of the variables in question, and the addition of more cases from around the globe. The latter strategy characterizes the reasoning behind cross-national variable-oriented studies. Research on the relationship between democracy and economic development (Lipset 1959; Cutright 1963; Cutright and Wiley 1969; Helliwell 1994); inequality and political stability (Bollen and Jackman 1985; Muller and Seligson 1987); and the stability of democratic institutions (Lijphart 1984; Powell 1982; Stepan and Skach 1993) all represent variable-oriented studies.

Case-oriented studies, on the other hand, suggest 'that there are distinct and singular entities (major features of countries, world regions, cultures, etc., or their histories) that parallel each other sufficiently to allow comparing and contrasting them' (Ragin 1994: 300). These distinct features are then examined through a careful, in-depth comparison of a few cases. Barrington Moore's (1973) classic study of the conditions for Fascism, communism, and liberal democracy is one example of this type of comparison. By comparing different historical contingencies in England, France, the United States, Germany, Japan, China, and India, Moore centres his study around four categories he considers crucial for determining

[2] For a discussion of these differences in method, see Ragin (1987), Rueschemeyer, Stephens, and Stephens (1992), Wickham-Crowley (1992: 302–3), and Faure (1994).

a country's route to modernity: economic change, state structure, state action, and social classes. In addressing Moore's failure to take into account the relative autonomy of the state and its susceptibility to international factors, Skocpol (1979) also employs a case-oriented research strategy in her study of revolutions in France, Russia, and China (Rueschemeyer, Stephens, and Stephens 1992: 20–4). Bendix's (1978) analysis of feudalism and its subsequent transformation offers another example of the case-oriented approach.

Case-oriented approaches are also associated with what has developed within the field of comparative politics as 'area studies', i.e. intra-regional studies that assume that the MSSD framework can be applied to certain political phenomena within a particular region. In *The Passing of Traditional Society*, Lerner (1963) limits his study of modernization to the Arab world. In *The Breakdown of Democratic Regimes,* Linz and Stepan (1978) develop a framework of conditions for democratic breakdown in Latin America through various case studies. Similarly, Collier (1979) collected case studies to develop an understanding of authoritarianism in Latin America as originally conceptualized by O'Donnell (1973). Subsequent comparative studies that use the case-oriented approach focus on the recent transitions away from authoritarian rule in Latin America and Southern Europe (O'Donnell, Schmitter, and Whitehead 1986), and on the process of democratic consolidation (Przeworski 1991; Higley and Gunther 1992; Mainwaring, O'Donnell, and Valenzuela 1992).

These different strategies of comparative research also tend to be aligned along a further schism in the literature: qualitative versus quantitative analysis. Despite the fact that both case-oriented and variable-oriented studies can employ either qualitative or quantitative methods (or both), most comparative studies use one or the other exclusively.[3] Case-oriented studies tend to use qualitative methods (small-N macro-historical comparisons), and variable-oriented studies tend to use quantitative methods (large-N cross-national comparisons). Qualitative practitioners argue that cross-national studies under-specify their models and therefore show nothing. Quantitative practitioners argue that qualitative comparisons are over-specified and therefore offer nothing more than 'story-telling'.

This division in the literature represents a false dichotomy.

---

[3] For examples that combine both approaches, see Paige (1975), Ragin (1987), Rueschemeyer, Stephens, and Stephens (1992), and Wickham-Crowley (1992).

Whether comparison uses qualitative methods, quantitative methods, or a combination of the two approaches, the goal of the comparative method is theory generation. This study is case-oriented and combines qualitative and quantitative methods in order to investigate the struggle for citizenship rights over time. It compares the four cases longitudinally by investigating variation within each case as well as across cases, and since it seeks commensurability (see Chapters 1 and 2), it employs measurable variables within a comparative framework. It compares instances of similar variation in similar cases which Faure (1994) calls the 'mirror-image' of MSSD. Within this framework it uses statistical analysis of variation over time rather than across cases, and so remains sensitive to the cultural specificities of the four cases. The commensurate elements in the cases outlined in Chapter 1 fall into two groups: (1) all the cases are instances of authoritarian regime that have experienced fluctuations in the guarantee of citizenship rights; and (2) all the cases exhibit a rise and fall of social mobilization over time. In sum, the study is a diachronic quantitative analysis that focuses on the contemporary processes of citizenship struggle in Brazil, Chile, Mexico, and Spain.

Measuring Citizenship

As suggested in Chapters 1 and 2, the study uses three measures of citizenship. Rights-in-principle are the legal and procedural rules a polity establishes in order to guarantee the civil and political rights of its citizens. They are the civil and political rights that are most frequently found in national constitutions, but they may also appear in statute laws (particularly those that affect labour), institutional acts (as in Brazil), emergency clauses (as in Chile and Spain), or transitory articles (as in Chile). Rights-in-practice are those civil and political rights actually enjoyed by citizens within the polity. Research on human rights assumes a difference between what a regime says, and what a regime does in relation to universal doctrines of human rights. This study focuses on this distinction between principle and practice at a national level, and develops quantitative measures to illustrate how rights-in-principle, rights-in-practice, and the variable gap between them, changes over time (see Chapter 4). The measures are then used to examine how those changes are related to social movement activity over time, in Chapter 6, and through time, in Chapter 7.

Measuring rights-in-principle

Rights-in-principle are encoded in national constitutions, statute laws, decree-laws, and the transitory articles of constitutions. Measuring them is a relatively simple procedure and has produced a plethora of scales and indices of civil and political rights too numerous to review here. Indeed, from 1954 to 1965, there were no fewer than 2,080 different indices of which only 28 per cent had been used more than once (Barsh 1993: 91). These indices are of two sorts. On the one hand, there are indices that measure a country's performance at a specific point in time (Bollen 1979; Nixon 1965), and on the other, those that are updated yearly for time-series analysis (A. S. Banks 1971, 1979, 1994). Since this study is concerned with longitudinal variation in the legal-institutional characteristics of regimes, the latter sort of index is more useful. Furthermore, existing indices are divided between those that measure pure institutional variation (i.e. rights-in-principle) and those that measure actual performance (i.e. rights-in-practice). Since the immediate focus is on rights-in-principle, an index of pure institutional variation is needed. In sum, the measure of rights-in-principle must be time-series and it must represent pure institutional variation.

One data set that comprises measures of pure institutional variation over time is the *Cross-Polity Time Series Data Archive*, compiled by Arthur S. Banks. The data set contains annual indicators for 115 countries from the nineteenth century to the present. In order to construct a measure of rights-in-principle, Banks's individual institutional scores are combined into a legal-institutional index (BANKSLII). BANKSLII is the sum of the measures for competitive nomination, executive effectiveness, legislative effectiveness (first and second chambers), legislative selection, and party legitimacy. The values for this combined index range from 1–17.[4] A score of one on BANKSLII indicates that the regime has no institutions in place that guarantee the protection of civil and political rights, and a score of seventeen indicates that the regime has institutions in place that give full protection to civil and political rights. For this study, Banks's data from 1950 to the present is used to illustrate the broader historical patterns of institutional variation in the four cases (see Chapter 4), and so serves as a benchmark for the indices developed in this study.

BANKSLII shows pure institutional variation, but does not depict lesser procedural changes in the four cases. For example, from

---

[4] See Appendix B for the values of each of these institutional measures.

1964 to 1978, the Brazilian military regime used its Institutional Acts in a quasi-legal fashion to alter the constitutional guarantees set out in the 1967 and 1969 constitutions (Alves 1985; Skidmore 1988). From 1980 to 1988, Augusto Pinochet used Transitory Article 24 to deny the civil and political rights guaranteed in the 1980 Constitution (Drake and Jaksic 1991; Loveman 1994). Despite the full civil and political rights guaranteed by the 1917 Constitution in Mexico, the Institutional Revolutionary Party (PRI) has manipulated labour and party rights since the late 1920s to maintain its hold on power (Bailey 1988; Cornelius and Craig 1991; Cornelius 1996). The rights guaranteed in authoritarian Spain by the series of Organic Laws of the State were compromised by Franco's use of 'state of siege' measures (Carr and Fusi 1981). These instances of procedural variation are not reflected in existing aggregate measures of rights-in-principle and require a more contextually sensitive institutional-procedural index.

An Institutional-Procedural Index

From a reading of the legal and institutional variation in the four cases, the study develops an institutional-procedural index (IPI). This reading targeted both constitutional changes (i.e. provisions for suffrage, elections, independent judiciary, equality, arbitrary arrest and detention, habeas corpus, and freedom of expression) and procedural changes (i.e. electoral rules, voter constraints, and party rules) over the years in question. A score sheet was developed consisting of core rights, contestation rights, and participation rights. Core rights are those civil rights that guarantee liberty of the person (see Chapters 1 and 2). The contestation and participation rights draw upon Dahl's (1971) notion of 'polyarchy' and represent the political rights of citizenship. The elements that compose each set of rights are coded for each year, and the resulting index can be aggregated and disaggregated to show how institutional-procedural rights vary over time. The score sheet is shown in Figure 3.1. The index ranges from 0 (no rights guaranteed) to 29 (full rights guaranteed). While coding, there is a natural tendency for a country to be penalized for known rights violations, even though those rights are still legally guaranteed. But the coding adheres strictly to the legal guarantee of civil and political rights. If a regime uses an exception clause to abrogate rights legally guaranteed elsewhere (e.g. the 1969 state of siege in Spain or the 1985 state of siege in Chile), the country is penalized for that year.

Core Rights	Score
Habeas corpus provisions	0–2
Assembly	0–1
Association	0–1
Speech/information	0–1
Exception clauses	0–1
Independent judiciary	2
No military tribunal	1
Military tribunal	0
Judicial review	0–1
Contestation	
Selection of legislature	0–2
Competitive nomination	1–2
Party competition	0–3
Largest party < 70%	2
Largest party > 70%	1
Trade unionism	0–3
Executive selection	0–1
Term limitation	0–1
Re-electin	1–2
Participation	
Suffrage	0–2
Elections exist	0–1
Fair procedure	0–1
TOTAL RANGE	**0–29**

FIGURE 3.1: *Coding sheet for the Institutional-Procedural Index (IPI)*

Thus, the study uses both Banks (BANKSLII) and an institutional-procedural index (IPI) for the measure of rights-in-principle. BANKSLII provides a general overview of the cases and IPI represents a more contextually sensitive reading of procedural and institutional variation. As might be expected, the indices share many of the same elements, and are significantly correlated in all four cases.[5] The descriptive trends of both indices are examined in the next chapter, but only IPI is used in the subsequent statistical analysis. Table 3.1 shows the data source, cases, and periods covered by the indices.

Measuring Rights-in-Practice

Rights-in-practice are those civil and political rights that citizens actually enjoy. It is notorious that civil and political rights have

---

[5] For Brazil, r = .45 (p = .02); for Chile, r = .65 (p = .003); for Mexico, r = .66 (p = .000); and for Spain, r = .93 (p = .000).

TABLE 3.1. *Rights-in-principle measures*

Data source	Cases	Dates
Banks (1971, 1979, 1994)	All cases	1950–1990
IPI	Brazil	1964–1990
	Chile	1973–1990
	Mexico	1963–1990
	Spain	1958–1983

been repeatedly violated in all four cases. But it is more difficult to measure rights-in-practice than rights-in-principle, for both ethical and methodological reasons. This difficulty is illustrated by the UNDP's *Human Development Report* of 1991, which linked economic development with human rights practice (Barsh 1993: 87) by using economic variables and a 'Human Freedom Index' (HFI) to show their positive correlation. The UNDP came under strong criticism both from member states of the UN and from methodologists. The states condemned the ethnocentric bias implicit in the use of Humana's (1983, 1986) *World Human Rights Guide*, while the methodologists criticized the reliance on impressionistic data from a single observer.

Human rights theorists and activists argue that it is dehumanizing to use statistics to analyse violations of human rights (Jabine and Claude 1992). Human rights reporting from organizations such as Amnesty International tends to give narrative accounts of the human drama of rights violations in various countries, but they make no attempt to quantify the violations. Similarly, the US State Department Reports summarize general impressions of rights violations. They use general terms such as 'improved', 'deteriorated', and 'remained the same as last year', which can prove intractable for coding purposes. There is merit in the ethical argument. Narratives of the conditions and victims of abuse illustrate human suffering in a way that promotes human rights activism. Statistical tables of individuals who are detained, imprisoned, tortured, and executed reveals very little of the experience of abuse. But statistics *do* capture the changes in the incidence of rights violations and provide a permanent record. Since raw numbers contribute to a description of regime behaviour, Chapter 4 includes the statistical data on rights violations.

The ethical questions aside, there are two difficulties in measuring rights-in-practice: the level of available information and the relativity of the measures. The information problem centres on reporting errors which can skew statistical results. Existing lists of violations only represent a small sample of actual violations. Bollen (1992: 198) argues that reportage of human rights violations exists at six levels: (1) an ideal level of all violations, recorded and unrecorded; (2) recorded violations; (3) known and accessible violations; (4) locally reported violations (nation-state); (5) internationally reported violations; and (6) the most restricted level of those violations reported in the United States. Most existing documentation of human rights abuse lies somewhere between the fourth and sixth levels. The second concern is one of relativity. In reporting raw violations, can one type of violation be compared to another? Can detentions be compared with political murders, or tortures with rapes? Similarly, raw numbers of violations are continuous measures that have no limit. Are sixty violations in one year better than one hundred in the next? An ideal society would have no violations, and any violation would be one too many.

There are several responses to these concerns. First, data reportage continues to be a problem in the social sciences overall. Simple micro-economic theory and game theory assume complete and free information, but the empirical testing of the theories uses the best numbers available. The economist recognizes measurement error and calculates a confidence interval accordingly. Survey data is equally suspect. Random sampling allows for inference, but 'doorstep opinion', non-responses, and deliberately incorrect responses can and do occur. Second, even if the problem of relativity cannot be overcome completely, it is possible to show the different repressive strategies of a regime by reporting different categories of rights violations. For example, the authoritarian regimes in this study often used executions during their early years and later developed elaborate police systems to routinely intimidate society, such as the National Intelligence Directorate (DINA) in Chile and the National Information Service (SNI) in Brazil.[6] International pressure on regimes to improve their human rights records often leads to more subtle and less recognizable forms of repression. Mass arrests and unlawful detentions replace 'disappearances'. Citizens are harassed by incessant phone calls through the night or followed in the streets by day. The change in strategy may maintain repression while making violations less obvious.

Chapter 4 illustrates the descriptive trends in civil and political

---

[6] For more on the DINA in Chile, see J. S. Valenzuela and Valenzuela (1986) and Oxhorn (1995). For more on the SNI in Brazil, see Alves (1985) and Kinzo (1988).

rights violations by reporting raw data in Brazil (Krane 1983; Dassin 1986; Cohen 1989; dos Santos 1990; Grzybowski 1990), Chile (Vicaría de la Solidaridad 1988; Americas' Watch 1988; Comisión Nacional de Verdad y Reconciliación 1991; Reiter, Zunzunegui, Quiroga 1992), Mexico (Amnesty International 1986, 1991; US State Department 1981, 1983, 1985, 1987; Americas' Watch 1991a, 1991b), and Spain (Anuario Estadístico de España 1952–1987). In selected years, the 'deaths from political violence' measure (Taylor and Jodice 1983) is used to complement the other sources of data, and build a more robust picture of civil and political rights violations. In addition, measures of newsprint consumption are included to illustrate general trends in the availability of printed information.

Abstract Measures of Rights-in-Practice

Raw data on rights violations is lumpy, incomplete, and difficult to integrate into the quantitative framework of this study. Consequently, abstract measures of rights-in-practice are used to construct a combined rights-in-practice index (CRI) that is used alongside the institutional-procedural index (IPI). Abstract indices rate countries on categorical and continuous scales that span high to low protection of civil and political rights. These indices lose the specificity of raw rights violation data, but have the advantage of being commensurate across different cases. The most popular time-series abstract measure of rights-in-practice was created by Raymond D. Gastil, who measures political liberties (PL) and civil liberties (CL) on a scale of one to seven, where a one denotes a democracy and a seven, a totalitarian state. Gastil is primarily interested in the rights of individuals as they vary across countries. His scale has been used as a measure of the 'repressiveness of the regime' (Muller and Seligson 1987), of the 'probability of political freedom' (Helliwell 1994), and of democracy (Stepan and Skach 1993), as well as a 'scale of polyarchy' (Coppedge and Reinicke 1988). In 1992, Freedom House took over the job of coding nations using the original Gastil scale (Ryan 1994). In its disaggregated form, it provides a guide to the relationship between political and civil liberties over time. In its aggregated form, it shows the broad patterns in regime behaviour over time.

There are many criticisms of the Gastil scale (Barsh 1993), and most object to the way in which the scores are calculated. Gastil (1990) claims he used a mental checklist that roughly scores political liberties, such as competitive elections, and civil liberties, such as freedom of the press and freedom of expression. Since these

TABLE 3.2. *Gastil's checklist for political and civil liberties*

Political liberties	Civil liberties
Chief authority recently elected by a meaningful process	Media/literature free of political censorship
Legislature recently elected by a meaningful process	Open public discussion
Fair Election Laws, campaigning opportunity, polling and tabulation	Freedom of assembly and demonstration
Fair reflection of voter preference in distribution of power	Freedom of political or quasi-political organization
Multiple political parties	Nondiscriminatory rule of law in politically relevant cases
Recent shifts in power through elections	Free from unjustified political terror or imprisonment
Significant opposition vote	Free trade unions, peasant organizations, or equivalent
Free of military or foreign control	Free businesses or cooperatives
Major group or groups denied reasonable self-determination	Free professional or other private organizations
Decentralized political power	Free religious institutions
Informal consensus, de facto opposition power	Personal social rights (property, internal and external travel, residence, marriage and family)
	Socio-economic rights (freedom from dependence on landlords, bosses, union leaders, or bureaucrats)

criteria have changed over the years, it is suggested that the scale cannot be used for longitudinal analysis (Barsh 1993: 105). But Burkhart and Lewis-Beck (1994: 904) argued that the scale represented a 'splendid opportunity' for their study of the connection between economic development and democracy. When Freedom House took over the coding, it published a complete checklist for both political and civil liberties (Ryan 1994), which are roughly the same as those employed by Gastil (see Table 3.2). Although this checklist may appear similar to the IPI, it must be emphasized that Gastil is concerned with the individual's experience of liberties or their lack. Moreover, such institutional contamination of his measures that does exist will gradually be diluted by the construction of a 'layered' or composite measure of rights-in-practice.

For the Latin American cases (Brazil, Chile, and Mexico), the

Gastil scale can be validated by comparison with other measures produced annually or at set intervals such as the Fitzgibbon-Johnson Image Index (FJII) which rates regimes according to the impressions of leading academics engaged in research on or in Latin America (Fitzgibbon 1967; Johnson 1976, 1977, 1981; Wilkie and Ruddle 1992). Every five years from 1945 to 1985 Fitzgibbon compiled questionnaire responses from the academics in order to achieve his ratings. The original questionnaire contained general social and political variables[7] which Fitzgibbon considered to be both preconditions and manifestations of democracy (Fitzgibbon 1967: 135). Each of the variables was scored on a scale from 1 to 5. Johnson revised the index in 1975 to include only political variables,[8] and then standardized it to a range of 1–20, where a one denotes the most democratic countries, and a twenty the least democratic. This *revised* and standardized index was used as one of the measures to describe regime behaviour in the Latin American cases.

The FJII can be complemented by other measures such as the repression measure from Duff and McCamant (1976) who have repression as one of their dependent variables. Since the measure is defined in similar terms to the notion of rights-in-practice,[9]

---

[7] These variables include: '(1) An educational level sufficient to give the political processes some substance and vitality, (2) A fairly adequate standard of living, (3) A sense of internal unity and national cohesion, (4) Belief by the people in their individual political dignity and maturity, (5) Absence of foreign domination, (6) Freedom of the press, speech, assembly, radio, etc. (7) Free and competitive elections—honestly counted votes, (8) Freedom of party organization; genuine and effective party opposition in the legislature; legislative scrutiny of the executive branch, (9) An independent judiciary—respect for its decisions, (10) Public awareness of accountability for the collection and expenditure of public funds, (11) Intelligent attitude toward social legislation—the vitality of such legislation as applied, (12) Civilian supremacy over the military, (13) Reasonable freedom of political life from the impact of ecclesiastical controls, (14) Attitude toward and development of technical, scientific, and honest governmental administration, (15) Intelligent and sympathetic administration of whatever local self-government prevails' (Fitzgibbon 1967).

[8] The revised political criteria include: free speech, free elections, free party organization, independent judiciary, and civilian supremacy (Wilkie and Ruddle 1992).

[9] Duff and McCamant (1976: 24) define repression as 'the use of government coercion to control or eliminate actual or potential political opposition. Coercion may come in the form of arrests and imprisonment or exile of individuals who oppose or are suspected of wanting to oppose the government. It may also come in the form of denial of due process to these individuals. The government may prevent opponents from associating and organizing. It may deny them the right to communicate through public media.'

TABLE 3.3. *Duff and McCamant repression criteria*

Component	0	1	2	3	4
Supension of constitutional rights	No report of suspension	Temporary suspension (< 30 days)	Suspension > 30 days, but < 9 months	Suspension > 9 months, judicial interference	Complete suspension of legal procedures
Arrests, exiles, executions	None	small-scale (< 10 per million)	Large number of temporary arrests	Mass arrests (> 50); assassination	Large number of political prisoners or exiles, opposition leaders dead
Political party restrictions	No restrictions	Extremes excluded	All but small extremes allowed, some harassment of other groups	Control prevents a majority party	No opposition allowed
Censorship	No restrictions	Minor restrictions	Long-term restrictions	Censorship of all political news, private ownership	Government directs what news is published

it can serve the broad purpose of tracing the evolution of citizen-ship rights. Like FJII and Gastil, the Duff and McCamant index (DUFFMC) is an impressionistic, abstract measure of rights. To code an index that fits their definition of repression, they score four components on a scale that ranges 0–4 (see Table 3.3), so producing a total range of 0–16.[10] A zero indicates that all rights are fully guaranteed, and sixteen a highly repressive regime. Duff and McCamant's coverage of the years 1950–1970 fills out the picture of the early years of the Brazilian and Mexican cases but fails to coincide with the relevant years of the Chilean case.

FJII and DUFFMC both enhance Gastil's picture of rights-in-practice but do not cover the Spanish case. Moreover, Gastil's scores do not start before 1972, and so omit a great number of relevant years for Spain. Consequently, the study required at least one other index covering all the cases. There are several time-series data sources that have some measures of civil and political rights in Spain. Taylor and Hudson (1972) have scores for electoral ir-regularities and government sanctions, but the sanctions vari-able is continuous and therefore impossible to code into an index. There are also claims about measurement error and bias (Bollen 1992: 194–5), which may also affect the civil and political rights variables in Taylor and Jodice (1983). Nixon (1960, 1965) and Lowenstein (1967) have very narrow measures, and only contain values for two separate years.

The more serviceable index is that of Arat (1991) who composed a statistical picture of political democracy along four dimensions (participation, inclusiveness, competitiveness, and government coer-civeness),[11] and although her index has been criticized both for its complexity and for its disregard of previous indices (Arat 1991; Barsh 1993: 108–9), its coverage makes it useful for the Spanish case and fills out the picture for the Latin American cases. Finally there is the Humana index (1983, 1986, 1992), which is calculated by scoring forty questions pertaining to political, civil, and social

[10] The Latin American cases included in the study (by order of repressiveness) are: Uruguay, Costa Rica, Chile, Mexico, Ecuador, Panama, Honduras, Peru, Brazil, Nicaragua, Colombia, El Salvador, Bolivia, Guatemala, Venezuela, Argentina, Cuba, Dominican Republic, Haiti, Paraguay (Duff and McCamant 1976: 39).

[11] Participation is scored by awarding points for an effective executive, effective legislature, and a competitive nomination procedure. Inclusiveness is awarded points for the level of suffrage. Competitiveness is scored by awarding points for party legitimacy and party competitiveness. Government coerciveness is the residual which results from regressing the number of sanctions employed by a regime on social unrest indicators. These four dimensions are combined to pro-duce an 'index of democraticness' (Arat 1991: 24–7).

TABLE 3.4. *Political rights from Charles Humana*

Freedom to associate
Freedom from serfdom, slavery, forced or child labour
Freedom from extrajudicial killings or disappearances
Freedom from torture or coercion by the state
Freedom from capital punishment
Freedom from indefinite detention without charge
Freedom from political censorship of the press
Freedom from censorship of mail or telephone tapping
Right to political opposition
Freedom for multi-party elections by secret and universal ballot
Freedom for legal and political equality of women
Freedom for independent newspapers
Freedom for independent book publishing
Freedom for independent radio and television networks
Freedom for all courts to total independence
Freedom for independent trade unions
Deprivation of nationality
Innocent until proven guilty
No secret civilian trials
Speedy trial
Inviolable home

rights on a scale of 0–3 with the final score transformed to 0–100 rating.[12] The Humana questions are drawn from the Universal Declaration of Human Rights, but the index was reduced to include only civil and political rights (see Table 3.4) In contrast to DUFFMC, the recoded Humana index is used to round out the latter part of the relevant periods.

These different studies provide a selection of rights-in-practice measures that can create a 'layered' view of the evolution of these rights over time in the four cases. Therefore, all the scales were transformed to a range of 0–1 in order to facilitate statistical and graphical comparisons. Since Gastil, FJII, and DUFFMC rate full rights protection as low and no rights as high, their scales were inverted before being transformed to the 0–1 range.[13] The Arat and

---

[12] The range is: *most free* = YES (coded as a 3); *moderately free* = yes (coded as a 2); *severe* = no (coded as a 1); and *most severe* = NO (coded as a 0). Gupta, Jongman, and Schmid (1994) argue that some rights in Humana's index are more important and should therefore be weighted; however, the weighting scheme they propose using discriminant analysis would only be useful for cross-national comparative analysis and does not significantly alter the scores for the four cases. For further comments, see Gupta, Jongman, and Schmid (1994).

[13] To convert Gastil, subtract the sum of the two raw scores from 14 and divide the

TABLE 3.5. *Rights-in-practice measures*

Data source	Dates covered	Cases covered
Gastil	1972–1990	Brazil, Chile,* Mexico, Spain
Fitzgibbon-Johnson	1945, 1950, 1955, 1960, 1965, 1970, 1975, 1980, 1985	Brazil, Chile, Mexico
Duff and McCamant	1950–1970	Brazil, Chile, Mexico
Arat	1948–1982	Brazil, Chile, Mexico, Spain*
Humana	1983, 1986, 1992	Brazil, Chile, Mexico, Spain

* Indicates full time-series coverage of case in question.

Humana indices rate democracies as high and non-democracies as low, so no inversion was needed. Since Arat's index ranges from 29 to 109, 29 points were subtracted from the raw scores before dividing them by 80. The recoded Humana index was divided by 100. None of these inversions or transformations alter the shape of the indices over time, but simply promote comparison on a common scale. The periods covered are FJII 1945–85 (at five-year intervals), Arat 1948–92, DUFFMC 1950–70, Gastil 1972–90, and Humana 1983, 1986, 1992 (see Table 3.5). There is considerable overlap among the different indices, and where this is extensive they are statistically correlated.[14]

Thus, prima facie it seems possible to combine the different measures to create a smoother line of rights-in-practice that covers the whole contemporary period. This measure will be called the Combined Rights Index (CRI). The simplest way to combine the measures is to average them for each year when there is a score. Clearly, in the years of heavy overlap the scores will tend to converge towards the average, while scores will be weighted more heavily in years with a single score or few scores. Methodologists

result by 12: converted Gastil = [14 − (PL + CL)]/12; see Helliwell (1994). To convert Fitzgibbon, subtract the raw score from 20 and divide the result by 19: converted FJII = [20 − FJII]/19. To convert Duff and McCamant, subtract the raw score from 16 and divide the result by 16: converted DUFFMC = [16 − DMRAW]/16.

[14] For Brazil, Arat and Gastil are correlated, r = .95 (p = .000); Arat and DUFFMC are correlated, r = .83 (p = .000). For Chile, Arat and Gastil are correlated, r = .95 (p = .000); Arat and FJII are correlated, r = .98 (p = .000); and Arat and DUFFMC are correlated, r = .65 (p = .002). For Mexico, Arat and DUFFMC are correlated, r = −.53 (p = .016). Finally, for Spain, Arat and Gastil are correlated, r = .94 (p = .000). See Chapter 4 for complete correlation matrices of these measures.

might also object to a manoeuvre that combines apples and avocados and calls them fruit. But since all these measures are somewhat subjective and abstract in nature, their combination appears warranted if it can provide a preliminary view of the evolution of rights-in-practice over time. Regrettably, more comprehensive or objective measures are not available at present.

Measuring the Gap

One of the main objectives in describing the movement of rights-in-principle and rights-in-practice over time is to measure the variation in the difference between them, the GAP. But before the gap can be measured the two indices have to be made directly comparable by transforming the rights-in-principle index (IPI) to a range of 0–1. Since it originally ranged from 0–29 (see Figure 3.1) , the raw score was simply divided by 29. With both indices on the same scale it was then possible to calculate the gap. Since there is a degree of 'institutional contamination' in the rights-in-practice index, the gap was calculated as the residuals that result from regressing the rights-in-practice index (CRI) on the rights-in-principle index (IPI) using ordinary least squares (OLS) (Duvall and Shamir 1980).

OLS regression produces residuals which are simply the difference between the predicted values of the dependent variable, in this case rights-in-practice (CRI), and its actual values. In short, the rights-in-principle index (IPI) is used as an independent variable to predict identical values of rights-in-practice. The predicted values represent what rights-in-practice ought to be given the rights-in-principle. The actual values, however, indicate the degree to which rights-in-practice exceed or fall short of their predicted values. The calculation assumes that all the variation in rights-in-practice will not be explained by the variation in rights-in-principle.[15] In short, the GAP represents the unexplained variance in rights-in-practice given a certain level of rights-in-principle. Assuming a linear relationship between the two indices which has a constant of zero and a positive slope of one, the equation that describes it appears as follows:

$$Y = X + \varepsilon$$

Where Y = the actual values of the CRI

[15] In quantitative terms, the GAP calculation assumes that $R^2 < 1.00$; an assumption which is supported by the results in the four cases (see Chapter 4).

X = the IPI

ε = GAP

The logical qualities of the GAP based on this equation can be illustrated with a simple X–Y chart (Figure 3.2). The CRI is represented along the Y-axis, the IPI is represented along the X-axis, and the diagonal line represents the predicted values of rights-in-practice (CRI) as a linear function of the effects of rights-in-principle (IPI). Values above the line constitute a positive GAP whereas values below the line represent a negative GAP. Under these conditions, a positive GAP means that practice is greater than principle, and citizens enjoy fuller rights than those that are legally guaranteed. A negative GAP means that principle is greater than practice, and citizenship rights are being denied or compromised. For values directly on the diagonal line, the GAP is zero, where rights-in-principle are equal to rights-in-practice. This tells us nothing about the quality of citizenship, since a zero GAP simply indicates a certain equivalence: a totalitarian polity with no rights protection and much repression, and a democratic polity with full rights protection and complete liberty may both have a zero GAP.

In reality, however, the relationship between rights-in-principle and rights-in-practice may not be so simple (see Chapter 4). The constant may be greater or less than zero,[16] and the slope may be greater or less than one,[17] as well as having values that are either positive or negative.[18] Since the GAP captures the unexplained variance (ε) in rights-in-practice beyond what is accounted for by rights-in-principle, it measures the 'repressive disposition of the regime' (Duvall and Shamir 1980: 161).[19] Many other independent factors may explain this unknown variance in rights-in-practice, such as international pressure, fluctuations in the domestic economy, the previous repressive disposition of the regime (see Chapter

[16] In this case, the constant represents the 'latent' rights-in-practice of the regime.

[17] This means that, on the one hand, for a slope greater than one, a one-unit increase in rights-in-principle will be accompanied by a much larger improvement in rights-in-practice; on the other hand, a slope less than one means that a one-unit increase in rights-in-principle will be accompanied by a much smaller improvement in rights-in-practice.

[18] It is possible for a polity to improve its rights-in-principle while continuing to deny rights-in-practice (Chapters 1 and 2).

[19] Duvall and Shamir (1980: 162–3) regress a 'government sanctions' variable on 'manifest conflict' (rebellion and turmoil measures) found in Taylor and Hudson (1972) to arrive at the repressive disposition of a regime. The GAP also captures this notion, since it represents the unexplained values of rights-in-practice given rights-in-principle.

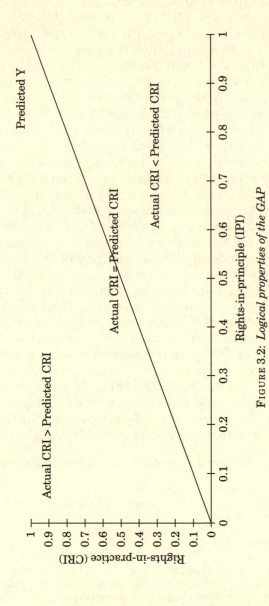

FIGURE 3.2: *Logical properties of the GAP*

6), and, most importantly for this study, moments of increased social mobilization (see Chapters 5–7).

The next chapter describes the evolution of rights trends using the three measures of the IPI, the CRI, and the GAP. The IPI is shown alongside BANKSLII to reveal the patterns in rights-in-principle over time. The CRI is presented with its different components to show the patterns of rights-in-practice over time, the contours of which are complemented by raw data on political and civil rights violations, deaths from political violence, and levels of newsprint consumption. Finally, the IPI, the CRI, and the GAP are brought together in each case to provide a full account of the changing profile of citizenship rights.

Measuring Social Movement Activity

The study treats labour mobilization and other social movement activity separately. This is justified by the historical importance of the labour movement, and by its long-term influence on the rights of citizenship (see Chapter 1). Data on labour activity is taken from the International Labour Organization (ILO) and other secondary sources. Data on social movement activity is generated by observing events, actors, and demands (see Chapter 2). Data from existing data archives, as well as an original coding protocol, were used to construct measures that describe the contours of social movement activity (Chapter 5). At a later stage, these measures contribute to the analysis of the relationship between waves of mobilization and changes in the provision of citizenship rights (Chapters 6 and 7).

Labour Activity

The primary source of labour movement data is the International Labour Organization's (ILO) *Statistical Yearbooks*, which include the number and magnitude of strikes in the four cases. The number of strikes in any one year is the strike rate. The total number of strikers involved in the total number of strikes provides the strike volume.[20] For years that are not covered by the ILO statistics, supplementary data was sought in the academic literature.[21] The

---

[20] For a review of strike data measurement, see Shorter and Tilly (1971), Hibbs (1976), Haimson and Tilly (1989), and Bordogna, Primo Celli, and Provasi (1989).

[21] Some examples of sources for the four cases include: for Brazil, Alves (1985) and Keck (1992); for Chile, Roddick (1989) and Frias (1989); for Mexico, Middlebrook (1982, 1989); for Spain, Maravall (1978).

secondary focus corroborated the primary events data, and provided information on the patterns of demand-making in the labour movement.

Other Social Movements: Existing Aggregate Data

Like measuring citizenship rights, measuring social movement activity raises questions of method. Tarrow identifies three approaches to measuring this activity, which are quantitative, textual, or a mixture of the two (Tarrow 1989: 357) . This study uses the mixture of methods to measure the events, participants, and the pattern of demand-making, as they develop over time. Available aggregate data sources provide quantitative measures of domestic conflict variables, which show broad patterns of social mobilization in the four cases. The two primary sources of this kind are the *World Handbook of Political and Social Indicators* (Taylor and Jodice 1983) and the *Cross-Polity Time Series Data Archive* (Banks 1994). Taylor and Jodice (1983) provide coverage of events from 1948 to 1977, and include data on demonstrations, political strikes, riots, armed attacks, and assassinations. Banks (1994) provides an accounting of events that were salient enough to appear in the *New York Times Index*. His data are for 1950 to 1990 and so cover the relevant years in all four cases. Banks has eight domestic conflict variables, of which four are most relevant: general strikes, riots, anti-government demonstrations, and assassinations. Summing the five measures from Taylor and Jodice (1983) and the four measures from Banks (1994) provides aggregate measures of social mobilization that are used alongside the other social movement events data developed in this study (see Chapter 5).

Other Social Movements: The Coding Protocol

A social movement activity coding protocol similar to that employed by Tarrow (1989) was developed to capture the main aspects of social movement activity other than labour activity.[22] Newspaper sources are suspect in the study of authoritarian regimes, since many acts of protest or dissent simply do not appear in the press. Hence, the enquiry surveyed the academic literature on social

---

[22] Tarrow (1989) used the *Corriere della Sera* to code events for Italy between 1965–75. Other studies that code events from national newspapers include: Klein (1984), Costain (1992), and Kriesi et al. (1995).

movements on the one hand, and primary documents, pamphlets, and ephemera produced by the movements themselves on the other, in order to code the elements of social movement activity. Much of the literature on social movements is concerned with general theoretical issues and the identities, strategies, and success of specific movements. This is certainly true of the literature on the four cases studied here (e.g. Davis 1992). Consequently, much of the work does not contain any events data, but some of it does. A substantial amount of information from the latter sources was collected and coded. Of the primary sources, two comprehensive microfilm collections of publications by the movements themselves exist for Brazil (Library of Congress 1988; Ballantyne 1988) and Chile (Princeton University 1985), and these provided information on events, participants, demands, and strategies.

General rules were established for coding data. First, social movement events were defined to include conferences, street demonstrations, marches, strikes, and public protests.[23] Tarrow (1989) noted that he did not code assemblies in Italy, unless they led to direct action. In authoritarian circumstances, however, assemblies and conferences often provoked repression by the state and qualify as mobilizing events. Second, a minimum threshold of data was established for registering an event, including the date of the event, the participants involved in the event, and the demands of the group participating in the event. Figure 3.3 shows the coding protocol, which is divided into quarter-years and contains the following categories: events, magnitude, forms of action (strike, non-strike, violent, non-violent), location (urban, rural), participants (workers, peasants, women, students, the poor), demands (material, economic, political, civil, other),[24] themes (e.g. land, water rights, housing, repression, voting), and links with unions and parties. Using the results of the protocol, Chapter 5 describes the contours

---

[23] For example, the *cacerolas* in Chile, where poor people living in the *poblaciones* of major cities pounded empty saucepans as a symbol of the food shortages that were due to Pinochet's austere economic programme (Oxhorn 1994).

[24] Material demands include: access to potable water and electricity, affordable housing, clean and functioning sewers, and day-care facilities and schools. Economic demands include: higher wages for work and lower prices for goods used in the home and small businesses. Political demands include: an end to repression, amnesty for political prisoners, political equality, and the free formation of political parties. Civil demands include legal title to land; the right to freedom of expression, association, conscience or belief; and the right to habeas corpus. Material and economic demands primarily address issues of physical survival (or the physical quality of life), whereas political and civil demands address issues of human dignity and integrity.

Category		Elements	1st Quarter	2nd Quarter	3rd Quarter	4th Quarter	Total for Year N
1	Events	N					
2	Magnitude	M					
3	Form of Action	Strike					
		Non-strike					
		Violent					
		Non-violent					
4	Location	Urban					
		Rural					
7	Participants	Workers					
		Peasants					
		Students					
		Women					
		Poor					
8	Demands	Material					
		Economic					
		Political					
		Civil					
		Other					
10	Themes	Water, housing, etc.					
11	Links	Unions, parties					

FIGURE 3.3: *Social movement coding protocol*

of social movement activity for the four cases. The protocol results are supplemented by secondary data and presented alongside data on the labour movement.

Summary

Since no complete and comprehensive measures of either social movement activity or citizenship rights were readily available, this study necessarily had to combine data from a variety of sources, in order to achieve the best measures it could. The resulting picture is something of a mosaic. Each piece of information that is coded adds a new tile to the mosaic, until the enquiry composes a full picture of citizenship rights and social movements. In this way, the study succeeds in operationalizing the main variables of citizenship and social movements (see Chapters 1 and 2). For citizenship rights, different sources of data were combined to measure rights-in-principle (IPI), rights-in-practice (CRI), and the gap between the two (GAP). For social movements, aggregate domestic conflict data, strike data, and the protocol data were combined to describe the waves of mobilization in the four cases. The next two chapters present the main trends, first in citizenship rights, then in social movement activity.

4

The Contours of Citizenship Rights

The previous chapter examined the sources and construction of the diverse measures and indicators that operationalize citizenship rights and social movements in this study. This chapter describes the trends and properties of the measures and indicators of citizenship rights. The next chapter will do the same for social movement activity. This chapter presents a succession of tables and figures which trace the evolution of citizenship rights over time. In this way, the different rights measures show the changes in rights provision both within and across cases. These measures comprise the rights-in-principle indicators (BANKSLII and the IPI), the rights-in-practice indicators (Gastil, FJII, DUFFMC, Arat, Humana, and the CRI), and the GAP indicator for the four cases over time. The three principal measures are presented for the four cases in the alphabetical order of Brazil, Chile, Mexico, and Spain. The chapter concludes with a discussion of the broad patterns of similarity and difference across the cases. These patterns will prove important to the subsequent analysis.

Rights-in-Principle

As outlined in the previous chapter, a longitudinal index of rights-in-principle was constructed from the data in the *Cross-Polity Time Series Data Archive* (Banks 1994), which represents pure institutional variation. BANKSLII covers the forty years from 1950 to 1990 and so amply accommodates the periods under study in all four cases. In this way, BANKSLII provides broad measures of rights-in-principle during and beyond the relevant periods of the enquiry. Since there are deficiencies and omissions in the aggregate data provided by Banks (1994), the IPI presents an index of pure institutional variation that is more sensitive to the procedural and legal changes that may affect citizenship rights. The three components of the index (core rights, contestation rights, and participation rights) may be viewed separately or combined to make a single index.[1] Here, the component parts are first presented separately, and then aggregated into a single index (IPI) for the purposes of comparing the four cases.

Brazil

Figure 4.1.1 shows the raw score[2] of BANKSLII for Brazil from 1950 to 1990. The slight dip and short rise that occurs in 1954 and 1955 indicates the end of the second administration of Getúlio Vargas and the brief military intervention that preceded the presidency of Juscelino Kubitschek. The steep dive in 1964 marks the military coup and the beginning of the authoritarian period. The slight rise in 1965–6 reflects Castelo Branco's declaration that the military intervention was only temporary. The next steep dive from 1966 to 1968 accompanies the passage of the 1967 Constitution and the Fifth Institutional Act (AI-5), after which Congress was suspended. The slight rise in 1982 responds to the return of directly elected governors. Finally, the small blip at the end of the period indicates the passage of the 1988 Constitution.[3] The procedural-institutional changes that are not reflected in the index include the 1978 abolition of AI-5 and the 1979 Party Reform Law, which rescinded the two-party model set up by the regime in 1966. IPI was constructed because BANKSLII overlooks institutional changes of this kind.

Figure 4.1.2 shows IPI's component parts for Brazil from 1964 to 1990. It was core rights which fluctuated most during the authoritarian period. AI-5 meant that such rights could be denied by the regime at any moment between 1968 and 1978. This potential is reflected in the steep dive of 1966–8 and the rise of 1978. The measure reaches its maximum in 1988 with the passage of the new Constitution. Contestation rights on the one hand remain quite

[1] The total raw score range for the index is from zero (0) to twenty-nine (29). The total raw score for core rights is ten (10); for contestation rights, is fifteen (15); and for participation rights, is four (4). See Figure 3.1 for these scores.

[2] Recall that this index ranges from 1 to 17. A score of one (1) indicates a regime with no institutions in place that guarantee the protection of citizen rights, and a score of seventeen (17) indicates full democratic institutions (See Chapter 3 and Appendix B).

[3] The much-studied democratic opening (*distensão*) begun under the leadership of President Geisel in 1974, does not appear to be represented by BANKSLII for the Geisel initiative was one of practice and not principle. Nothing changed in a pure institutional sense in 1974. In contrast, the main measure of rights-in-practice, the CRI, does reflect the *distensão*.

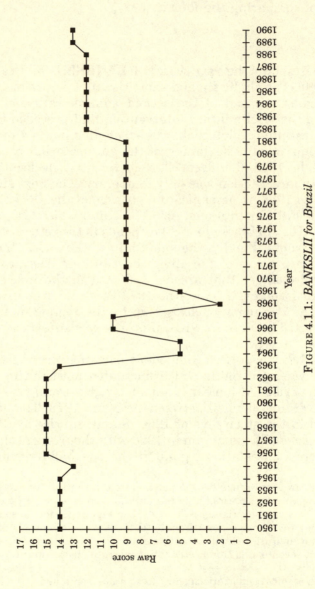

FIGURE 4.1.1: *BANKSLII for Brazil*

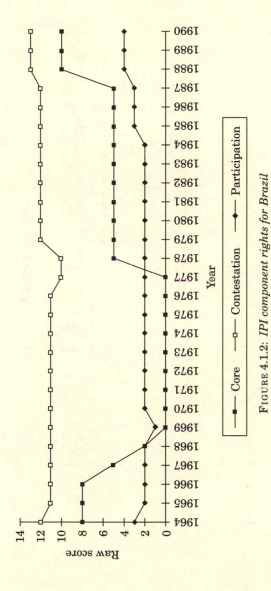

FIGURE 4.1.2: *IPI component rights for Brazil*

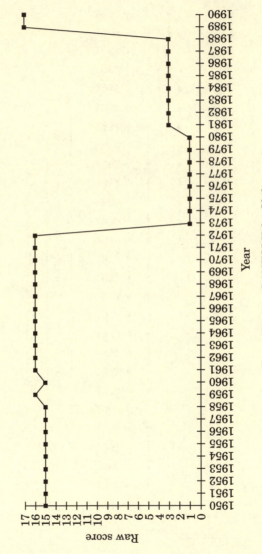

FIGURE 4.2.1: *BANKSLII for Chile*

high throughout the period (a mean of 12 out of 15), owing to the presence of the Congress, a functioning opposition party (the MDB), and limited trade unionism. Moreover, IPI is sensitive to the 1979 Party Reform Law, which ended the period of two-party rule. Finally, participation rights were curtailed throughout the period. Although the regime permitted regular elections, they were manipulated to maintain the military's hold on power. Only in 1985 did the regime begin to re-establish full participation rights. The 1988 Constitution extended the suffrage to illiterates. It is therefore clear that the fluctuations in the IPI in Brazil were mainly owing to changes in core rights. Despite the apparent protection of contestation rights, the core rights of citizenship were curtailed, especially between 1968 and 1978.

Chile

Figure 4.2.1 shows BANKSLII for Chile. It is clear that Chile enjoyed strong democratic institutions for many years before the 1973 coup. After the coup, the ruling four-man junta suspended the Constitution, dissolved the Congress, outlawed Popular Unity parties, banned all other political parties, disbanded labour unions, removed elected officials, suspended habeas corpus provisions, stopped all elections, and assumed all power in the junta. Authoritarian rule continued and was legalized in a number of Constitutional Acts in 1976. With a plebiscite recording 67 per cent popular support, the 1980 Constitution was approved. Ostensibly, this was a liberal democratic constitution, but contained within it a number of emergency clauses (particularly Transitory Article 24) which allowed the regime to continue its arbitrary suspension of citizenship rights (Drake and Jaksic 1991; Garretón 1989b; J. S. Valenzuela and Valenzuela 1986). The slow return to liberal democratic institutions is apparent in Figure 4.2.1. But the figure fails to capture the state of siege declared in November 1984 which suspended all citizenship rights for six months.

Figure 4.2.2 shows IPI's component parts for Chile from 1973 to 1990. In contrast to Brazil, all three rights components were curtailed by the Pinochet regime. Core rights were rescinded by the coup, but were ostensibly restored in 1976 with the passage of the Constitutional Acts. The 1980 Constitution guaranteed all liberal democratic rights, but contained the emergency clauses that could deny rights, as they did during the 1985 state of siege. The steep dive in core rights in 1985 marks the state of siege. Not until the 1988 plebiscite and the election of Patrício Aylwin were core rights

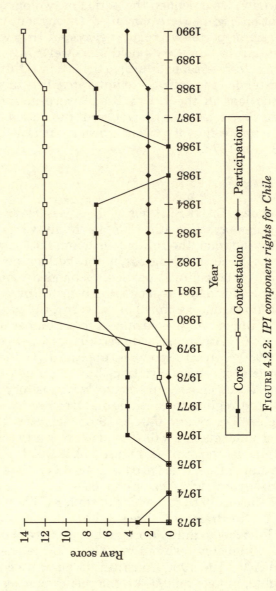

FIGURE 4.2.2: *IPI component rights for Chile*

fully protected. Contestation and participation rights were partially restored in 1980, and fully restored in 1989.

Mexico

Figure 4.3.1 shows BANKSLII for Mexico. The striking flatness of this figure seems to suggests that Mexico made no institutional changes over the period. Rights-in-principle in Mexico are difficult to measure. A succession of amendments to the 1917 Constitution has resulted in broad powers being given to the president (Garrido 1989). Beyond the powers established by these amendments, the president enjoys discretionary powers that are not contained in constitutional provisions.[4] Banks's measures (A. S. Banks 1994) do not reflect this growth of executive power. But they are sensitive to the relative power of the three branches of government, and the consequence is the relatively low raw score for the period (12 out of 17). De La Madrid's 'moral renovation' of 1982 and the greater fidelity of the electoral returns in major metropolitan areas in 1983 is the only change reflected in BANKSLII.

Figure 4.3.2 shows IPI's component parts for Mexico from 1963 to 1990. It is apparent that many of the procedural and electoral reforms carried out by the ruling party often escape the categories designed for the purposes of comparative enquiry. One such reform is the 1963 Party Deputy Reform which lowered the minimum age for members of Congress, and eased requirements for party registration (Bailey 1988). But IPI does capture some reforms. In 1970, the ruling party lowered the voting age from 21 to 18 and suppressed Article 145–2 of the Penal Code so reinstating the constitutional right to political assembly. In 1977 the Federal Law on Political Organizations and Electoral Processes (LOPPE) promoted party registration,[5] made grants available for party organization, and enlarged the chamber of deputies to 400 seats. Three hundred of these seats are elected by single member districts, and 100 proportionally, with the caveat that any minor party getting

---

[4] These include the power: (1) to amend the constitution, (2) to act as the chief legislator, (3) to act as the ultimate authority in electoral matters, (4) to designate presidential successors, (5) to designate state governors, members of PRI majorities in Congress, and state representatives, (6) to remove officials at the federal, state, and local level, (7) to impose views on both chambers of Congress, (8) to assume jurisdiction in judicial matters, (9) to impose authority over state governors, (10) to influence municipal government (Garrido 1989: 422–5).

[5] Parties that achieve 1.5 per cent of the vote for three elections, or that have 65,000 members, constitute a viable party organization (Hellman 1983).

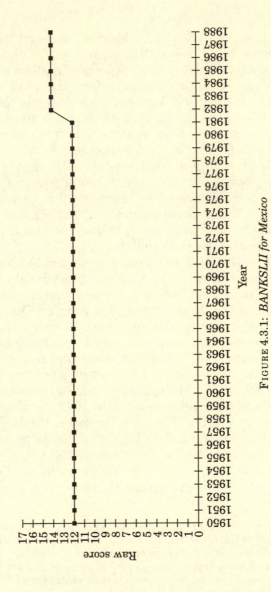

FIGURE 4.3.1: *BANKSLII for Mexico*

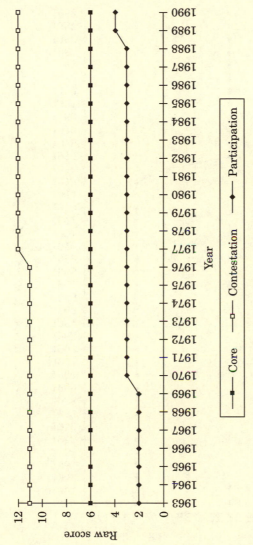

FIGURE 4.3.2: *IPI component rights for Mexico*

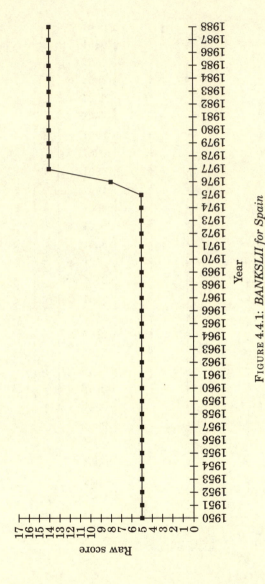

FIGURE 4.4.1: *BANKSLII for Spain*

more than 90 seats, gets half of those seats stripped away.[6] The LOPPE reforms ensured the dominance of the ruling party, while encouraging the competition of minor parties like the Mexican Communist Party (PCM), the Mexican Democratic Party (PDM), and the Socialist Worker's Party (PST) (Hellman 1983: 131). The LOPPE alters the measure of contestation rights. Finally, in 1989, changes to the Electoral Code increased participation rights. In contrast to Brazil and Chile, core rights in Mexico remain unchanged throughout the period. Thus, the 1970 reforms affected participation rights, the 1977 reforms affected contestation rights, and the 1989 reforms again affected participation rights.

Spain

The Francoist state did not have a single document that could be called a constitution. Rather, both the institutions of the state and the rights and duties of Spanish citizens were established by a series of Organic Laws that extend from 1938 to 1967.[7] The Francoist state was corporatist-authoritarian with all power concentrated in the executive. Unlike a Fascist state, however, it did not require mass mobilization and support, but only passive acceptance (Linz 1964). Citizens were given rights similar to those found in liberal democratic constitutions by the Fuero de Españoles, but these rights could be denied at any time by executive emergency powers. Figure 4.4.1 shows BANKSLII for Spain. The peculiar collection of Organic Laws that made up the Francoist Constitution restrict Spain's score to 5 until the death of Franco in 1975, when representative institutions were restored. A fully liberal democratic constitution was promulgated in 1978.

The IPI for Spain is shown in Figure 4.4.2. The 1969 state of siege reduces all scores to zero in that year. The state of siege was sanctioned by the emergency clauses and the 1967 Organic Law. The passage of the Statute of Associations in 1974 legalized autonomous political organizations for the first time since the Civil War. The statute permitted political organizations to participate

---

[6] A later reform in 1987 increased the Congress to 500 seats, but this reform does not affect the index (Hellman 1983: 131).

[7] These laws include: The Labour Law (9 March 1938); the Cortes Law (17 July 1942); the Fuero de Españoles (17 July 1945); the Law Referendum (22 October 1945); the Law of Succession (26 July 1947); the Principles of the National Movement (17 May 1958); and finally, the Organic Law (10 January 1967). For a complete set of these laws, see *Fundamental Laws of the State: The Spanish Constitution* (1972).

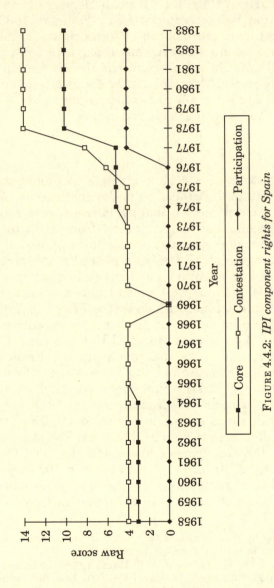

FIGURE 4.4.2: *IPI component rights for Spain*

TABLE 4.1. *Descriptive summaries and correlations of rights-in-principle indicators*[†]

	Mean	Std. dev.	Var.	Range	Min.	Max.	Corr.
Brazil							
Banks	.63	.20	.04	.81	.06	.88	.45*
IPI	.65	.17	.03	.57	.43	1.00	
Chile							
Banks	.58	.43	.18	1.00	.00	1.00	.65**
IPI	.48	.34	.11	.97	.00	.97	
Mexico							
Banks	.71	.05	.00	.13	.69	.81	.66***
IPI	.73	.02	.00	.07	.71	.79	
Spain							
Banks	.43	.26	.07	.56	.25	.81	.93***
IPI	.43	.30	.09	1.00	.00	1.00	

[†] Indicators range from 0 to 1; Pearson's r reported.
* p < .05   ** p < .01   *** p < .001

in elections. But the regime only recognized those organizations with a membership of 25,000 or more. Nonetheless, eight associations were established within nine months (Carr and Fusi 1981: 201). This law leads to a slight rise in the core rights component of the index. In 1976 contestation rights were altered by two important laws. In January, the Political Associations Bill legalized all political associations with no minimum membership requirement. The law originally excluded totalitarian parties but was amended in April to include the Communist Party. The Law for Political Reform dissolved the Francoist Assembly and opened the way for general elections (López-Pintor 1987). In March of the following year unions became legal. Finally, the 1978 Constitution brought full citizenship rights to Spain after almost forty years of dictatorship.

Figures 4.1.1 to 4.4.2 show BANKSLII and the three components of IPI for the four cases over time. Table 4.1 offers a comparison of summary statistics for BANKSLII and the IPI across the four cases. The three component parts of the IPI have been aggregated into a single index, and both BANKSLII and the IPI have been converted to a common scale ranging from 0 to 1, where a zero (0) signifies no rights guaranteed and a one (1) means full rights are guaranteed. In addition to the descriptive statistics provided in the table, bivariate correlations for BANKSLII and IPI are reported.

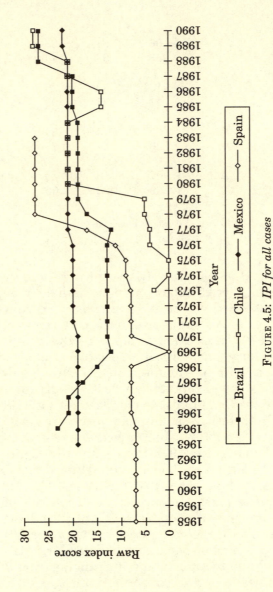

FIGURE 4.5: *IPI for all cases*

Of the four cases, Mexico appears as the most democratic of regimes in principle, and the one that has varied its institutional-procedural guarantees the least. Chile has the widest range of values, followed by Spain and Brazil in that order. Moreover, it is clear that BANKSLII and the IPI are significantly correlated for all the cases. Although the IPI covers fewer years, the overall correlations are significant and support the use of the IPI as a measure of pure institutional-procedural variation, or of variation in rights-in-principle. As comparison of the aggregated index demonstrates (Figure 4.5), the IPI assumes a similar shape in the four cases: after initial low scores and occasional dips, it tends to rise. All the regimes have made improvements in rights-in-principle and Mexico has the lowest IPI score by the end. Turning to rights-in-practice, the next figures describe the components of the combined rights index (CRI). The figures are supported by the available data on rights violations.

Rights-in-Practice

The last chapter outlined the five measures of rights-in-practice used to compose the combined rights-in-practice index (CRI), which include Gastil (1987, 1989), Freedom House (1995), Fitzgibbon (1967), Johnson (1977, 1981), Duff and McCamant (1976), Arat (1991) and Humana (1983, 1986, 1992). Of these five, only Arat, Gastil, and Humana cover all four cases, with the two remaining measures addressing only the Latin American cases.[8] The following figures present both the separate measures and the combined index, or CRI, and are accompanied by bivariate correlations of the measures. The statistical evidence and the correlation matrices and figures lend support to the visual representation of the figures, and both of them defend the construction of the CRI, which is the arithmetic mean of the separate measures (see Chapter 3). Raw data on rights violations is used to supplement the abstract measures in each case and serve to confirm more general impressions. The CRI is then compared across the four cases.

Brazil

Table 4.2 is a bivariate correlation matrix of the rights-in-practice measures for Brazil. Three out of the five measures are significantly

---

[8] See Table 3.5 for dates of coverage.

TABLE 4.2. *Correlation matrix of rights-in-practice measures for Brazil* (Pearson's r)

	Duff-McCamant	Fitzgibbon-Johnson	Gastil	Humana
Arat	.82**	.33	.95**	—
Duff-McCamant		.73	—	—
Fitzgibbon-Johnson			—	.33
Gastil				—

— No correlation due to too few cases.
* p < .05   ** p < .01   *** p < .001

correlated. This means that the measures reach similar results by different means (see Chapter 3), and that the CRI is a faithful expression of the overall trend in rights-in-practice for Brazil. Figure 4.6.1 shows both the component rights-in-practice measures and the composite CRI, which follows the bold black line. Since the different measures are so closely correlated, the CRI achieves a good visual 'fit'. The 1964 coup, the period of political liberalization, and the gradual transition to civilian rule are clearly visible.

According to Alves, the initial years of the Brazilian military regime were characterized by three cycles of repression. The first cycle of 1964 targeted those individuals politically linked to the populist past, but direct physical violence was limited to workers and peasants (Alves 1985: 103). During the military's Operação Limpeza, some 50,000 people were arrested including trade union leaders, peasant leaders, intellectuals, teachers, students, and lay organizers of the Catholic movements in the universities and in the countryside (Alves 1985: 34–8).[9] The second cycle of 1965–6 extended the first, but 'it did not include direct widespread use of violence' (Alves 1985: 103). The third cycle of 1968–9 began with the passage of the Fifth Institutional Act (AI-5) and its extensive purges were 'accompanied by large-scale military maneuvers using physical violence against all classes indiscriminately' (Alves 1985: 103). The evidence presented in Figure 4.6.1 appears to confirm the argument. The CRI takes an initial dive in 1964, rises slightly during the second cycle, and then dives deeply again during the third cycle.

[9] This number of 50,000 is an estimate that 'was reached after compiling data from interviews with different political actors who dealt closely either with lists of political prisoners that were reported in the press or with their defense' (Alves 1985: 305 n. 17).

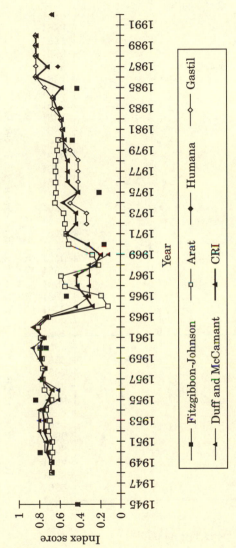

FIGURE 4.6.1: *Rights-in-practice measures for Brazil*

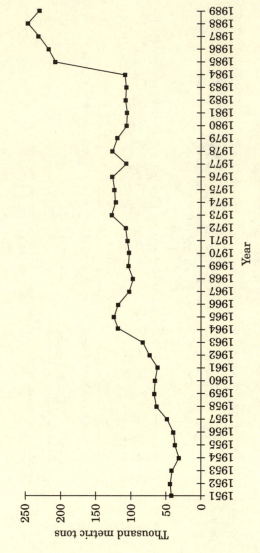

FIGURE 4.6.2: *Newsprint consumption in Brazil (1951–1989)*

Other sources also support the Alves argument. Dassin (1986) and Y. Cohen (1989) demonstrate the increases both in the number of deaths sanctioned by the military regime between 1969 and 1973, and in the political disappearances from 1971 to 1975. The deaths from political violence measure (Taylor and Jodice 1983) also rises from 1970 to 1974. Krane (1983) and dos Santos (1990) show that political purges of the national congress, state assemblies, city councils, state governorships, and mayorships were most intensive between 1967 and 1970.[10] These observations are supported by P. J. King's (1989) summary of findings from Amnesty International and the International Commission of Jurists on the total number of deaths, political prisoners, and exiles over the period.[11] The only exception is found in the rural sector. Despite the positive trend in the CRI after 1974, rural assassinations reach their peak between 1980 and 1985 (Grzybowski 1990). The patterns of violence in rural Brazil are buttressed by traditional forms of patrimonialism or *coronelismo*, which place large landowners beyond the law (Panizza 1993). Hence, the violence is seen as a consequence of a culture of 'paralegality' (Zac 1989; Panizza 1993).[12] Rural assassinations are one form of rural violence perpetuated by rogue landowners who operate free of effective government control.

Finally, Figure 4.6.2 shows newsprint consumption levels from 1951 to 1989. It is assumed that under conditions of press censorship newsprint consumption will vary with the changing disposition of the regime. In this case, newsprint consumption reaches its first peak before the coup, and then slumps until 1969. The plateau from 1973 to 1976 marks the initial period of political liberalization. The sharp dip in 1976 responds to the increased censorship which followed repeated MDB victories but which is soon corrected by the new policy on press censorship in 1977.[13] A final surge in newsprint consumption occurs after 1985, the year official press censorship was ended.[14] Although newsprint consumption is often

[10] During the Castelo Branco administration (1964–7) 224 political offices were purged, and during the Costa e Silva administration (1967–70) 349 political offices were purged. During the Médici administration (1970–3) the figure dropped to 10, and for the Geisel years (1974–9) the figure was 12.

[11] P. J. King (1989) reports 354 dead, 25,000 detainees, and 10,000 exiles.

[12] 'It is not so much, as in the past, a case of the patrimonial state blurring the dividing lines between the public and private domains but the blurring of the frontier between legality and illegality by the emergence of a culture of paralegality' (Panizza 1993: 211).

[13] This law is known as the Lei Falcão, named after Armando Falcão, the federal Justice Minister (Skidmore 1988: 189; Alves 1985: 164).

[14] Article 19 (1991: 77).

TABLE 4.3. *Correlation matrix of rights-in-practice measures for Chile* (Pearson's r)

	Duff-McCamant	Fitzgibbon-Johnson	Gastil	Humana
Arat	.65**	.99**	.95**	—
Duff-McCamant		—	—	—
Fitzgibbon-Johnson			−.50	.33
Gastil				—

— No correlation due to too few cases.
* p < .05 ** p < .01 *** p < .001

taken as an indicator of economic development, it did not increase dramatically during the 'miracle' growth rate of the early 1970s. But its close relationship with political liberalization is supported by its correlations with both the IPI and the CRI over the years 1964–89.[15]

Chile

There is broad agreement in the interpretation of rights-in-practice in Chile with four out of the five measures significantly correlated (see Table 4.3). The graph of these measures and of the composite CRI (Figure 4.7.1) confirms this agreement. There is a stark contrast between the Pinochet years and the period preceding the coup. The slight dip in 1985 marks the state of siege and the sharp rise of 1988 marks the moment of the plebiscite and the beginning of Chile's return to democracy.

As in the Brazilian case, raw data on rights violations supports the trajectory described by the CRI. Like the Archdiocese of São Paulo, the Catholic Church in Chile, and the Vicaría de la Solidaridad in particular, documented cases of human rights abuse and helped those who were persecuted by the regime. More data is available in reports from Amnesty International and the International Commission of Jurists. The Truth and Reconciliation Commission has listed state-sanctioned deaths for each year of the regime, confining the list to deaths that are fully documented with names, dates, and locations. The reports are summarized in graphic

[15] For IPI, r = .63, p = .001; for CRI, r = .71, p = .000.

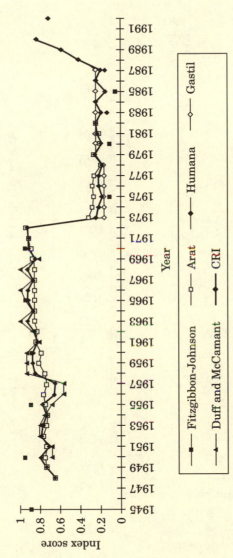

FIGURE 4.7.1: *Rights-in-practice measures for Chile*

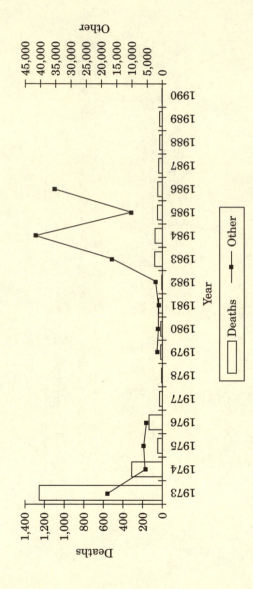

FIGURE 4.7.2: Raw rights violations in Chile (1973–1990)

form in Figure 4.7.2.[16] The deaths line represents the documented cases of deaths, while the other line represents a summary of detentions, tortures, and intimidation. Extreme repression declined during the late 1970s, rose sharply during the 1983–6 protests, and declined again before and during the plebiscite and democratic transition. Although outright killing was kept to a minimum during the latter part of the period, arbitrary detention and torture were the two forms of repression most used by the regime.[17]

With regard to newsprint consumption (Figure 4.7.3) in Chile, the trend is paradoxical. It declines during the Allende years (1970–3), then rises in the first years of the military dictatorship. The decline in the Allende years is owing to his battles with the conservative press.[18] The initial rise under Pinochet levels off until 1982, and then surges upward during the 1980s. Freedom of the press was established by the 1980 Constitution,[19] but it was repeatedly violated by the military under their emergency powers. Despite these violations, publication, circulation, and dissent do not appear to have diminished.[20] Institutionally, Chile was slowly making a transition to fuller protection of political and civil rights. Freedom

[16] Although not used in the figure, the deaths from political violence measure (Taylor and Jodice 1983) supports the evidence assembled by the organizations mentioned above.

[17] In 1984, 38,000 people were detained without a formal charge being levelled, and over 1,500 were tortured. In 1986, some 33,000 were detained and over a 1,000 were tortured. These figures illustrate a cycle of repression carried out by the regime that continued right up to within a year of the 1988 plebiscite (Reiter, Zunzunegui, and Quiroga 1992: 116–20).

[18] During the Allende years, the owners of the conservative newspaper *El Mercurio* owned paper production factories, under control of Augustín Edwards. To combat a rising tide of negative press, President Allende attempted to nationalize the Compañía Manufacturera de Papeles y Cartones (La Papelera) to give the government a monopoly over paper production. His bid failed, but he froze paper prices below market equilibrium causing great losses in the paper industry and a slowing of production (Kaufman 1988: 60–114).

[19] Article 19, clause 12 of the 1980 Constitution provided for freedom of expression and private operation of the press. However, Article 41 allows suspension and restriction of information during a declared state of emergency (hence the small dip in 1986), and Transitory Article 24 permits the President to restrict information generated by the 'founding, editing, or circulating of new publications' (Article 19 1988: 73–4).

[20] 'Despite harsh legal restrictions . . . with the shutdown of several opposition publications; despite severe (and often violent) repression in practice, including the September 1986 death squad murder of a leading journalist, José Carrasco Tapia; and despite frequent jailings and prosecutions, the Chilean press has been remarkably resilient. In this sense, Chile presents a contradiction: it is simultaneously a country that treats dissent with extreme harshness and one in which, under duress, the expression of dissent flourishes' (Article 19 1988: 75).

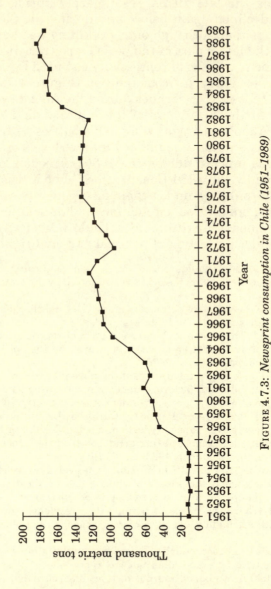

FIGURE 4.7.3: *Newsprint consumption in Chile (1951–1989)*

TABLE 4.4. *Correlation matrix of rights-in-practice measures for Mexico* (Pearson's r)

	Duff-McCamant	Fitzgibbon-Johnson	Gastil	Humana
Arat	−.53*	.45	.05	—
Duff-McCamant		—	—	—
Fitzgibbon-Johnson			.87	—
Gastil				—

— No correlation due to too few cases.
* p < .05   ** p < .01   *** p < .001

of the press was among the first rights to be protected. Newsprint consumption is highly correlated with the IPI and weakly correlated with the CRI.[21]

Mexico

There is only one significant correlation among the five rights-in-practice measures for Mexico (Table 4.4), and that correlation is negative. Clearly there is little academic agreement about rights provision in Mexico. Duff and McCamant respond to the 1968 Tlatelolco massacre, whereas Arat ignores the event entirely. Duff and McCamant's trajectory descends while Arat's tends to rise. But, as Figure 4.8.1 shows, most measures register a decline in values from the mid-1970s, with the CRI itself descending rapidly throughout the 1980s.

The documentary evidence on political and civil rights abuse in Mexico supports this picture of decline. Amnesty International and Americas' Watch both conclude that human rights abuse is especially high in rural areas, and that land disputes can often lead to murder. There were 351 assassinations between 1971 and 1986, and 93 per cent were of peasants (Amnesty International 1986; Concha 1988; Americas' Watch 1991*a*). These deaths may have little to do with government authorities, but Amnesty alleges that some local authorities have been directly involved in political killings (Concha 1988; Nagengast, Stavenhagen, and Kearney 1992). Besides corroborating these cases, the US State Department's *Country Reports on Human Rights* (1981) claims that 500 people have disappeared without a trace since 1969. There were at least

[21] For IPI, r = .66, p = .004; for CRI, r = .42, p = .09.

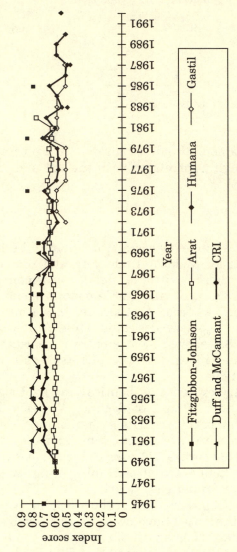

FIGURE 4.8.1: *Rights-in-practice measures for Mexico*

nineteen disappearances during the de la Madrid administration (Amnesty International 1991: 35), and some thirty-three journalists were assassinated (Amnesty International 1991: 113). Activists of the Party of the Democratic Revolution (PRD) claim that 250 of their supporters were assassinated by PRI supporters following the hotly contested 1988 elections (Amnesty International 1991: 41–8; *La Jornada*, 11 May 1993).

In addition to deaths and disappearances, there is a high incidence of torture and physical abuse of detainees in local prisons, as well as unfair trials and the incarceration of prisoners of conscience (Nagengast, Stavenhagen, and Kearney 1992: 9; Amnesty International 1991; Americas' Watch 1991*b*). After the 1985 earthquake in Mexico City, which destroyed the Attorney General's building, bodies were found showing marks of torture (US State Department 1985). More recently, it was alleged that the Salinas administration was 'one of the bloodiest in the recent history of the country', with widespread assassinations of 'common delinquents, exalted politicians, social activists, Catholic ministers, prominent drug traffickers, peasants, workers, rebellious prisoners, political bosses and other members of society' (*Proceso*, 3 October 1994: 6). Although *Proceso* gives no global figures, it is abundantly clear from the narrative that the accumulated dead run into the hundreds.

Besides these more blatant abuses, there are also strong indications that other basic rights, like freedom of assembly or freedom of speech, are less securely protected than the benign accounts of Mexican politics might suggest. The constitutional guarantee of freedom of the press, for example, is often abrogated by the 'conscious use of economic and political mechanisms' (Article 19 1988: 94; Amnesty International 1991: 73–81). Press companies depend on advertising and subsidies to fund their papers. Private corporations can penalize papers by withholding lucrative advertising contracts as they did from *Excélsior* between 1972 and 1974. More importantly, two-thirds of all advertising is paid by the government (Article 19 1988: 99) which can itself withhold advertising contracts from newspapers with which it disagrees. Since the government also controls paper production, is has de facto control of the press.[22] Newsprint consumption shows a rapid increase for the

[22] The state owns 90 per cent of the shares in the Productora e Importadora de Papel, SA (PIPSA) and '[t]hrough PIPSA, the state is not only able to pressurize a newspaper into changing its editorial policy, but also to provoke its disappearance by not supplying it with paper or not supplying it on time' (Article 19 1988: 100). Although President Salinas announced that PIPSA would be privatized, it remained under government control.

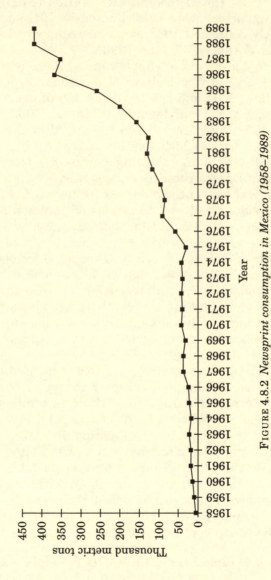

FIGURE 4.8.2 *Newsprint consumption in Mexico (1958–1989)*

mid-1970s onwards (see Figure 4.8.2), and it is more highly correlated with the IPI than in the other cases, but negatively correlated with the CRI.[23]

Spain

The only measures covering Spain are Arat, Gastil, and Humana, and Humana's intermittent coverage (1982, 1987, 1992) means that only Arat and Gastil are correlated. Arat extends from 1948 to 1982 and Gastil from 1972 to 1990. For the ten years that they overlap, the correlation is both high and significant, suggesting that they read the democratic transition in Spain in much the same way (r = .94, p = .000). Gastil may have anticipated Arat in some degree (see Figure 4.9.1), but it is clear that the big change in rights-in-practice in Spain is concentrated in the years of the transition itself. Rights-in-practice continue to improve in the years following the 1978 Constitution.

Despite the lack of systematic studies of rights violations in Spain under Franco, there is some evidence in support of this picture. The government's prison records in the *Anuario Estadístico de España* include the total prison population by year as well as the population incarcerated for offences against national security. These records are presented in Figure 4.9.2, where the bars indicate the number of national security prisoners, and the line their ratio to the entire prison population. The number of national security prisoners declines up to the passage of the 1967 Organic Law, but increases sharply during the state of siege of 1969, in both absolute and relative terms. Their number and proportion decreases dramatically with the democratic transition, only to rise again owing to the terrorist campaign of the Basque Separatists. The State Department's *Country Reports* on Spain have focused on the treatment of terrorist suspects.[24] Not surprisingly, the ratio of national security prisoners to the total prison population is negatively correlated with the IPI and the CRI.[25]

The deaths from political violence in Spain, as reported by Taylor and Jodice (1983) cluster in the years of the democratic transition. There were 57 deaths between 1948 and 1968, but 159 between 1969 to 1977 (Taylor and Jodice 1983: 49). The measure of newsprint consumption (as shown in Figure 4.9.3) also emphasizes the

[23] For IPI, r = .73, p = .000; for CRI, r = −.61, p = .001.
[24] See, for example, the discussion of the 10-day detention period in the 1983 *Country Report*, 1088.
[25] For IPI, r = −.58, p = .002; for CRI, r = −.64, p = .000.

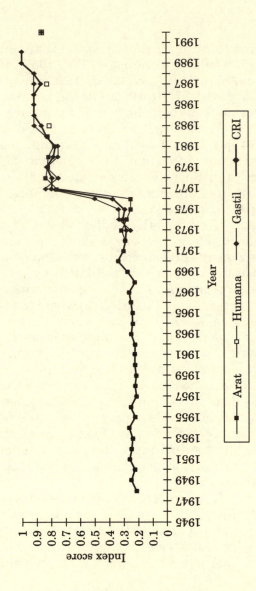

FIGURE 4.9.1: *Rights-in-practice measures for Spain*

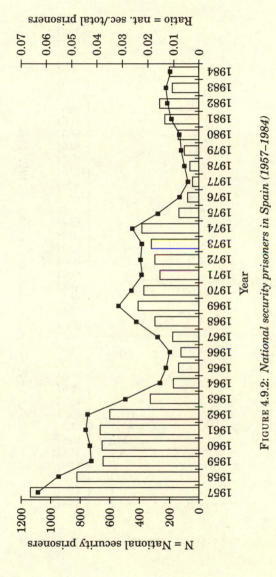

FIGURE 4.9.2: *National security prisoners in Spain (1957–1984)*

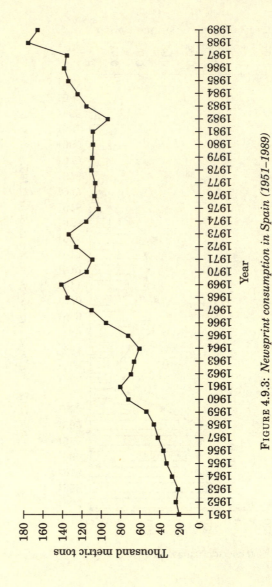

FIGURE 4.9.3: *Newsprint consumption in Spain (1951–1989)*

importance of the 1969 state of siege, with consumption dropping without interruption from the late 1960s to the early 1980s. During the state of siege, most civil and political rights were suspended and the practice of prior censorship was reintroduced (Hollyman 1974: 60–9).[26] Newsprint consumption is not significantly correlated with the IPI but is significantly correlated with the CRI.[27]

Summary

This review has created a clear, comparative picture of the evolution of rights-in-practice. In all cases there were 'waves of repression', characterized by a large number of extrajudicial killings, political executions, prolonged detentions, torture, and broad patterns of press censorship. These measures cannot capture all rights violations, nor are all these violations perpetrated by the state. But the measures, and especially the CRI, do describe the general condition of rights-in-practice as it changes over time. In this way, they can highlight the moments when individual citizens were not free to associate or express dissent and were not free from persecution.

A comparative picture of the evolution of the CRI (Figure 4.10) reveals a clear contrast between Chile and Spain, on the one hand, and Brazil and Mexico, on the other. The former experienced concentrated and rapid transitions back to fuller protection of rights-in-practice, effectively meeting the standards set out in their new constitutions, whereas Brazil underwent a slow and protracted transition through incremental changes in both rights-in-practice and rights-in-principle. But the most striking result is that Mexico has the lowest scores for both rights-in-principle (Figure 4.5) and rights-in-practice (Figure 4.10) by the end of the period. Despite incremental improvements in rights-in-principle Mexico's rights-in-practice show a secular decline over the period which leaves it with the worst overall performance.

The Gap

The indices of rights-in-principle (IPI) and rights-in-practice (CRI) measure the variation of these two aspects of rights provision over time. This variation can also be measured by the difference between the two indices, which is the GAP. The statistical values of

---

[26] Articles 12, 14, 15, 16, and 18 of the Fuero de Españoles were suspended, which guaranteed rights to expression, residence, home, association, and freedom from illegal arrest.   [27] For IPI, $r = .17$, $p = .399$; for CRI, $r = .57$, $p = .001$.

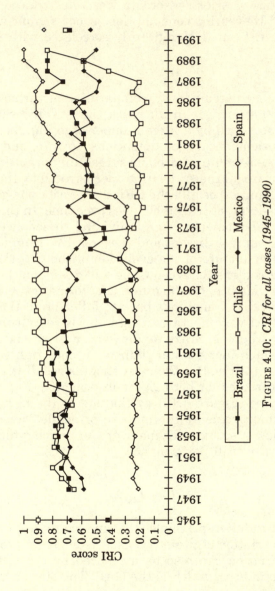

FIGURE 4.10: *CRI for all cases (1945–1990)*

the GAP are the residuals that result from regressing the CRI on the IPI. In Chapter 3, it was assumed for logical purposes that the relationship between rights-in-principle and rights-in-practice would be positive, have a slope of one, and a constant of zero (see Figure 3.2). In reality, this relationship may be different as the figures in this section will show. In particular, the slope of the relationship may be positive or negative, and may be less than one. The constant may be greater than zero and the overall explanatory power of rights-in-principle may be less than 100 per cent. It is this unexplained variance in rights-in-practice that is captured by the GAP. A positive GAP means there are more rights-in-practice, and a negative GAP fewer rights-in-practice, than might have been predicted by the level of rights-in-principle. In short, the GAP measures the repressive disposition of the regime. The statistical relationship between the GAP and measures of social mobilization will be examined in Chapters 6 and 7. Here, the GAP will simply be described and related to the IPI and the CRI.

Brazil

The values of the GAP for Brazil over the period 1964–90 can first be shown as a scattergram (Figure 4.11.1) It is evident that the positive and negative values of the GAP are evenly distributed around the regression line. This means that the number of years the GAP is negative (1971, 1974, 1976–8, 1983–4, and 1986–9) is roughly equal to the number of years it is positive (1964–1970, 1979–82, and 1985) (see Figure 4.11.2). Although the relationship between rights-in-principle and rights-in-practice is positive and significant, with both improving over time,[28] the R^2 value of .24 obtained from calculating the GAP suggests that institutional-procedural improvements (IPI) cannot explain all the variation in rights-in-practice (CRI). The unexplained variance is thus captured by the GAP.

Prima facie, the years during which the GAP is negative are also moments of increased social mobilization and political contestation (see Chapter 5). In 1968 workers carried out a general strike in the industrial cities of Osasco and Contagem; and 1968–70 were years of urban terrorism which provoked the regime's violent repression. In 1979–82 new labour organizations became

---

[28] The equation for the regression line in Brazil is CRI = .19 + .55*IPI (t = 3.083; p = .005), which means that for every positive unit of change in rights-in-principle, rights-in-practice improve roughly by one-half.

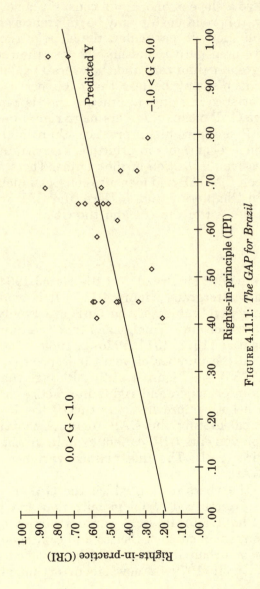

FIGURE 4.11.1: *The GAP for Brazil*

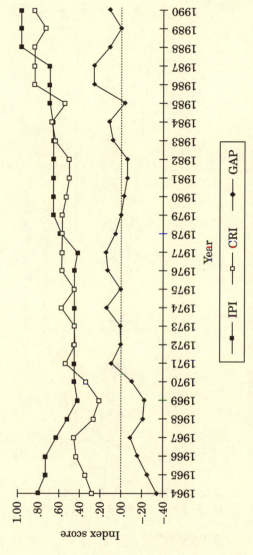

FIGURE 4.11.2: *IPI, CRI, and GAP in Brazil (1964–1990)*

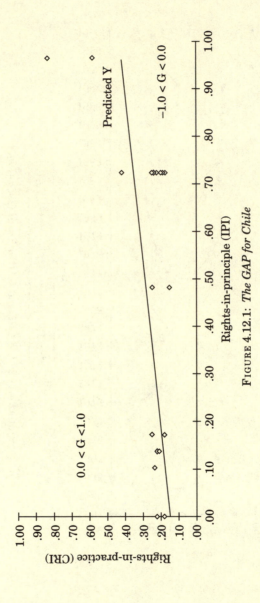

FIGURE 4.12.1: *The GAP for Chile*

active in Brazil's industrial heartland, urban social movements spread through the cities of Rio and São Paulo, and newly formed political parties entered the electoral arena at the municipal level. In 1984–5 there was widespread mobilization around the direct election campaign of *diretas já* and the democratic transition itself. Chapter 5 sets out to measure these waves of mobilization, while their statistical relationship with the GAP is explored in Chapters 6 and 7.

Chile

As in Brazil, the GAP values in Chile fall above and below the regression line (Figure 4.12.1) where it is negative for nine years (1978, 1980–7) and positive for eight years (1973–7, 1979, 1988–90) (Figure 4.12.2). As in Brazil, the relationship between rights-in-principle and rights-in-practice is positive and significant.[29] But, once again, the R^2 of .25 suggests that institutional-procedural changes cannot entirely explain the variance in rights-in-practice. On the contrary, the Pinochet regime impaired rights-in-practice while guaranteeing them in principle in the years following the 1980 constitutional plebiscite, and the GAP remains negative throughout the 1980s until the second plebiscite in 1988.

With the exception of the 1985 state of siege, rights-in-principle tend to improve after 1979, whereas rights-in-practice remain precarious until the late 1980s. This difference between principle and practice in part produces the negative GAP between 1980 and 1987. Once again, this is the period where social mobilization and political contestation are concentrated. Labour mobilization rises sharply in both 1979 and 1987. Overall social mobilization peaks in 1983–4 (Chapter 5). The relationship between the changes in individual rights provision and waves of social mobilization is examined in Chapters 6 and 7.

Mexico

The values of the GAP for the period 1963–90 show that although there were relatively few legal-institutional changes that could

---

[29] The equation for the regression line in Chile is CRI = .15 + .28*IPI (t = 2.607; p = .02), which means that for every one-unit increase in rights-in-principle, rights-in-practice improves by just over one-quarter.

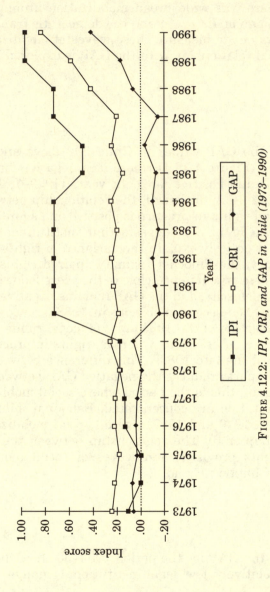

FIGURE 4.12.2: *IPI, CRI, and GAP in Chile (1973–1990)*

be construed as extending rights-in-principle, the GAP remains negative for the greater part of the period. In stark contrast to Brazil and Chile, the relationship between rights-in-principle and rights-in-practice is *negative* and significant[30] producing a regression line of predicted CRI values that slopes down and to the right (Figure 4.13.1). This negative relationship indicates that, even while the regime tried to extend rights-in-principle by improving its institutional design, its record on rights-in-practice went on deteriorating. Moreover, the R^2 value is .49, indicating that about half of the variance in the actual values of rights-in-practice is explained by rights-in-principle themselves. But a negative GAP still means that there are fewer rights-in-practice than might be expected from the prevailing level of rights-in-principle.

The combination of the negative coefficient with the R^2 value suggests some interesting hypotheses about the evolution of rights over this period. On the one hand, it is possible that the institutional improvements that extended rights-in-principle made the regime more confident about denying or offending rights-in-practice; or that the extension of rights-in-principle was designed to disguise a deterioration of rights-in-practice. On the other hand, it is possible that the extension of rights-in-principle called forth increased mobilization and contestation around demands stated in the language of rights which, in turn, entailed higher levels of repression and the denial of rights.[31]

The second hypothesis seems especially compelling in the context of an increasingly contested electoral arena. This suggests another and possibly more accurate way of stating the hypothesis: as political rights are extended (and, in particular, as mobilization around these rights moves squarely into the electoral arena) so the record on civil rights deteriorates as these rights are increasingly curtailed or denied. Since the construction of the CRI does not permit its disaggregation into civil and political rights, it is impossible to test this hypothesis directly, but strong circumstantial evidence in its support is suggested by juxtaposing the IPI, the CRI, and the GAP (Figure 4.13.2). It is evident from the figure that whenever political contestation increases (1968, 1976, 1983, and

---

[30] The equation for the regression line in Mexico is CRI = $1.70 - 1.54 \times$ IPI ($t = -5.19$; $p = .000$), which means that for every one-unit increase in rights-in-principle there is approximately a one-and-a-half unit decrease in rights-in-practice.

[31] A third possibility, more simply, is that information on the denial of rights-in-practice becomes available with improved reporting and scrutiny by international agencies. This possibility might weaken the suggested hypotheses, but would not render them entirely spurious.

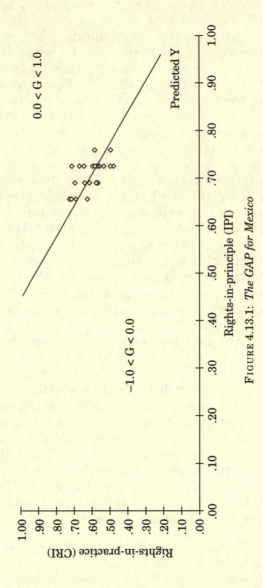

FIGURE 4.13.1: *The GAP for Mexico*

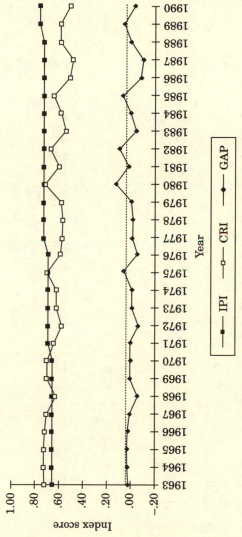

FIGURE 4.13.2: *IPI, CRI, and GAP in Mexico (1963–1990)*

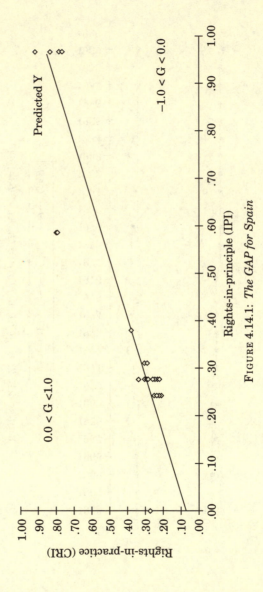

FIGURE 4.14.1: *The GAP for Spain*

1987–8) the (negative) GAP rapidly widens,[32] and this observation may go some way towards explaining these contradictory effects of the citizenship process in Mexico. It remains for Chapters 6 and 7 to explore this connection between the changes in individual rights provision and waves of mobilization.

Spain

Finally, Spain presents a fascinating case of 'we mean what we say'. The majority of GAP values are close to zero (Figure 4.14.1), suggesting that Franco carefully constructed his authoritarian regime and then stuck closely to his rules. As in Brazil and Chile, the relationship between rights-in-principle and rights-in-practice is positive and significant.[33] But the unusually high R^2 value of .86 indicates that changes in rights-in-principle explain most of the variance in rights-in-practice, so differentiating Spain from the other three cases. In authoritarian Spain, rights were denied. In democratic Spain, rights were protected. The two positive spikes in the GAP reflect the 1969 state of siege and the period immediately preceding the 1978 Constitution, which are both moments when rights-in-practice exceed rights-in-principle.

Although the dramatic change in rights provision is clearly concentrated in the years of democratic transition (Figure 14.14.2), social mobilization and the pursuit of rights began in the early 1960s. Successive waves of mobilization throughout the 1960s and early 1970s finally peaked in 1976–7 (Chapter 5). For most of this time the struggle for rights was led by the labour movement, and especially the Worker's Commissions inside the regime's Vertical Syndicate. The statistical analysis in Chapter 6 addresses the relationship between these waves of mobilization and rights provision, while Chapter 7 reveals the mutual impact of individual rights and social mobilization in the moment of democratic transition.

[32] 1968 was the year of the students' movement. 1976 marked the culmination of the struggle of the Sole Union of Electrical Workers of the Mexican Republic (SUTERM) and the formation of the National Coordinating Committee 'Plan de Ayala' (CNPA). 1983 saw a significant electoral mobilization by the opposition, and its electoral victory in several metropolitan districts. 1987–8 saw the rise of the National Democratic Front (FDN), the debacle of the July elections, and the ensuing months of mobilization and protest.

[33] The equation for the regression line in Spain is CRI = .07 + .81*IPI (t = 12.608; p = .000). In Spain the correspondence between IPI and CRI is the highest of the four cases as it is closest to unity.

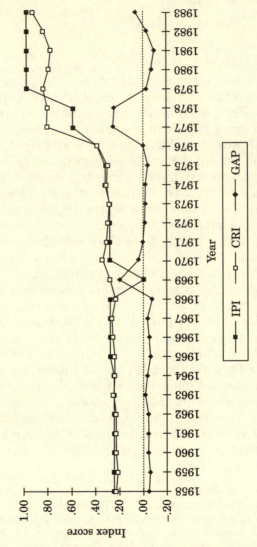

FIGURE 4.14.2: *IPI, CRI, and GAP in Spain (1958–1983)*

Individual Rights and Authoritarian Regimes

There are common patterns of rights provision across the four cases which place them squarely in the MSSD framework outlined in Chapter 3. First, all the cases show an improvement in rights-in-principle. With the possible exception of the two states of siege in Chile and Spain, once rights-in-principle are established, they tend not to be rescinded. Second, all the cases show visible fluctuations in rights-in-practice. Third, all the cases show shifts between a negative and positive GAP. These common patterns begin to describe the characteristics of the individual rights of citizenship in authoritarian or semi-authoritarian conditions.

But there are also differences between the cases that can begin to structure the comparative argument. With regard to rights-in-principle (IPI), an initial dip in Brazil is followed by improvement throughout the period. The Chilean index remains static until the Constitution of 1980, but this rise is reversed by the state of siege. Mexico shows a steady improvement from 1970 onward. And like Chile, Spain's index remains static until its dramatic rise during the democratic transition. With regard to rights-in-practice, Brazil's index follows rights-in-principle until 1979, when principle and practice diverge. In contrast, the rights-in-practice indices in both Chile and Spain remain static for the duration of the Pinochet and Franco regimes, and then rise rapidly. In Mexico alone does the rights-in-practice index exhibit a distinctive decline over the period, with the result that Mexico has the lowest final score of the four cases.

Finally, with regard to the GAP, Brazil has moments when the GAP is negative, reflecting the controlled political liberalization carried out by the military. The negative GAP in Chile through most of the 1980s reflects the continuing repressive inclination of the regime. The recurrently negative GAP in Mexico reflects the regime's attempt to contain the mobilization of opposition, especially in the electoral arena. Finally, the GAP hovering close to zero in Spain reflects the tight control of the Francoist state which only begins to loosen after the death of the dictator.

It is the premiss of this study that fluctuation and comparative differences in citizenship rights shown in this chapter are related to the rise and fall of social mobilization. On the one hand, an increase in individual rights protection may lead either to an increase in social mobilization, as a result of greater freedom to act, or to a decline, as the *raison d'être* of social movement activity is removed. On the other hand, social mobilization in the pursuit of individual rights may lead to an extension of rights provision, or may provoke increased repression or a loss of rights. The next chapter describes these waves of mobilization through a focus on the events, actors, and demands of social movement activity across the four cases. Chapters 6 and 7 examine in what ways and in what degree these waves of mobilization are related to the evolution of the individual rights of citizenship.

The Contours of Social Movements

The previous chapter described the trends in the measures and indicators of citizenship rights in the four cases. This chapter does the same for social movement activity. Like citizenship rights, there are no comprehensive studies of social movement activity, and so this chapter pieces together primary and secondary source material on social movements to provide a picture of waves of protest. The chapter is organized into three sections. The first section describes both labour and other social movement events, drawn from the coding protocol, the ILO, and the secondary literature. Using these same sources the second section shows the trends in labour and other social movement demands over time. Finally, the third section describes three further aspects of social movement activity—sectors, participants, and forms of action—which serve to complement the events and demands trends described in the first two sections.

Events

The first set of figures in this section (5.1.1–5.1.4) draws on the coding protocol (cf. Chapter 3) to show the trajectory of social movement activity (SMA). The data represents the events that have received most attention in the literature and composes a time-series measure of the waves of mobilization in the four cases. The second set of figures (5.2.1–5.2.4) describes the two most useful measures of labour movement activity. The strike rate (SR) is simply the number of strikes, and the strike volume (SV) the total number of workers involved in all strikes, in any given year.[1] Since the strike rate is the most salient measure of labour activity and can be compared directly to social movement activity, it is central to the statistical analysis in Chapters 6 and 7. Although the strike volume provides a less comparable measure (since volume

---

[1] A third measure, the strike size, is derived by dividing the volume by the rate.

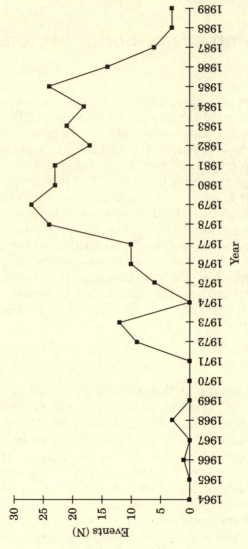

FIGURE 5.1.1: Social movement activity in Brazil

measures for other social movements are difficult to obtain), it is incorporated in the preliminary analysis of Chapter 6. The third set of figures (5.3.1–5.3.4) compares SMA and SR over time in all the cases and is complemented by a final set of figures (5.4.1–5.4.4) which shows 'domestic conflict' measures (Taylor and Jodice 1983; A. S. Banks 1994).

Social Movement Activity (SMA)

The social movement events in Brazil (Figure 5.1.1) reach three peaks of activity over the period 1964–89. The first peak occurs in 1973, one year before the political opening. The second peak in 1979 coincides with the passage of the Party Reform Law and the dramatic rise in labour activity in the 'ABC' strikes (compare Figure 5.3.1). The third peak in 1984–5 marks the year of the *diretas já* campaign and the year of the transition to civilian rule. Throughout the years of the military regime, there was a growth in both urban residents' and professional associations, and rural and urban trade unions, that formed the basis of much of this social movement activity.[2] There was an average number of 1,798 urban trade unions during the military period (Alves 1985), but the number of rural unions grew from 4 in 1960 to 2,586 in 1986.[3] The popular mobilization of the 1980s, which is clearly shown in the figure, drew upon this prolific growth of popular organizations.

In the case of Chile, the events data (Figure 5.1.2) reveal the sharp rise in social movement activity during the 1983–4 days of national protest. The wave of mobilization ended in the six-month state of siege in 1984–5. There is a second but smaller peak just prior to the 1988 plebiscite. As in Brazil, popular organizations developed throughout the period. Popular Economic Organizations (OEPs) in Santiago and other urban areas flourished during the late 1970s and 1980s, and dedicated their energies to setting up workshops (*talleres*), committees of unemployed workers, consumer groups, soup kitchens, housing committees, health groups,

---

[2] From 1964 to 1978, the number of middle and upper class residents' and professional associations in Rio de Janeiro increased from 1 to 5, but the lower class associations decreased from 70 to 28. The trend was reversed in 1979–81, when the total of 30 middle and upper class associations was overtaken by 136 lower class associations (Boschi 1987*b*). Urban associations in Belo Horizonte grew from 3 in 1964 to 40 in 1980, reaching a peak of 46 in 1978 (Somarriba, Valadares, and Afonso 1984).

[3] Rural unionization was driven by the state under its plan of *assistencialismo* in an attempt to incorporate and control rural workers. But, as the final section of this chapter shows, rural mobilization increased throughout the period.

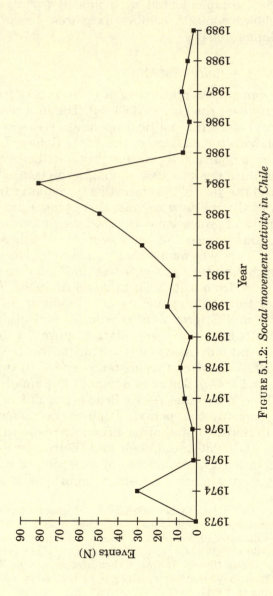

FIGURE 5.1.2: *Social movement activity in Chile*

and independent workers' unions. The number of such organizations grew from 2 in 1973 to 456 in 1985 (Razeto et al. 1986) despite their selective repression by the regime (Razeto et al. 1986; Leiva and Petras 1988).[4] These urban organizations provided the foundation for social movement activity and, in particular, for the groups which mobilized during the national days of protest (Oxhorn 1995).

The events results for Mexico (Figure 5.1.3) show four peaks of social movement activity. The first peak occurs in 1974–5 and reflects rural mobilization for agrarian reform and land distribution. The second peak in 1981–2 coincides with the onset of economic crisis. The National Coordinating Committee of the Urban Popular Movements (CONAMUP) was the most active group during the years surrounding this second peak (Ramirez Saiz 1986).[5] The third peak occurs in the aftermath of the 1985 earthquake and is largely owing to the activity of the Coordinating Committee for Earthquake Victims (CUD). The final peak of 1988 marks the electoral challenge to the ruling party led by the National Democratic Front (FDN) of Cuauhtémoc Cárdenas (see Chapter 4).

The lack of quantitative studies of social movement activity in Spain under Franco led to a reliance on coded narratives of the opposition to him, combined with two measures from Taylor and Jodice (1983), namely political strikes and demonstrations.[6] It is clear that social movement activity in Spain (Figure 5.1.4) gradually increases over the period, before surging dramatically after the death of Franco in 1975. Maravall's (1978) account of student opposition to the regime over the period 1963–74 corroborates the picture of social movement events in general.

Castells's (1983) in-depth study of the Citizens Movement of Madrid[7] also supports these trends. This movement emerged after the 1969 state of siege, when the political opposition learned the painful lesson that 'direct confrontation with the dictatorship was

[4] For the early 1980s, 30 per cent of the OEPs were workshops, 18 per cent were canteens, and 14 per cent were consumer cooperatives. Soup kitchens only represent 6 per cent of the OEPs during this period.

[5] In the late 1970s Mexico began to experience a growth in the number of Urban Popular Movements (MUPs). There were approximately 159 MUPs distributed throughout Mexico by the mid-1980s with the majority of them concentrated in Mexico City (12 per cent) and the Federal District (46 per cent). CONAMUP is the umbrella organization for the MUPs in Mexico.

[6] The Taylor and Jodice (1983) data come from the *New York Times*, which can be expected to have covered the most important events in Spain over the period.

[7] Castells (1983) codes 23 neighbourhood associations according to levels of mobilization, to which he relates the geographical distribution of the associations, their socio-economic and political characteristics, and their links with other groups.

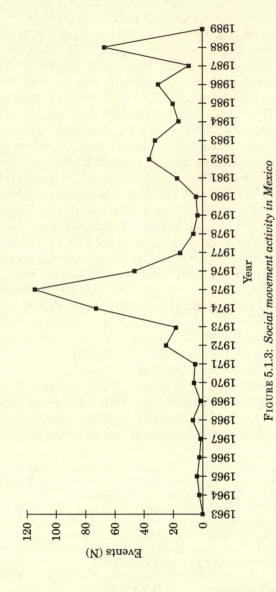

FIGURE 5.1.3: *Social movement activity in Mexico*

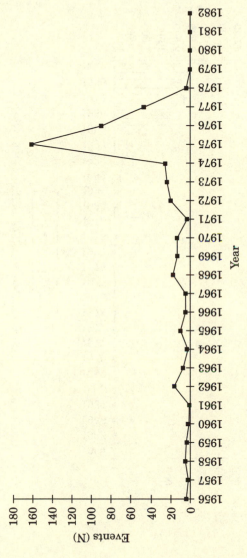

FIGURE 5.1.4: *Social movement activity in Spain*

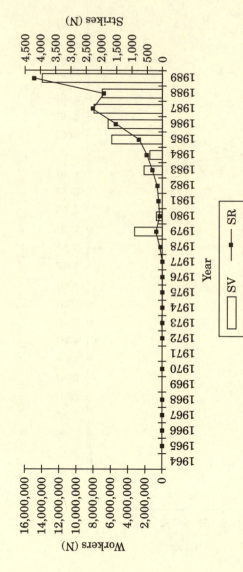

FIGURE 5.2.1: *Strike rate and strike volume in Brazil (1964–1989)*

suicidal' (Castells 1983: 234). At that time the neighbourhood associations were still illegal, since all associations except the Falange
were banned. Yet, the movement managed to consolidate its support
in the shanty towns and public-housing areas during the early
1970s and went on to fight for legal recognition as 'part of the final
popular assault to end authoritarian rule' (Castells 1983: 235–6).
It continued to grow during the late 1970s and by 1977 it comprised
110 associations, with 60,000 members and 5,000 militants. It led
waves of mobilization mostly in the shanty towns and in middle-
class residential neighbourhoods and estates (Castells 1983: 226–
8). Similarly to the urban associations in Brazil, the OEPs in Chile,
and the MUPs in Mexico, the movement provided a platform for
popular opposition to the regime.

Labour Movement Activity (SR and SV)

Figure 5.2.1 shows the strike rate (SR) and strike volume (SV)
measures for Brazil, from 1964–89. The data in the figure are the
averages of measures found in ILO reports and other secondary
sources (Humphrey 1979; Alves 1985; Payne 1991; and Antunes
1994).[8] There was little visible labour opposition to the regime
during the years immediately after the coup (Y. Cohen 1989), but
it grew throughout the period and dramatically so after 1978.[9]
This year saw the beginning of the 'ABC' strikes, centred in the
industrial heartland of Brazil, and initially concentrated in the
metallurgical, medical, and educational sectors. As the wave of
mobilization built in 1979, strike volume exceeded strike rate, with
an average strike size of 17,818 workers (twice the average for the
following year and over four times the average for the 1983–9
period).[10] Both the rate and volume of strikes steadily increases
throughout this period, with the volume exceeding the rate until

[8] These sources do not cover all the years. ILO data is for 1980–9, Alves (1985)
for 1978–80, Payne (1991) for 1983–8, and Antunes (1994) for 1978–88.
[9] Strikes in 1968 occurred in the metallurgical sector in the cities of Contagem
and Osasco (Weffort 1972). Eleven strikes occurred in 1973 at the Indústria Villares
plant in São Paulo, and at three motor company factories, including Volkswagen,
General Motors, and Ford. In the next year, 19 strikes were led by unions in the
metallurgical, energy, textile, and electrical power sectors (Humphrey 1979, 1982).
[10] There is no reason for the strike rate and strike volume to coincide and it is
common for the 'shape' of labour mobilization to change over time (Shorter and
Tilly 1971; Hibbs 1976), suggesting that strikes can be small and more frequent
in some periods, and large and less frequent in others. Those peaks that do coincide suggest an increase in the number of strikes that also mobilize more workers.

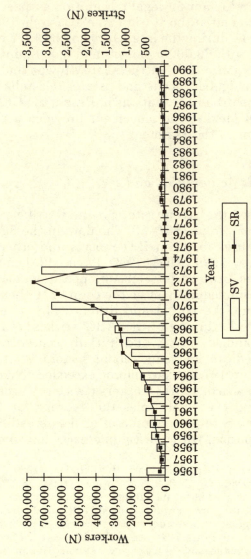

FIGURE 5.2.2a: *Strike rate and strike volume in Chile (1956–1990)*

1987. Despite the differences between rate and volume, they are highly correlated, suggesting a steadily growing labour movement.[11]

Since labour activity plummeted after the military coup in Chile, two figures are required to describe the trends in strike rate and strike volume (Figures 5.2.2a and 5.2.2b). The average of 980 strikes per year in the 1956–73 period dropped to an average of 48 strikes between 1973 and 1990, while the average strike volume dropped from 229,215 to 12,329 workers, and the average strike size from 307 to 179 workers.[12] Although Figure 5.2.2a seems to indicate that labour activity ceased altogether after 1974, Figure 5.2.2b successfully describes the new wave of labour mobilization from 1979 to 1990. During this wave the strike rate peaks twice, once in 1980, the year of the constitutional plebiscite, and once in 1990. Early in the period strike volume exceeded strike rate, but they move closer together during the 1980s, and the two are strongly correlated.[13]

In Mexico it is apparent that labour is quiescent during the 1960s and early 1970s (Figure 5.2.3),[14] and there is little strike activity accompanying either the doctors' movement of 1965–6 or the student movement of 1968. Labour mobilization accelerates with the López Portillo administration (1976–82) and the strike rate peaks in 1982. In this year, the country defaulted on its international debt repayments, and entered a profound economic crisis, which temporarily stopped the labour movement in its tracks. For the remainder of the 1980s strike volume exceeded strike rate, indicating that strikes were both large and infrequent. Average strike size rose from 60 workers before 1982 to 483 after that year, as a result of mobilization by the large unions in the Confederation of Mexican Workers (CTM) and the Federation of the Public Service Workers' Unions (FSTSE) against the austerity measures implemented to contain the crisis. In contrast to Brazil and Chile, strike rate and strike volume are not significantly correlated.[15]

In Spain strike rate far exceeded strike volume for the years 1962–76 (Figure 5.2.4),[16] indicating that strikes tended to be small but frequent. The average strike size was 367 workers for this period, against 1,624 for the years 1977–85. The strike rate peaked in 1976, one year after Franco's death, and three years before

[11] $r = .97$; $p = .000$.   [12] These data are from the ILO and Frias (1989).
[13] $r = .84$; $p = .000$.   [14] The data are from the ILO and Middlebrook (1982).
[15] $r = -.008$; $p = .97$.
[16] The data are from Blanc (1966), Maravall (1978), and the ILO (1969), which was allowed into Spain in 1962 to conduct an assessment of labour conditions subsequent to Spain's application for membership to the EC.

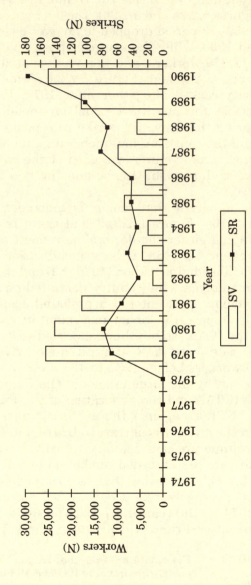

FIGURE 5.2.2b: *Strike rate and strike volume in Chile (1974–1990)*

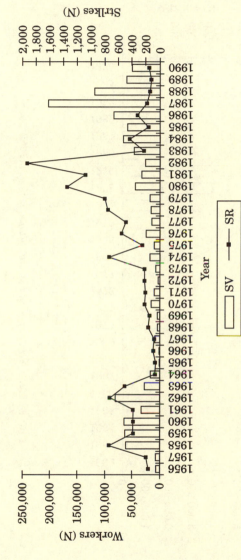

FIGURE 5.2.3: *Strike rate and strike volume in Mexico (1956–1990)*

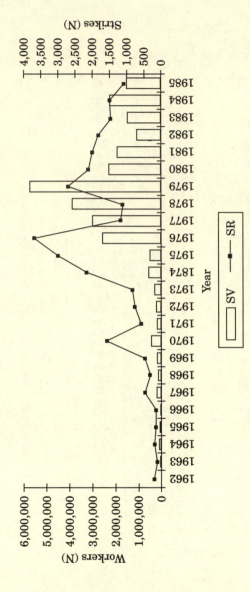

FIGURE 5.2.4: *Strike rate and strike volume in Spain (1962–1985)*

the peak in strike volume of 1979. The average strike size for the latter year is 2,132 workers, or some six times the average of the years preceding Franco's death. Before 1976 labour mobilization was largely led by the clandestine Worker's Commissions, and the dramatic increase in average strike size follows the legalization of trade unions in that year. Like Brazil and Chile, strike rate and strike volume are significantly correlated, but the correlation is not so strong.[17]

Waves of Protest (SMA and SV)

It is now possible to compare the events measures for social movement activity (SMA) with the events measures for labour mobilization (SR) in order to decribe the waves of protest that occurred in the four cases (Figures 5.3.1–5.3.4). In all the cases, labour mobilization tends to *precede* other social movement activity, indicating that it was the labour movement which mounted the first challenge to these regimes. In Brazil, the enormity of labour compared to other mobilization (Figure 5.3.1) required the strike rate to be scaled by a factor of 100. The difference between labour and non-labour mobilization demonstrates the preponderance of the labour movement. The 19 strikes (SR) and 12 social movement events (SMA) in 1973, had risen to 180 and 27 respectively in 1979. A ratio of labour to non-labour mobilization of 330:21 in 1983 had increased to 843:24 by 1985. In other words, labour mobilization is both larger and more frequent than other mobilization and tends to precede it.

It is clear that labour mobilization also precedes other social mobilization in Chile (Figure 5.3.2), with the 1980 peak in labour mobilization preceding other mobilization by four years. In contrast to Brazil, the strike rate did not have to be scaled, since the incidence of each kind of mobilization is comparable.[18] In Mexico too, where the strike rate has been scaled by a factor of ten, labour organizations are the first to mobilize (Figure 5.3.3), with the 1974 peak in the strike rate narrowly preceding the 1975 peak in non-labour mobilization. The 1980 peak in labour activity again precedes a rise in non-labour mobilization, but both culminate in the 1982 wave of protest, the year the economic crisis broke. The pattern

---

[17] $r = .56$; $p = .005$.
[18] The comparatively low strike rate in Chile reflects both the effectiveness of the military's repression and its policy of de-industrialization.

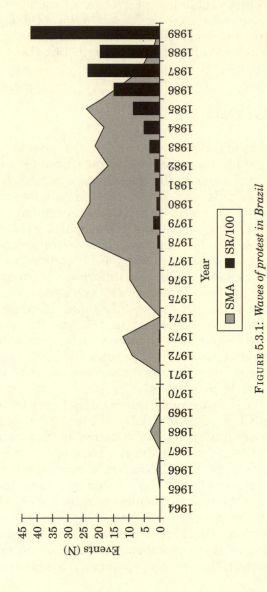

FIGURE 5.3.1: *Waves of protest in Brazil*

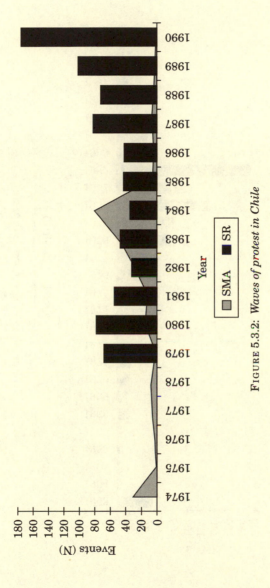

FIGURE 5.3.2: *Waves of protest in Chile*

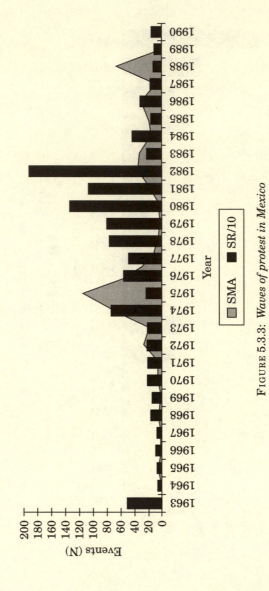

FIGURE 5.3.3: *Waves of protest in Mexico*

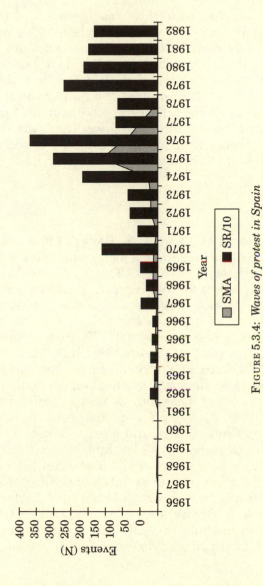

FIGURE 5.3.4: *Waves of protest in Spain*

continues until 1988 when non-labour mobilization peaks without a concurrent peak in labour activity, demonstrating that the contested election campaign provoked high levels of mobilization without causing major strikes in industry.

In Spain, where the strike rate was again scaled by a factor of ten (Figure 5.3.4) protest events in the late 1950s and the early 1960s were evenly distributed between labour and other social movements. By 1962, however, labour begins to exceed non-labour activity by 216 events to 16, and the 1967 peak in the strike rate precedes the small swell of protest from other social movements. Similarly, peaks of labour activity in 1970 and 1974 precede other social mobilization, so conforming to the general pattern. The exception to the rule occurs in 1975, when the peak of social movement activity precedes the labour peak by one year.

Domestic Conflict

Taylor and Jodice (1983) and A. S. Banks (1994) provide aggregate data on social mobilization which complements the patterns described in Figures 5.1.1–5.3.4. The Taylor and Jodice (1983) data contains measures for five domestic conflict variables, namely demonstrations, political strikes, riots, armed attacks, and assassinations.[19] Figure 5.4.1 shows the sum of the five variables for the four cases over the period 1968–77. Spain appears to have the highest level of conflict, followed by Chile, Mexico, and Brazil. A. S. Banks (1994) uses similar domestic conflict variables, namely general strikes, riots, demonstrations, and assassinations. Figure 5.4.2 shows the sum of these four domestic conflict variables over the period 1950–90, where Spain again appears to have more conflict, followed by Chile, Brazil, and Mexico. The two measures are strongly correlated in Spain, Chile, and Mexico.[20]

The relationship between these domestic conflict measures and the social mobilization measures (SMA and SR) varies from case to case. For Brazil and Mexico, neither the Taylor and Jodice (1983) nor the A. S. Banks (1994) data are correlated with either SMA or SR, and in Chile the only correlation is between Banks and SMA. But for Spain, Taylor and Jodice are correlated with

---

[19] Note that two of these measures are used for SMA in Spain.

[20] For Chile, $r = .76$; $p = .01$; for Mexico, $r = .96$; $p = .001$; and for Spain, $r = .70$; $p = .023$. The lack of significant correlation for Brazil ($r = .48$; $p = .163$) indicates a possible error in reportage or different sources of information.

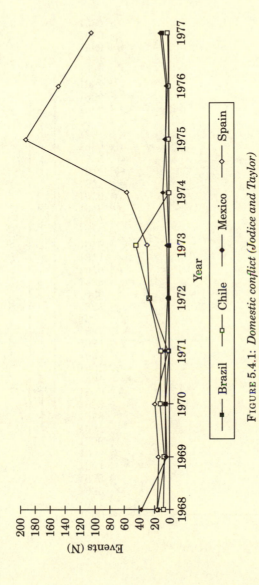

FIGURE 5.4.1: *Domestic conflict (Jodice and Taylor)*

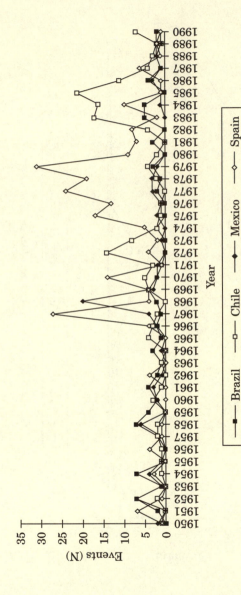

FIGURE 5.4.2: *Domestic conflict (Banks)*

TABLE 5.1. *Critical years of social mobilization*

Case	Social movement events (SMA) Figures 5.1.1–5.1.4	Strike rate (SR) Figures 5.2.1–5.2.4	Strike volume (SV) Figures 5.2.1–5.2.4	Domestic conflict Figures 5.4.1–5.4.2
Brazil	1968, 1973, 1979, 1983, 1985	1982, 1987, 1990	1979, 1983, 1985	1968–1969, 1977–1978, 1984
Chile	1980, 1984, 1989	1980, 1987, 1990	1979–1981, 1989–1990	1973, 1982–1985
Mexico	1968, 1972, 1975, 1982, 1986, 1988	1962, 1974, 1982	1962, 1987	1968, 1976–1977, 1985–1986
Spain	1958, 1962, 1965, 1968, 1975	1962, 1970, 1976, 1979	1979, 1984	1967, 1972–1977

both SMA and SR, and Banks is correlated with SR.[21] The very partial correlations between SMA and SR, on the one hand, and the Banks, and Taylor and Jodice, on the other, suggest that the latter measures may capture political violence rather than domestic conflict.[22] But the domestic conflict measures do capture the concentrated moments of mobilization of the Spanish democratic transition and the 1983–4 protests in Chile to some degree. This is evident from Table 5.1 which summarizes the critical years of domestic conflict (Figures 5.4.1 and 5.4.2) alongside the peak years of mobilization apparent in the social movement measures.

This first section of the chapter has focused on social movement events, which, as one of the most salient features of social mobilization, will be incorporated into the statistical analysis of Chapters 6 and 7. SMA, SR, and their sum (SMA + SR) will be used to examine the relationship between social movement activity and citizenship rights over time in Chapter 6. Subsequently, the critical years of mobilization listed in Table 5.1 will be used to examine their relationship through time in Chapter 7. The next section examines the composition and evolution of social movement and labour demands across the four cases.

[21] For Chile, $r = .50$; $p = .04$. For SMA and Taylor and Jodice in Spain, $r = .96$; $p = .000$; for SMA and Banks, $r = .29$; $p = .14$; for SR and Taylor and Jodice, $r = .84$; $p = .002$; and for SR and Banks, $r = .46$; $p = .02$. The fact that SMA in Spain is composed of two measures found in Taylor and Jodice explains the high correlation.

[22] Moreover, the Taylor and Jodice data stops in 1977, which effectively excludes the three Latin American cases and may provide a further reason for the low correlations.

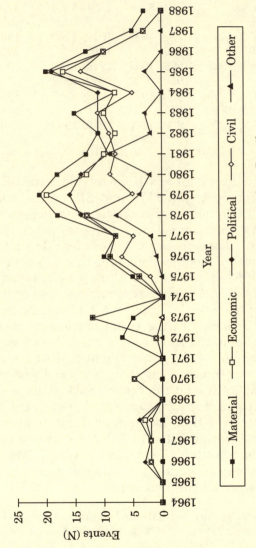

FIGURE 5.5.1a: *Social movement demands in Brazil*

TABLE 5.2. *Demand patterns in Brazil* (percentages)

Period	Material	Economic	Political	Civil
1964–1973 (n = 34)	35	74	79	35
1974–1982 (n = 140)	74	61	61	41
1982–1989 (n = 86)	57	44	50	37

Demands

Social movement demonstrations, marches, sit-ins, and strikes often carry with them particular demands that are chanted, written down, or voiced in some other way by the movements. The coding protocol contains four general types of demands: material, economic, political, and civil (see Chapter 3). This section describes the overall trends in demands, their patterns across periods of years derived from the trends, and the ratio of political and civil demands to material and economic demands. The main aim of the section is to describe the development of the language of rights over time by identifying the principal shifts in the patterns of demand-making.

Of the 260 total events recorded for the whole period in Brazil (Figure 5.5.1a), material demands are made in 69 per cent of the events, economic demands in 61 per cent, political demands in 64 per cent, and civil demands in 43 per cent.[23] But these summary statistics tend to obscure how the composition of demands changes over time. Hence, periods were derived from the waves of protest to reveal the main changes. The cells in Table 5.2 are the percentage of total events for each period in which different types of demand are made. Reading across the cells shows that economic and political demands dominated the events of the first period, since these were the most repressive and authoritarian years of the regime. In the period of political liberalization, from 1973 to 1982, material demands displaced the previous dominance of economic and political demands. Material demands continued to dominate the third period (1982–9), but political and civil demands

---

[23] The total of these percentages exceeds 100, since different types of demand could be made in each event.

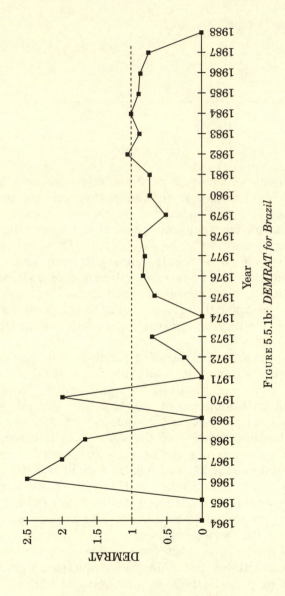

FIGURE 5.5.1b: *DEMRAT for Brazil*

became proportionately more important, demonstrating a shifting composition of demands in which the discourse of the political and civil rights of citizenship becomes more pronounced.

Material demands peak in 1979, when they appear in 74 per cent of the events. Political demands are numerous during the 1984 *diretas já* campaign (61 per cent), but peak one year later during the transition to civilian rule (79 per cent). When the ratio of political and civil demands to material and economic demands (DEMRAT) is plotted for the whole period, the shifts in demand become clearer. When DEMRAT > 1 (1965–8, 1970, 1982, and 1984), political and civil demands *exceed* material and economic demands (Figure 5.5.1b).[24]

In contrast to Brazil, political demands dominate the entire period in Chile (Figure 5.5.2a). Of the 262 events coded, material demands are made in 44 per cent of the events, economic demands in 49 per cent, political demands in 71 per cent, and civil demands in 53 per cent. As in Brazil, dividing these years into separate periods (1973–82 and 1983–9) clarifies the shifting composition of demands (Table 5.3). In the first period, material and economic demands are more important than political and civil demands, but in the second period the relationship is reversed. After the economic crisis of 1982 political and civil demands exceed material and economic demands. Material and economic demands peak in 1982, whereas political and civil demands peak in 1984 at the height of the national days of protest. The plot of DEMRAT for Chile makes this shift in composition clearer (Figure 5.5.2.b). DEMRAT is greater than one in three separate periods, 1975–9, 1983–4, and 1986–9. The peak of mobilization in 1984 is dominated by political and civil over material and economic demands by a ratio of 10:1.

The pattern of demands in Mexico is similar to the one found in Chile (Figure 5.5.3a). Of the total of 560 events, material demands are made in 67 per cent of the events, economic demands in 47 per cent, political demands in 57 per cent, and civil demands in 26 per cent. Dividing the overall trajectory of demands into three separate periods (1964–77, 1978–82, and 1983–8) again clarifies their evolution (Table 5.4). Reading across the cells in the table shows that material and economic demands are made in more events

---

[24] In Chapter 7 Boolean algebraic analysis is used to explore the necessary and sufficient conditions for the impact of social movement activity on rights provision, and vice versa. DEMRAT is included in this analysis as POLD, or political demands, which are deemed to be present whenever DEMRAT > 1.

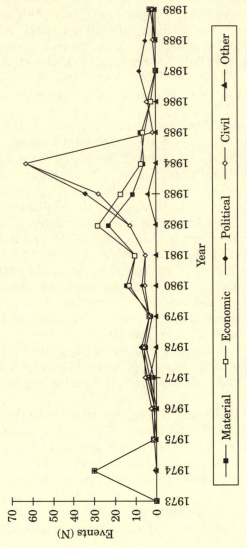

FIGURE 5.5.2a: *Social movement demands in Chile*

TABLE 5.3. *Demand patterns in Chile* (percentages)

Period	Material	Economic	Political	Civil
1974–1982 (n = 105)	83	90	67	39
1983–1989 (n = 157)	17	22	75	62

than political and civil demands during the first period. But political demands dominate the second and third periods. Hence, material demands peak in 1975 and 1982, whereas political demands peak in 1982 and 1988. DEMRAT is greater than one (Figure 5.5.3b) in 1967–8, the year of the student movement; in 1981–4, the years of growing mobilization against austerity policies; and 1988, the year of the National Democratic Front's challenge to the ruling party.[25]

Demands in Spain throughout the period were predominantly political and civil (Figure 5.5.4a), with any early economic demands giving way to political and civil demands in later moments of mobilization. This pattern is consistent with Castells's (1983) analysis of demand-making in the urban context. The urban movement erupted in 1970, and mobilized hundreds of thousands of residents in Madrid, Barcelona, and other major cities around diverse demands such as the right to association, and the right to enjoy street parties (Castells 1983: 215). The concerns of the Citizens Movement of Madrid included housing, schooling, public health, transportation, more open space, preservation of the historical city, and improvement of social life, while its political demands centred on the right to organize voluntary organizations, to elect board members, call meetings, and stage mass rallies (Castells 1983: 224). Furthermore, Castells argues that there was a clear tendency for these demands to become more political over time.[26]

---

[25] For 1988, political and civil demands actually exceeded material and economic demands by a ratio of 68:1, which was scaled down to 6.8 for purposes of presentation.

[26] We should emphasize that the expression of these demands developed in a distinctive way: a given neighbourhood, when successful, tended to shift from defensive demands (resistance against gentrification and displacement) to offensive demands (public redevelopment for the benefit of residents), in order to assert a local culture (fairs, celebrations, support of local networks), and then to press for institutional reform (asking for participation in the local government) (emphases added) (Castells 1983: 225).

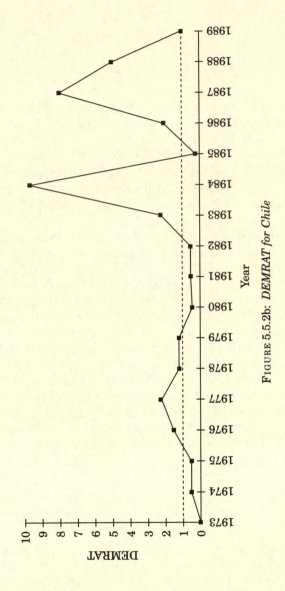

FIGURE 5.5.2b: *DEMRAT for Chile*

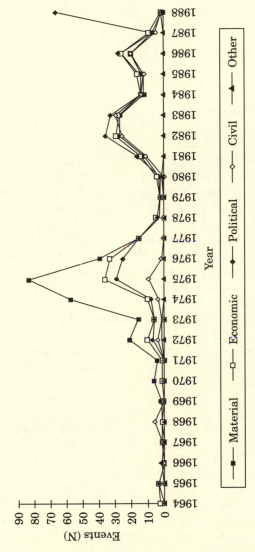

FIGURE 5.5.3a: *Social movement demands in Mexico*

TABLE 5.4. *Demand patterns in Mexico* (percentages)

Period	Material	Economic	Political	Civil
1964–1977 (n = 320)	77	37	31	8
1978–1982 (n = 66)	73	80	89	55
1983–1989 (n = 174)	44	53	93	47

Since there are fewer secondary sources on social movements in Spain than in the other cases, demands of the labour movement found in Blanc (1966), the ILO (1969), and Maravall (1978) are substituted. In the first wave of strikes in the early 1960s, Blanc (1966) shows that economic demands made between 1962 and 1964 are increasingly accompanied by demands centred on solidarity and the right to strike: the latter demands were made in 10 per cent of the 426 strikes in 1962, and in 18 per cent of the 628 strikes in 1964 (Blanc 1966: 274).[27] The 1969 ILO Report on labour conditions in Spain suggests that political and legal demands were not made until 1967, when they appeared in 55 per cent of the 501 strikes. Maravall's (1978) data (summarized in Table 5.5) shows a distinctive shift in the composition of demands from 1963 to 1974 that is similar to the patterns in the other cases. If Maravall's data is converted into a ratio similar to DEMRAT (Figure 5.5.4b), it is clear that later mobilizations become increasingly dominated by political demands, with the ratio exceeding one in 1967, 1970, 1972, and 1974.

Sectors, Participants, and Forms of Action

The first two sections of this chapter have examined the trajectories and demands of labour and non-labour movements across all the cases. The trajectories, or events data, will be integral to the statistical analysis of the next two chapters. The remainder of the chapter considers three further aspects of social movement activity, namely its sectors (rural and urban), its participants (workers, peasants, students, women, and the poor), and its forms of action (violent or non-violent and strikes or non-strikes).

[27] Solidarity demands, although not explicitly political or civil, do evoke a concern with the right to association, which was illegal at the time.

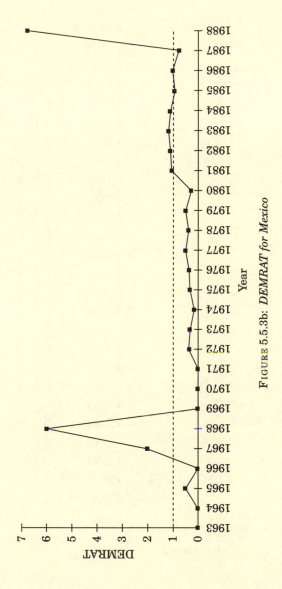

FIGURE 5.5.3b: *DEMRAT for Mexico*

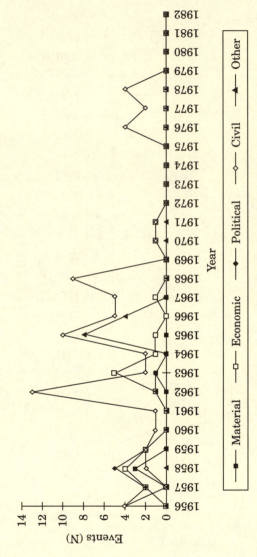

FIGURE 5.5.4a: *Social movement demands in Spain*

TABLE 5.5. *Demand patterns in Spain* (percentages)

Period	Material	Economic	Political	Civil
1963–1969 (n = 298)	NA	43	23	10
1970–1974 (n = 1257)	NA	30	39	21

Sectors

In Brazil, 66 per cent of the events over the period occurred in the urban sector. In Chile, urban social movement activity far outweighs rural activity with 92 per cent of the events, and the days of national protest (1983–4) were concentrated mostly in the urban areas, where direct confrontation with the regime was more visible. In Mexico, the 1960s were dominated by urban mobilization, the 1970s by rural mobilization, and the 1980s by urban mobilization again. From 1970 to 1980, there was an average of 22 events per year in the rural sector, and six in the urban sector; whereas from 1980 to 1989, there were 7 events per year in the rural sector and 18 in the urban sector. In Spain, events were concentrated in the urban areas where workers, students, and low-income residents were responsible for most of the mobilization against the regime (Maravall 1978; Castells 1983).

Participants

Four figures illustrate the participants in the social movements activity (SMA) described in the events section (Figures 5.6.1–5.6.4).[28] Of the total of 260 events in Brazil, 50 per cent of them involved workers, 27 per cent peasants, 32 per cent women, 16 per cent students, and 46 per cent the poor (Figure 5.6.1). For workers and peasants, mobilization peaked in 1979; for the poor, 1981; and for women, 1985. Of the total of 262 events in Chile, 46 per cent of them involved workers, 1 per cent peasants, 23 per cent women, 28 per cent students, and 44 per cent the poor (Figure 5.6.2). Women's mobilization peaked in 1984 and 1987. Mobilization by both students and the poor peaked in 1984, during the days of

[28] Worker activity appears only where the secondary literature shows that workers had participated in events alongside others in marches, demonstrations, and rallies, outside their capacity as workers. All explicit strike activity (i.e. industrial activity) is placed separately in the section on the labour movement.

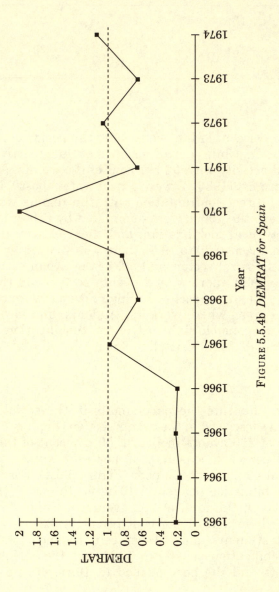

FIGURE 5.5.4b *DEMRAT for Spain*

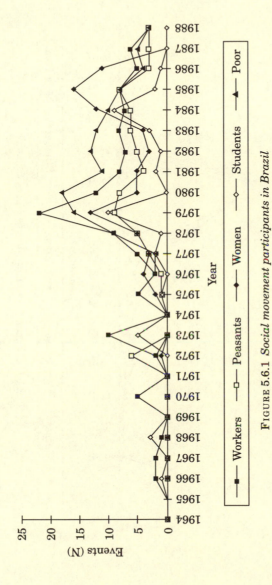

FIGURE 5.6.1 Social movement participants in Brazil

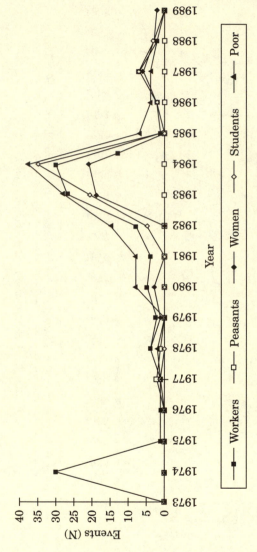

FIGURE 5.6.2: *Social movement participants in Chile*

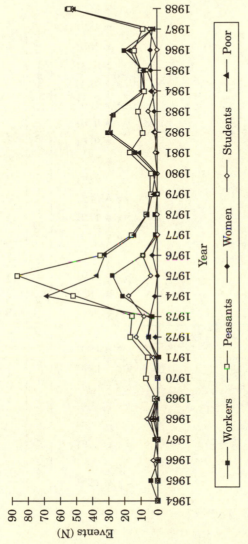

FIGURE 5.6.3: *Social movement participants in Mexico*

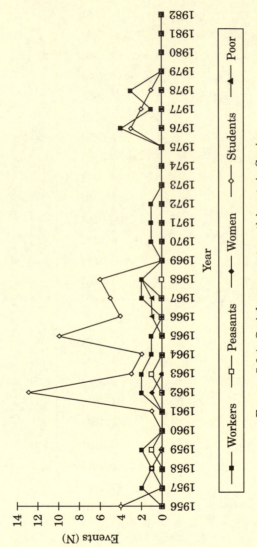

FIGURE 5.6.4: Social movement participants in Spain

national protest, after which total mobilization declined.[29] High levels of mobilization from all sectors did not recur until the weeks leading up to the 1988 plebiscite (LASA 1989).

In Mexico, workers participated in 42 per cent of the total of 560 events, peasants in 66 per cent, women in 13 per cent, students in 22 per cent, and the poor in 58 per cent (Figure 5.6.3). The early mobilizations consisted mainly of peasants and the poor, both of which peaked in 1975. The second wave of protest from 1981 to 1984 consisted mainly of workers and the poor, who were most hurt by the 1982 economic crisis. The 1986 mobilization comprised mainly workers, peasants, and the poor, with a greater role for women than during the previous four years. The 1988 mobilization encompassed all of these sectors and was characterized by a dramatic rise in the participation of women. The data presented in Figure 5.6.4 for Spain[30] tends to confirm that workers and students were the main force of opposition to the regime (Vilar 1976: 26–55; Maravall 1978; and Foweraker 1989).

Forms of Action

Social movement activity can be categorized as strike or non-strike, and as violent or non-violent. Events with arrests or detentions are coded as violent, since this type of result tends to require physical force of some kind. Clearly, violence can be a consequence of aggressive behaviour by movement participants, of repressive behaviour by the regime, or of a combination of the two. Street demonstrations may be repressed violently, even though mounted with peaceful intentions, and defensive actions, like building barricades in a shanty town, can provoke repressive responses.

For all events in Brazil, 23 per cent are strikes and 22 per cent are violent (Figure 5.7.1). Just 5 per cent are strikes and 17 per cent are violent in the period 1964–77, but these increased to 29 per cent strikes and 24 per cent violent in the subsequent years, 1978–88. In contrast to Brazil, Chilean events (Figure 5.7.2) tend

---

[29] Leiva and Petras (1987, 1988) argue that unions distanced workers from the mobilizations, as did centre political parties (e.g. the Christian Democratic Party) which disagreed with the more radical strategies of the parties on the left (the Communists and Socialists).

[30] The Taylor and Jodice (1983) data included in Figure 5.1.4 is not included in Figure 5.6.4, since this data consisted only of events. In the total of 82 events coded from the secondary literature workers participated in 32 per cent, peasants in 2 per cent, women in 4 per cent, students in 67 per cent, and the poor in 5 per cent.

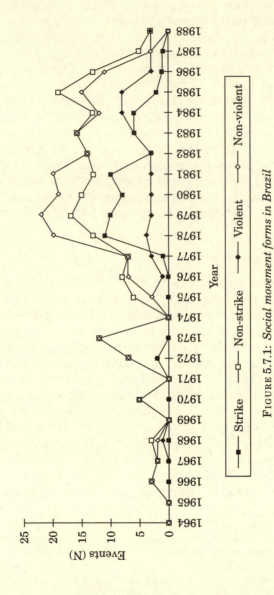

FIGURE 5.7.1: *Social movement forms in Brazil*

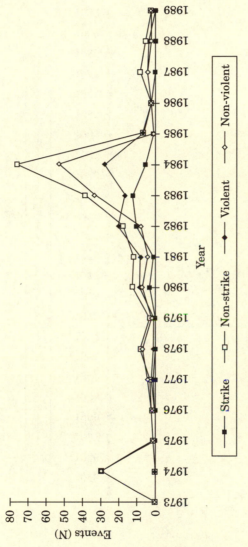

FIGURE 5.7.2: *Social movement forms in Chile*

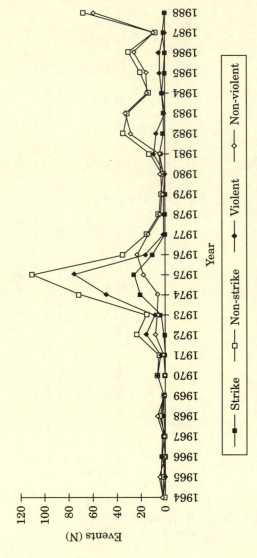

FIGURE 5.7.3: *Social movement forms in Mexico*

to be more violent (38 per cent), although the proportion of strikes is similar (25 per cent). Forty-three per cent of events are strikes and 38 per cent of events are violent for 1973 to 1982, but the proportion of strike events drops in the following years (13 per cent) with the proportion of violent events remaining the same.[31] As in Chile, Mexican events (Figure 5.7.3) tend to be more violent than those in Brazil (38 per cent). Between 1964 and 1980, 22 per cent of events are strikes, 56 per cent are violent, but there is a dramatic decrease to 4 per cent strikes and 12 per cent violent during the 1980s.[32] No clear pattern emerges from the forms of action in Spain (Figure 5.7.4). But the violence measures from Taylor and Jodice (1983) indicate that 69 per cent of the total of 442 violent events (1968–77) were concentrated in the three years after Franco's death.[33]

Waves of Protest under Authoritarian Conditions

As in the previous chapter, the comparative evidence and common patterns that characterize the four cases place them squarely in the MSSD framework. All the cases experience waves of protest which have distinct beginnings, peaks, and declines. In all cases labour mobilization tends to precede other social movement activity. In all cases the composition of demands shifts away from material and economic demands to political and civil demands. Nearly all the waves of protest were located primarily in the urban sector, where workers, students, women, and the urban poor all contributed to the proliferation of urban and neighbourhood movements.

Yet, there are differences that will inform the comparative argument. In Brazil, labour is the first to mobilize massive numbers, and its mobilization continues to rise throughout the 1980s, after other social movement activity has peaked in the mid-1980s. In

---

[31] Much of the violence took place during the eleven national days of protest, with 71 people killed (which includes the immolation of two students), 747 people injured, and 5,366 people detained (Tironi 1989: 187–202).

[32] These figures appear to contradict the downward trend in rights-in-practice (Chapter 4). But it is quite possible for the protection of individual rights to decline at the same time that social mobilization is itself less confrontational, and is met with less immediate repression.

[33] Until 1972 there are more non-violent actions per year than violent actions, but after 1972 (with the exception of 1975) violent actions become preponderant. The increase in violence is owing to regime behaviour before 1974 and to increased activity by the ETA and right-wing terrorist groups after that date.

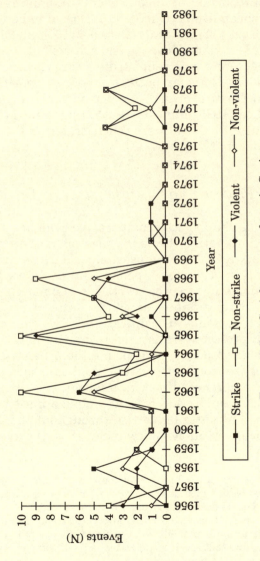

FIGURE 5.7.4: *Social movement forms in Spain*

Chile, labour mobilization peaked before the 1983–4 protests led by other social movements, and did not rise so far again until the end of the decade. In Mexico, early labour mobilization in the mid-1970s is soon followed by other social mobilization. The next peak of labour activity in 1982 is followed by rising non-labour mobilization from the mid-1980s through the rest of the decade. Finally, early labour mobilization in Spain is joined by other social movement activity, with the latter peaking in 1976, a year prior to the final peak in labour activity.

The previous and present chapters have described the main trends in citizenship rights and social movements across the four cases. These trends can inform initial observations on the relationship between rights and movements in each case. The gradual liberalization of citizenship rights over time in Brazil was accompanied by an increase in social movement activity. Citizenship rights in Chile remained relatively static until the 1988 plebiscite, but the struggle for those rights began in the late 1970s. The increasing divergence between rights-in-principle and rights-in-practice in Mexico was punctuated by peaks of labour and other social movement activity. Despite growing social mobilization in Spain in the 1960s, citizenship rights were denied until the beginning of the democratic transition, and the massive upsurge in mobilization that accompanied it. But these observations remain general, and can only support rather crude comparisons. The study will therefore proceed to submit the main indicators of rights (IPI, CRI, and GAP) and movements (SMA, SR, SMASR) to statistical analysis in order to make the observations more specific and the comparisons more exact. This analysis sets out to test the principal propositions about the relationship between rights and movements developed in the first chapters.

Relating Citizenship Rights and Social Movements over Time

The previous two chapters have described the general contours of citizenship rights and social movement activity across the four cases under comparison. The argument now proceeds to address the relationship between rights and social movements, and deploys a variety of quantitative methods in order to examine this relationship both within and across cases. These methods carry the enquiry forward in three separate stages. First, the three rights measures (IPI, CRI, and the GAP) are correlated with the four measures of social movement activity (SMA and SR, SV, and SMA + SR) to reveal the 'first order' or descriptive associations that may exist between rights and social movements. Second, multiple regression is used to model the unidirectional and causal mechanisms that may configure the relationship both between rights and movements and between movements and rights. At this stage the scope of the enquiry is broadened to include economic variables in addition to the rights and social movement variables. Third, a non-recursive model of simultaneous regression equations is used to test the assumption that citizenship rights and social movements are 'mutually constitutive' (see Chapter 2), or, less boldly, that their presence and progress condition each other in mutual fashion.

It is well known that simple correlations cannot support causal statements of any kind. But the first stage of the enquiry does begin to build a general (if still hypothetical) picture of the relationship between rights and movements by referring the correlation results for the four cases to their respective institutional and historical contexts. Multiple regression, on the other hand, can support causal inferences, but both the quality of the data and the constraints of the methods suggest that such inferences must be drawn with due caution. Yet, in combination, the correlation and regression results do succeed in measuring the degrees of association and mutual

TABLE 6.1.1. *Bivariate correlations between citizenship rights and social movements in Brazil* (Pearson's r)

	GAP	IPI	SMA	SR	SV	SMASR
CRI	.85***	.52**	.25	.70***	.64*	.70***
GAP		.00	.27	.36	.34	.34
IPI			.03	.72***	.71*	.72***
SMA				−.23	−.44	−.22
SR					.97***	1.0***

* p < .05   ** p < .01   *** p < .001

influence of citizenship rights and social movements for the four cases. Finally, since the methods are applied to time-series data, their results necessarily describe the relationship between rights and movements over time. But it is not until the following chapter that the enquiry attempts to reveal how the relationship develops through time by focusing on the annual changes in the relationship over the relevant periods.[1]

Correlating Citizenship Rights and Social Movements

Brazil

Brazil's correlation results tend to highlight the importance of the labour movement in that country, both to the overall shape of social movement activity and to the development of citizenship rights. The strong correlations between strike volume (SV) and strike rate (SR) suggest the presence of a broad-based movement, and the lack of correlation of either strike measure with other social movement activity (SMA) cannot corroborate, but is certainly consonant with the earlier finding (see Chapter 5) that labour protest tends to precede other forms of social protest. Turning to the correlations between social movement and rights measures, it is clear that both SR and SV track both rights-in-principle (IPI), or vice versa, and rights-in-practice (CRI), or vice versa (whereas SMA is not associated with either the IPI or CRI measures), suggesting that either the labour movement extends formal rights and has a strong impact on regime behaviour, or that it takes advantage

[1] To do so it combines a variation of multiple regression, multiple interrupted times-series analysis (MITS), with a form of Boolean algebraic analysis (see Chapter 7).

TABLE 6.1.2. *Bivariate correlations between citizenship rights and social movements in Chile* (Pearson's r)

	GAP	IPI	SMA	SR	SV	SMASR
CRI	.84***	.55*	−.14	.80***	.50*	.40
GAP		.00	−.43	.48*	.28	−.32
IPI			.32	.77***	.51*	.85***
SMA				−.09	−.21	.50*
SR					.81***	.83***

* p < .05   ** p < .01   *** p < .001

of such formal rights that are conferred, and that regime behaviour is effective in encouraging and discouraging labour activity. Furthermore, the strong correlations of SMASR with both the IPI and the CRI, which hardly differ at all from those of the SR alone, again suggest the overwhelming preponderance of the labour movement in overall protest against the regime and its policies.

Chile

In most respects the Chilean results appear to replicate the Brazilian ones. The measures of strike volume and strike rate are strongly correlated, but show no association with other forms of social movement activity, which is again consistent with the earlier finding that labour protest precedes the rise of other social movements. The subsequent correlations reveal that the relationship between rights and movements is also similar in Chile and Brazil, insofar as both SR and (to a lesser degree) SV track both rights-in-principle (IPI), or vice versa, and rights-in-practice (CRI), or vice versa; whereas, once again, other social movement activity (SMA) is not associated with either of the rights measures. It is therefore clear that in both Chile and Brazil it is mainly labour activity which either influences or responds to citizenship rights, formal and real. However, the negative, if neither strong nor significant, correlation of SMA and the GAP in Chile may suggest that its regime was especially intolerant of protest that spilled onto the streets.

Mexico

In Mexico, very differently from Brazil and Chile, there appears to be no association between strike rate and strike volume (although

TABLE 6.1.3. *Bivariate correlations between citizenship rights and social movements in Mexico* (Pearson's r)

	GAP	IPI	SMA	SR	SV	SMASR
CRI	.70***	−.71***	−.10	−.06	−.58***	−.01
GAP		.00	.05	.41*	−.30	.44*
IPI			.21	.32	.51**	.52**
SMA				.08	.10	.13
SR					−.08	1.0***

* p < .05   ** p < .01   *** p < .001

both continue to show little correlation with other social movement activity). In fact, the incidence of strikes (SR) was high during the *insurgencia sindical* of the 1970s and early 1980s, which was led by 'dissident' movements; while strike volume (SV) increased massively during the 1980s, as the 'official' union corporations of the ruling party began to protest against its austerity policies. Thus, the particular profile of labour protest in Mexico is a result of the dual character of that protest, which may be led either by state-chartered unions or independent movements of different kinds (Foweraker 1993: chapters 1 and 3). This dual character also influenced the relationship of the labour movement and citizenship rights. Neither strike rate (SR) nor other social movement activity (SMA) appears to be associated with either rights-in-principle (IPI)[2] or rights-in-practice (CRI), but strike volume (SV) is positively associated with the IPI and negatively associated with the CRI, suggesting that the period of high strike volume in the 1980s coincided both with important institutional changes and with a declining record of rights-in-practice. Finally, the positive correlations between the sum of labour and other social movement activity, on the one hand, and both the IPI and the GAP, on the other, may indicate either that it is the combination of labour and other protest that induced the regime to alter the institutional rules or concede more rights in practice, or that such government initiatives tended to encourage labour and other movements to act in consort.

Spain

The labour movement in Spain looks different from either the Brazilian and Chilean or the Mexican movements, insofar as strike rate

[2] The correlation between SR and IPI is weakly positive at p = .09.

TABLE 6.1.4. *Bivariate correlations between citizenship rights and social movements in Spain* (Pearson's r)

	GAP	IPI	SMA	SR	SV	SMASR
CRI	.36	.93***	−.09	.41*	.73***	.46*
GAP		.00	.08	−.06	.32	−.06
IPI			−.13	.50*	.67**	.50*
SMA				.55**	−.02	.58**
SR					.56**	1.0***

* p < .05   ** p < .01   *** p < .001

and strike volume are moderately associated, with the strike rate showing a further association with other social movement activity (SMA). In fact both SR and SMA increased over the early years of the 1970s, while strike rate and volume moved closer together from the mid-1970s (the rate having far exceeded volume in conditions of pure dictatorship). Turning to the rights measures, both rights-in-principle (IPI) and rights-in-practice (CRI) are associated with the strike rate and, yet more strongly, with strike volume, but bear little relation to other social movement activity. This suggests that it was the labour movement that had most impact on citizenship rights, or vice versa, but that neither labour nor any other social actor had much impact at all until the moment of the democratic transition in the mid-1970s. As in the Brazilian case, the moderate correlations of both the IPI and the CRI with the sum of social movement activity (SMASR) simply express the preponderance of the labour movement in social movement activity in general.

Summary

Despite the huge effort dedicated to theorizing new forms and sectors of social movement activity (Foweraker 1995), it appears that it is the labour movement which is most closely associated with citizenship rights. Labour is both the biggest actor and the first to enter the political arena. Moreover, although the correlations can tell us nothing about the direction of the relationship between labour activity and rights, the strength of the association does invite some interesting hypotheses. In Brazil it seems possible that labour protests succeeded in influencing both regime configuration and regime behaviour (rights-in-principle and rights-in-practice); while in Chile it may appear more plausible that labour took whatever advantage it could from periods of mitigated repression. In Spain the labour movement may have both precipitated and responded to the moment of democratic transition (which itself tends to 'concentrate' these two-way effects), even if its often powerful protests failed to have much impact on rights until that moment. Finally, the labour movement in Mexico is divided between official and dissident strands and so behaves differently; and it may be the combination of labour and other social movement protest (especially in the electoral arena) that influences rights-in-principle and -practice.

However, there are reasons to be cautious about these conclusions. On the one hand, the apparent preponderance of labour may be owing, in part, to measurement bias: the data on strike activity is relatively complete in relation to the more spotty data on other social movement activity. On the other, correlations cannot tell the whole story, and it may be the case that the labour movement mimics the effects of underlying economic variables such as inflation or economic growth, with which it is itself highly correlated. These considerations are pertinent to the next stage of the statistical analysis which will both clarify the hypothetical possibilities and test the strength of the associations arising from the correlation results by modelling the relationship between social movements and rights, and vice versa, through multiple regression.

Unidirectional Modelling

Methodological Considerations

The second stage of the statistical enquiry into the relationship between social movements and citizenship rights seeks to model this relationship in unidirectional fashion by looking separately both at the causal connections between movements and rights, and at those between rights and movements. These two relationships are illustrated as follows:

$$\text{Social Movements} \rightarrow \text{Rights} \quad [1]$$

$$\text{Rights} \rightarrow \text{Social Movements} \quad [2]$$

For the first relationship, the dependent variable is citizenship and is represented by the three rights measures, IPI, CRI, and GAP. The independent variable is social movement activity, represented by SMA and SR. The enquiry also considered the effects of the aggregate variable of social movement activity, SMASR, and results are reported for Mexico, the one case where the aggregate measure seems to make a significant difference to the results (and so advances the analysis). At the same time, measures of GDP growth, inflation, and energy consumption[3] are included as independent variables for modelling purposes. It is plausible to argue that the three rights measures describe the pattern of regime behaviour, and there is little doubt that economic conditions will influence that behaviour in some degree. Since economic conditions will also influence social movement activity, the second relationship maintains these independent economic variables, but switches the rights and social movement measures, making rights independent and movements dependent.[4]

For the first relationship [1] the three indicators of citizenship require parameter estimates for the following three separate equations per case:

$$IPI = \alpha + \beta_1 SMA + \beta_2 SR + \beta_3 GDP + \beta_4 Inflation + \beta_5 Energy + \varepsilon \qquad [3]$$

$$CRI = \alpha + \beta_1 SMA + \beta_2 SR + \beta_3 GDP + \beta_4 Inflation + \beta_5 Energy + \varepsilon \qquad [4]$$

$$GAP = \alpha + \beta_1 SMA + \beta_2 SR + \beta_3 GDP + \beta_4 Inflation + \beta_5 Energy + \varepsilon \qquad [5]$$

Where, α is the constant; $\beta_{1\ldots5}$ are the estimated coefficients; SMA, SR, GDP, Inflation and Energy are the independent variables, and ε is the error or disturbance term. In the Mexican case, the three equations are re-estimated by substituting the aggregate measure of social movement activity, SMASR, for the separate variables, SMA and SR, so producing three further equations:

$$IPI = \alpha + \beta_1 SMASR + \beta_2 GDP + \beta_3 Inflation + \beta_4 Energy + \varepsilon \qquad [6]$$

$$CRI = \alpha + \beta_1 SMASR + \beta_2 GDP + \beta_3 Inflation + \beta_4 Energy + \varepsilon \qquad [7]$$

---

[3] Energy consumption is the million metric tons of coal equivalent consumed by a nation in any given year. The figure represents total energy consumption, including solid and liquid fuels; domestic and imported gas; hydroelectric, nuclear, and imported electricity.

[4] The literature on the connections between economic growth and regime types has dominated much of comparative political science since the seminal work of Seymour Martin Lipset (1959, 1960), who has recently defended his original arguments (Lipset 1994). Enquiries into the specific connections between economic growth and democracy (reviewed by Rueschemeyer, Stephens, and Stephens 1992: 2–39) continue to accumulate (cf. Helliwell 1994). There is distinct literature which examines the relationship between economic development and social mobilization (e.g. Gurr 1970; Tilly 1978; Brand 1990; Tarrow 1994*b*).

$$\text{GAP} = \alpha + \beta_1\text{SMASR} + \beta_2\text{GDP} + \beta_3\text{Inflation}$$
$$+ \beta_4\text{Energy} + \varepsilon \qquad [8]$$

In similar fashion the two disaggregated measures of social movement activity require two principal equations to model the second relationship [2], while the aggregate measure, or combined term SMASR, requires a third equation for the Mexican case. These equations are written as follows:

$$\text{SMA} = \alpha + \beta_1\text{IPI} + \beta_2\text{CRI} + \beta_3\text{GAP} + \beta_4\text{GDP} + \beta_5\text{Inflation}$$
$$+ \beta_6\text{Energy} + \varepsilon \qquad [9]$$

$$\text{SR} = \alpha + \beta_1\text{IPI} + \beta_2\text{CRI} + \beta_3\text{GAP} + \beta_4\text{GDP} + \beta_5\text{Inflation}$$
$$+ \beta_6\text{Energy} + \varepsilon \qquad [10]$$

$$\text{SMASR} = \alpha + \beta_1\text{IPI} + \beta_2\text{CRI} + \beta_3\text{GAP} + \beta_4\text{GDP} + \beta_5\text{Inflation}$$
$$+ \beta_6\text{Energy} + \varepsilon \qquad [11]$$

As suggested above, the social movement measures (SMA, SR, and SMASR) are now the dependent variables and the rights measures (IPI, CRI, and GAP) are now the independent variables, having been switched to the right-hand side of the equation. The economic variables used in equations [9], [10], and [11] are identical to those found in equations [3–8].

Before estimating the parameters for these nine equations the enquiry must address two potential problems of regression analysis, namely autocorrelation and multicollinearity. In the analysis of time-series data, in particular, the results can be distorted by autocorrelation. In other words, in each of the nine equations [3–11], the disturbance term for any year (ε_t) may be correlated with the disturbance term for the previous year (ε_{t-1}). Since these disturbance terms can 'trend' on each other over time, the use of the standard ordinary least squares regression technique (OLS) can produce biased results,[5] in the form of inflated coefficients and underestimated standard errors. If this leads to the validation of a false hypothesis, a Type II error will have been committed.[6] One way to achieve the best linear unbiased estimates (BLUE) for

[5] This condition is described as serially correlated error, where the error term of one year is a function of the error term in a previous year: $\varepsilon_t = p\varepsilon_{t-1} + \upsilon_t$, where ε_t and ε_{t-1} are the systematic errors from an OLS time-series regression and υ_t is a randomly distributed, or genuine error term. See Sanders and Ward (1994) for a discussion of the problem of serial correlation in time-series regression.

[6] In a Type I error, the analyst rejects a null hypothesis which is true. In a Type II error, the analyst accepts a null hypothesis which is not true. See Sanders and Ward (1991) for a full review of time-series techniques and the problems of autocorrelation. For more general points about biased estimates and Type I and II errors, see Gujarati (1988: 655).

time-series data is to use the lagged endogenous method of OLS, which simply includes a lagged term of the dependent variable on the right-hand side of the equation.[7] Although this method certainly eliminates the problem of autocorrelation, the results of estimating the present parameters in this way produced such highly significant coefficients for the lagged term that they eliminated all other independent effects that the equations sought to test.[8]

The difficulties created by the lagged term led to its rejection in favour of the autoregressive method, which is designed to estimate the parameters of time-series models and so reveal the distinct effects of separate independent variables. It does this by deriving an autoregressive term from the error terms themselves, and by including this new term on the right-hand side of the equation. In this way the independent effects of the other variables in the equation are allowed full expression. By controlling for autocorrelation this method seeks to ensure that coefficients are not inflated, that standard errors are not deflated, and that the tests for significance are therefore sound.[9] These advantages dictated the choice of autoregression as the preferred method for estimating the parameters of the present equations.

Multicollinearity, on the other hand, arises where some or all of the independent variables are correlated with each other, and may remain a problem in the autoregressive method. All regression analysis assumes that the independent variables are not so correlated, and there is no doubt that high degrees of collinearity can produce biased estimates. Hence, it is just as important to monitor and avoid the effects of multicollinearity as it is to control for the effects of autocorrelation.[10] In the present equations the rights

[7] A recent application of this method using pooled cross-sectional time-series data is found in Poe and Tate (1994).

[8] The results lead to conclusions that past values of regime behaviour or social movement activity affect their future values. This conclusion is neither surprising nor useful—if it eliminates other independent effects. The observation that past political practices induce present practices fails to explain why changes occur. Similarly, the suggestion that past social movement activity leads to future activity simply indicates the kind of trend that has already been demonstrated in Chapter 5.

[9] See Sanders and Ward (1991) for discussion of the autoregression technique. Autoregressive models have been criticized for taking autoregression into account without explaining it. But if the autoregressive term is employed instrumentally to assess the relative strength of specific explanatory variables (as it is here) there is no real advantage in explaining the term itself.

[10] However, there is some doubt and debate about whether multicollinearity violates the assumptions of regression analysis, or not. For further discussion, see Gujarati (1988: 288–95).

measures are often highly correlated both with each other and with the several economic variables.[11] Similarly, the economic variables are sometimes correlated both with each other and with the social movement variables. These potentially problematic independent variables were first included and then excluded from successive parameter estimates in order to monitor for possible effects of multicollinearity.[12]

Results

The reporting of the results will follow the order and numbering of the regression equations in each case. Thus, the reporting will begin with the first relationship [1] and the parameter estimates for the three equations [3], [4], and [5], and proceed to the second relationship [2] and the parameter estimates for the two equations [9] and [10]. In the Mexican case, the enquiry into [1] will *also* include estimates for the three equations [6], [7], and [8] (six equations altogether), and, similarly, the enquiry into [2] will include equation [11] (three equations altogether). Furthermore, all tables of results will take the same form, listing the independent variables in the first column on the left and the dependent variables along the top row. In each case the reporting will seek to emphasize the strongest connections between the rights measures and the social movement measures, without entirely ignoring the independent effects of the economic variables.

Brazil

It is clear from the results of model [1] (as reported in Table 6.2.1) that both the labour movement and social movement activity in general have a significant and positive impact on rights-in-principle (IPI), while labour also has a positive influence on the delivery of rights-in-practice (CRI). These positive results are made more

[11] As a rule of thumb, correlations higher than $r = .70$ are deemed to create concerns of multicollinearity. Tables 1–4 show that, for Brazil, Chile, and Mexico, CRI and GAP are correlated at $r > .70$, while for Spain, CRI and IPI are correlated at $r > .70$. Since the GAP is a function of the CRI (and the IPI) only the CRI will be included in the equations that estimate model [2] in Brazil and Chile. In the case of Mexico the GAP will be used, since IPI and CRI are negatively correlated ($r = -.7$), and their inclusion would violate the assumptions of regression analysis.

[12] The specific statistical procedures used in this monitoring are spelled out in the footnotes to the tables which report the results of autoregression for the various cases.

TABLE 6.2.1. *Parameter estimates for model [1] in Brazil*
(equations [3], [4], [5])[†]

Ind. var.	IPI	IPI (w/o inflation)	CRI	CRI (w/o inflation)	GAP	GAP (w/o inflation)
Constant	.85	.87	.225	.14	−.41	−.47
	(10.85)**	(11.58)**	(3.26)**	(1.63)	(−5.47)**	(−5.16)**
SMA	.01	.01	−.004	−.006	−.009	−.009
	(4.15)**	(4.19)**	(−1.84)[a]	(−2.02)[b]	(−3.28)**	(−2.76)**
SR	.0002	.0002	.00009	−.00001	.00001	−.00009
	(4.41)**	(7.36)**	(2.32)*	(−.47)	(.25)	(−2.63)*
GDP	−.015	−.015	−.002	−.0008	.005	.007
	(−4.60)**	(−5.10)**	(−.75)	(−.23)	(1.39)	(1.70)
Inflation	.00009		−.0003		−.0004	
	(.71)		(−2.69)**		(−2.91)**	
Energy	−.005	−.005	.005	.006	.007	.008
	(−3.82)**	(−3.97)**	(4.34)**	(4.52)**	(5.70)**	(4.99)**
AR	−.66	−.64	−.36	.05	−.10	−.04
	(−2.76)**	(−2.87)**	(−1.24)	(.16)	(−.31)	(−.15)
Res.	21	21	21	21	21	21
DF	14	15	14	15	14	15
LL	25.75	25.56	30.20	27.02	29.48	24.76

Note: Reported values are unstandardized coefficients; t-values appear in parentheses; Res. = number of residuals; DF = degrees of freedom; LL = log likelihood.

[†] Since inflation is highly correlated with the strike rate (r = .91), two columns of results are reported for each equation, one with inflation and one without.

* p < .05   ** p < .01   [a] p = .09   [b] p = .06

impressive by the generally negative effect of the economic variables on the same rights measures (energy and GDP on rights-in-principle and inflation on rights-in-practice). Yet social movements in Brazil still had to struggle to secure these rights from an authoritarian and often hostile regime, and the significant and *negative* impact of the two social movement measures on the GAP demonstrates that their protests were frequently met by more repression. If the aggregate social movement measure SMASR is included in the modelling (not reported here), this picture remains much the same.

The picture which emerges from the results of model [2] (as reported in Table 6.2.2) is equally evocative. It will be recalled that in this model the independent and dependent rights and movement variables have been switched, and it now appears that rights-

TABLE 6.2.2. *Parameter estimates for model [2] in Brazil (equations [9] and [10])*[†]

Ind. var.	SMA	SR
Constant	−15.86	−2290.03
	(1.54)	(−4.79)**
IPI	22.15	1184.89
	(1.55)	(1.76)[a]
CRI	−34.25	3807.96
	(−2.63)*	(4.85)**
GDP	.11	31.53
	(.37)	(1.98)[b]
Inflation	−.02	2.17
	(−3.22)**	(5.93)**
Energy	.46	−7.22
	(4.50)**	(−1.80)[c]
AR	.42	−.63
	(1.44)	(−2.78)**
Res.	24	23
DF	17	16
LL	−70.6	−163.34

Note: Reported values are unstandardized coefficients; t-values appear in parentheses; Res. = number of residuals; DF = degrees of freedom; LL = log likelihood.

[†] Since the CRI and the GAP are highly correlated (r = .85), the GAP was excluded from the equation.

* p < .05   ** p < .01   [a] p = .10   [b] p = .06   [c] p = .09

in-practice (CRI) have a significant and positive impact on labour activity, and a significant but negative effect on other forms of social movement activity. In other words the variation of rights-in-practice appears capable both of encouraging labour activity and discouraging other movements. (If the combined term SMASR is substituted for the disaggregated movement measures, it emerges that rights-in-principle also have a positive effect on social movement activity overall).[13] At the same time inflation also appears to encourage labour activity, as might be expected, and discourage other social movements—possibly by eroding their already exiguous resources. Economic growth, on the other hand, as measured by energy consumption, seems to stimulate these movements.

[13] The equation is: $SMASR = -4417.55** + 4121.78_{IPI}** + 3855.98_{CRI}* + 59.89_{GDP} - 1.24_{Energy} - .50_{AR}$.

TABLE 6.2.3. *Parameter estimates for model [1] in Chile*
(equations [3], [4], [5])[†]

Ind. var.	IPI	IPI (w/o energy)	CRI	CRI (w/o energy)	GAP	GAP (w/o energy)
Constant	−.59	.27	−.66	.18	−.65	−.07
	(−1.61)	(2.52)*	(−4.60)**	(2.26)*	(−3.42)**	(−1.04)
SMA	.004	.004	−.0002	−.00003	−.001	−.001
	(2.85)*	(2.25)*	(−.37)	(−.02)	(−1.72)	(−1.28)
SR	.003	.006	−.001	.002	−.002	.0002
	(1.46)	(3.72)**	(−1.89)[a]	(1.41)	(−2.27)*	(.22)
GDP	−.01	−.007	−.001	.003	.003	.005
	(−2.23)*	(−1.09)	(−.62)	(.61)	(.90)	(1.22)
Inflation	−.001	−.0009	.0001	.00007	.0002	.0004
	(−3.56)**	(−2.37)*	(−.91)	(.27)	(1.23)	(1.76)
Energy	.09		.09		.06	
	(2.38)*		(5.77)**		(3.12)**	
AR	.13	.15	−.26	.30	−.29	−.03
	(.03)	(.53)	(−.82)	(.80)	(−.89)	(−.07)
Res.	16	16	16	16	16	16
DF	9	10	9	10	9	10
LL	13.92	10.45	27.66	16.67	23.06	17.90

Note: Reported values are unstandardized coefficients; t-values appear in parentheses; Res. = number of residuals; DF = degrees of freedom; LL = log likelihood.

[†] Since SR and energy consumption are highly correlated (r > .70), the equations both include and exclude energy consumption.

* p < .05   ** p < .01   [a] p = .09

These results tend to confirm the conclusion drawn from the correlations (see Table 6.1.1) that it is the labour movement in Brazil which is central to the development of citizenship rights. But the regression analysis also clarifies the causal direction of the different correlations by showing that social movement activity (labour and other movements) actually succeeds in actively extending the formal rights of citizenship, while the real behaviour of the regime, as measured by rights-in-practice, is equally effective in encouraging labour activity and discouraging other social movement activity. The additional positive impacts of labour on rights-in-practice and of rights-in-principle on aggregate social movement activity support the overall impression that the relationship between social movements and citizenship rights in Brazil is indeed 'mutually constitutive'. In other words, there is little room to doubt that the progress of citizenship rights and the rise of social movement activity elicit and reinforce one another over time.

Chile

Similarly to Brazil, the modelling of the first relationship for Chile [1] (as reported in Table 6.2.3) shows that both the labour movement and social movement activity in general have a significant and positive effect on rights-in-principle (IPI). On the other hand, labour's impact on rights-in-practice is weak. A rather liberal interpretation of the significant but negative effect of labour mobilization on the GAP (before controlling for multicollinearity) may just suggest that labour protests do not so much enhance rights as increase repression. This impression is confirmed by the estimates for the economic variables. Economic growth (as measured by energy consumption) clearly improves both orders of rights performance, but inflation's significant but *negative* influence on rights-in-principle may reflect a repressive political order committed to combatting inflation by suppressing wage demands and labour protests.[14] Substituting the combined term SMASR does not alter the overall profile of the results in any important respect.[15]

The economic variables are less salient in the results from model [2] (as reported in Table 6.2.4), which reveal that both rights-in-principle (IPI) and rights-in-practice (CRI) have a significant and positive impact on labour activity, while rights-in-principle also appear to affect other forms of social mobilization (SMA)—but only before controlling for multicollinearity. Together the two sets of regression results tend to confirm the strong associations observed in the correlations (see Table 6.1.2) between labour protest (SR) and the rights measures; and, despite the lack of significant correlations between these measures and other social movement activity (SMA), they reveal that this activity does condition rights-in-principle (IPI), and may even be conditioned by them in some small degree. It is therefore possible that this activity increased in

---

[14] This argument is popular in the literature on Chile in particular and on authoritarian regimes in general. For this type of discussion on Chile, see J. S. Valenzuela and Valenzuela (1986), and Drake and Jaksic (1991). For the more general discussion, see O'Donnell (1973), Collier (1979), and Sheahan (1987).

[15] For rights in principle, the equation is: $IPI = -.45 + .004_{SMASR}{}^{**} - .01_{GDP}{}^{*} - .001_{Inflation}{}^{**} + .08_{Energy}{}^{*} - .05_{AR}$. For the GAP, the equation is: $GAP = -.57 - .002_{SMASR}{}^{*} + .003_{GDP} + .0002_{Inflation} + .05_{Energy}{}^{**} - .24_{AR}$.

TABLE 6.2.4. *Parameter estimates for model [2] in Chile*
(equations [9] and [10])[†]

Ind. var.	SMA	SMA (w/o energy)	SMA (w/o inflation)	SR	SR (w/o energy)	SR (w/o inflation)
Constant	172.2	−.28	15.21	−185.62	−23.09	−26.25
	(1.25)	(−.01)	(.94)	(−2.25)*	(−1.16)	(−2.26)*
IPI	102.32	51.71	29.87	18.15	60.46	65.49
	(2.92)*	(1.61)	(1.34)	(.48)	(1.83)[a]	(3.19)**
CRI	122.47	−68.32	−56.23	−153.50	143.22	139.70
	(1.30)	(−1.02)	(−.88)	(−1.39)	(3.24)**	(3.56)**
GDP	1.35	.50	.13	−.15	.54	.65
	(1.69)	(.56)	(.15)	(−.14)	(.53)	(.73)
Inflation	.144	.07		−.07	−.01	
	(2.22)*	(1.01)		(−1.01)	(−.20)	
Energy	−22.45			23.34		
	(−2.38)*			(−2.15)*		
AR	.35	.27	.22	−.07	−.02	−.03
	(1.25)	(.93)	(.82)	(−.20)	(−.07)	(−.11)
Res.	17	17	17	16	17	17
DF	10	11	12	9	11	12
LL	−69.92	−73.40	−73.90	−66.45	−75.27	−75.06

Note: Reported values are unstandardized coefficients; t-values appear in parentheses; Res. = number of residuals; DF = degrees of freedom; LL = log likelihood.
[†] Since inflation is highly correlated with IPI ($r = -.70$), and energy consumption is highly correlated with CRI ($r = .88$) estimates are run both with and without inflation and energy consumption in order to monitor the effects of collinearity.
* $p < .05$ ** $p < .01$ [a] $p = .09$

response to the constitutional change of 1980, and probable that the mass mobilization and intense protests of 1983–4 did have a medium-term impact on later regime liberalization.

Thus, even in the extreme conditions of Pinochet's dictatorship, there is some evidence to suggest that social movement activity influences citizenship rights just as rights encourage social mobilization. Nonetheless, the relationship between movements and rights is very different in Chile than in Brazil, where the labour movement was successful in extending rights-in-practice just as rights-in-practice were a potent stimulus to labour protest. In Chile, on the contrary, rights-in-practice remain entirely insensitive to both labour and other social movement activity, and are themselves ineffective in evoking social movement activity overall (when the combined term, SMASR, is substituted for the disaggregated movement measures in model [2] the significant effect of rights-in-practice is eliminated, leaving only rights-in-principle to explain the mobilization).[16] In other words, although social movements might have influenced the institutional configuration of the regime in the longer term, the regime was never prepared to concede rights-in-practice in response to social protest, and, equally, such concessions could never encourage social mobilization.

Mexico

In the Mexican case the regressions reveal a different profile than those of Brazil and Chile. The results from the first model [1], running the equations with disaggregated social movement measures (equations [3], [4], and [5] as reported in Table 6.2.5), show that neither measure has any visible effect on either rights-in-principle or rights-in-practice. Indeed, only economic growth, as measured by energy consumption, seems to have any positive impact on these rights. But labour activity does have a positive and significant effect on the GAP. When the combined term for social movement activity, SMASR, is substituted for the disaggregated measures, the results (equations [6], [7], and [8] as reported in Table 6.2.6) are broadly the same. It appears that the strongest effect of social movement activity in Mexico is to widen the gap between the rhetoric and reality of citizenship rights, leaving rights-in-practice ever less protected than might be expected from the prevailing level of rights-in-principle (cf. Chapter 3).

The results for model [2] are yet more distinctive. When the parameters are estimated for the disaggregated social movement measures (equations [6] and [7], as reported in Table 6.2.7), the results indicate that none of the explanatory variables has any kind of significant connection to either measure (with the possible exception of a positive but rather weak effect of the GAP on labour activity). But when the combined term for social movement activity, SMASR, is substituted for the disaggregated measures (equation [11], as reported in Table 6.2.8), the results indicate that both rights-in-principle (IPI) and the GAP have a significant and positive impact on social movement activity in general. These results both confirm and clarify the conclusions derived from the correlations (see Table 6.1.3), which suggested no association between the disaggregated measures of social movement activity and the rights measures, but a firm association between the combined term, SMASR, and both rights-in-principle and the GAP. But it is now clear that it is government initiatives (IPI) and regime behaviour

---

[16] The equation for SMASR without inflation and energy consumption is: $SMASR = 9.59 + 100.22_{IPI}{}^{**} - 10.48_{CRI} + .72_{GDP} + .09_{AR}$.

TABLE 6.2.5. *Parameter estimates for model [1] in Mexico*
(equations [3], [4], [5])[†]

Ind. var.	IPI	IPI (w/o inflation)	CRI	CRI (w/o inflation)	GAP	GAP (w/o inflation)
Constant	.64	.68	.69	.70	−.03	−.03
	(48.01)**	(47.20)**	(13.06)**	(13.60)**	(−.72)	(−.67)
SMA	−.00008	−.00007	.0003	.0003	.0001	.00009
	(−.86)	(−.83)	(.58)	(.56)	(.27)	(.26)
SR	−.000001	−.0000001	.00004	.00005	.00004	.00006
	(−.19)	(−.03)	(1.06)	(1.58)	(1.43)	(2.35)*
GDP	−.0007	−.0005	.0008	.002	.0009	.003
	(−.97)	(−.85)	(.16)	(.50)	(.21)	(.78)
Inflation	−.00008		−.0004		−.0005	
	(−.57)		(−.47)		(−.77)	
Energy	.0007	.0007	−.001	−.001	.0002	−.0002
	(4.25)**	(4.91)**	(−1.21)	(−2.84)**	(.35)	(−.52)
AR	.65	.68	.13	.11	−.16	−.17
	(3.24)**	(3.59)**	(.59)	(.44)	(−.72)	(−.76)
Res.	25	25	25	25	25	25
DF	18	19	18	19	18	19
LL	83.41	83.38	39.21	39.23	42.96	42.74

Note: Reported values are unstandardized coefficients; t-values appear in parentheses; Res. = number of residuals; DF = degrees of freedom; LL = log likelihood.

[†] Since inflation is negatively correlated with GDP and positively correlated with energy consumption beyond the threshold for multicollinearity ($r > .70$), estimates for GDP and energy are run both with and without inflation.

* $p < .05$ ** $p < .01$

(GAP) which stimulate the labour movement and other social movements to act in consort in Mexico; and, in particular, that social movements react to the *perceived* gap between the rights they hold in principle and those they enjoy in practice, and mobilize to close this gap. These specificities of the Mexican case probably reflect the struggle for political rights waged by social movements within the electoral arena.

Spain

The regression results for model [1] in Spain (estimates for equations [3], [4], and [5], as reported in Table 6.2.9)[17] appear difficult

[17] The statistical construction of the table is complicated both by multicollinearity and by the nature of the data. On the one hand, energy consumption is highly

TABLE 6.2.6. *Parameter estimates for model [1] in Mexico (w/SMASR)*
(equations [6], [7], [8])

Ind. var.	IPI	IPI (w/o inflation)	CRI	CRI (w/o inflation)	GAP	GAP (w/o inflation)
Constant	.64	.64	.71	.71	−.02	−.03
	(51.05)**	(49.94)**	(14.22)**	(14.72)**	(−.73)	(−.69)
SMASR	−.0000008	1.00E-7	.00004	.00005	.00005	.00006
	(−.15)	(.01)	(1.12)	(1.66)	(1.51)	(2.45)*
GDP	−.0006	−.0004	−.0009	.002	−.0008	.003
	(−.77)	(−.64)	(.09)	(.41)	(.20)	(.80)
Inflation	−.00008		−.0004		−.0009	
	(−.53)		(−.43)		(−.78)	
Energy	.0007	.0006	−.001	−.001	.0003	−.0003
	(4.40)**	(5.18)**	(−1.29)	(−2.95)**	(.35)	(−.54)
AR	.61	.64	.15	.06	−.09	−.13
	(2.92)**	(3.24)**	(.35)	(.25)	(−.78)	(−.82)
Res.	25	25	25	25	25	25
DF	19	20	19	20	19	20
LL	83.10	83.07	39.24	39.26	43.12	42.87

Note: Reported values are unstandardized coefficients; t-values appear in parentheses; Res. = number of residuals; DF = degrees of freedom; LL = log likelihood.

[†] Since inflation is negatively correlated with GDP and positively correlated with energy consumption beyond the threshold for multicollinearity (r > .70), estimates for GDP and energy are run both with and without inflation.

* $p < .05$ ** $p < .01$

to decipher, insofar as both the labour movement and other social movement activity have a significant but *negative* effect on the GAP, with non-labour activity repeating this *negative* effect on rights-in-principle. The only positive effect is that of the labour mobilization on rights-in-principle. If the combined term for social movement activity is substituted for the disaggregated measures (not reported here), the picture remains substantially unchanged. When the direction of the relationship is reversed in model [2] (equations [9] and [10], as reported in Table 6.2.10) the estimates

correlated both with inflation (r = .74) and with labour activity (r = .83), and to maintain consistency across cases energy is included in the first column of the table but then excluded. On the other, not only are labour (SR) and other social movement (SMA) activity correlated in some degree (r = .56), but the events data for SMA was taken from Taylor and Jodice (1983) and hence (differently from the other cases) may include labour activity (see Chapter 5). Consequently the third column of each equation shows parameter estimates without SMA.

TABLE 6.2.7. *Parameter estimates for model [2] in Mexico* (equations [9] and [10])[†]

Ind. var.	SMA	SMA (w/o energy)	SR	SR (w/o energy)
Constant	314.91	83.40	807.74	−1483.72
	(.85)	(.32)	(.14)	(−.59)
IPI	−458.87	−78.68	−1055.41	2718.09
	(−.79)	(−.21)	(−.12)	(.76)
GAP	90.81	105.57	2242.20	2561.97
	(1.01)	(1.19)	(1.39)	(1.76)[a]
GDP	−2.02	−1.67	−4.47	−2.89
	(−1.07)	(−.90)	(−.14)	(−.01)
Inflation	−.07	.10	−1.82	.12
	(.369)	(.31)	(−.37)	(.03)
Energy	.47		4.81	
	(.85)		(.55)	
AR	.61	.56	.36	.38
	(3.20)**	(2.95)**	(1.83)	(2.04)*
Res.	25	25	27	28
DF	18	19	20	22
LL	−112.22	−112.52	−196.80	−203.68

Note: Reported values are unstandardized coefficients; t-values appear in parentheses; Res. = number of residuals; DF = degrees of freedom; LL = log likelihood.

[†] Since rights in principle and rights in practice are negatively correlated ($r = -.70$), the equations include only IPI and the GAP. Since energy consumption is positively correlated with inflation and rights in principle, it is included in the first and third columns of the results.

* $p < .05$ ** $p < .01$ [a] $p = .09$

reveal that the two significant impacts, of the GAP on the labour movement and rights-in-principle on non-labour activity, are again *negative*. As in model [1], substituting the combined term, SMASR, for this activity makes no difference to the results.

In general, the Spanish case is characterized by the way the relationship between citizenship rights and social movements is concentrated into, and distorted by the moment of democratic transition. This is the clue to resolving the apparent contradiction between the *positive* correlation results (see Table 6.1.4) and the *negative* regression results. The correlations showed a moderate level of association between citizenship rights and labour activity in the form of the strike rate (SR), and a much stronger association between these rights and strike volume (SV). This is because, although the

TABLE 6.2.8. *Parameter estimates for model [2] in Mexico (w/SMASR) (equation [11])*[†]

Ind. var.	SMASR	SMASR (w/o energy)
Constant	−3393.25	−7627.69
	(−.75)	(−3.42)**
IPI	5046.57	11947.46
	(.70)	(3.62)**
GAP	2471.0	3256.01
	(1.53)	(2.20)*
GDP	−14.73	−12.35
	(−.51)	(−.43)
Inflation	−9.0	−2.78
	(−1.80)	(−1.47)
Energy	8.17	
	(1.08)	
AR	−.01	−.04
	(−.06)	(−.18)
Res.	25	25
DF	18	19
LL	−178.51	−179.11

Note: Reported values are unstandardized coefficients; t-values appear in parentheses; Res. = number of residuals; DF = degrees of freedom; LL = log likelihood.

[†] Only the IPI and GAP are included since IPI and CRI are negatively correlated ($r = -.70$).

* $p < .05$ ** $p < .01$

labour movement grew in strength during the dictatorship, it could make no impact on either rights-in-principle or rights-in-practice until the years of the transition itself—when strike volume increased massively (see Chapter 5).[18] This goes some way towards explaining the negative regression results. Far from changing its rights performance, the Franco regime stuck rigorously to its own repressive rules (see Chapter 4) and even exceeded them in most

[18] In addition to the evidence presented in Chapter 5, simple scatterplot analysis between SMA and IPI or SR and IPI shows that the overall relationship is positive, but for the crucial years between 1976–8, both SMA and SR are declining while IPI is rising. These critical years of change produce the negative effects evident in the regression results. Social mobilization increased massively over the eighteen months following Franco's death, but then declined dramatically once trade unions and political parties were legalized and a new constitution approved.

TABLE 6.2.9. *Parameter estimates for model [1] in Spain (equations [3], [4], [5])*

Ind. var.	IPI	IPI (w/o energy)	IPI (w/o SMA)	CRI	CRI (w/o energy)	CRI (w/o SMA)	GAP	GAP (w/o energy)	GAP (w/o SMA)
Constant	-.27	.41	.56	.05	.60	.60	.13	.10	.09
	(-.71)	(1.80)	(1.46)	(.17)	(2.20)*	(2.29)*	(.77)	(.98)	(.89)
SMA	-.003	-.005		-.002	-.0005		.0006	.0005	
	(-2.75)*	(-3.10)**		(-1.98)[a]	(-.77)		(.89)	(.87)	
SR	.0001	.0002	.00004	.00002	-.00004	-.00005	-.0001	-.0001	-.0001
	(2.69)*	(2.21)*	(1.05)	(.36)	(-1.45)	(-1.79)[b]	(-2.53)*	(-3.66)**	(-3.62)**
GDP	.03	-.03	.01	.0007	-.01	-.01	-.03	-.02	-.02
	(2.30)*	(-1.37)	(.87)	(.06)	(-1.00)	(-1.23)	(-2.25)*	(-2.70)*	(-2.60)*
Inflation	.008	.004	-.01	.01	-.003	-.002	.006	.009	.009
	(.54)	(.35)	(.92)	(1.08)	(-.29)	(-.22)	(.63)	(1.29)	(1.35)
Energy	.006			.004			.0005		
	(1.22)			(1.06)			(.20)		
AR	.86	-.20	.94	.83	.94	.94	.52	.60	.61
	(6.09)**	(-.78)	(11.22)**	(5.74)**	(12.35)**	(12.16)**	(1.72)	(2.83)**	(2.82)**
Res.	18	20	20	18	20	20	18	20	20
DF	11	14	15	11	14	15	11	14	15
LL	15.46	7.70	12.55	19.59	19.55	19.27	23.00	26.59	26.25

Note: Reported values are unstandardized coefficients; t-values appear in parentheses; Res. = number of residuals; DF = degrees of freedom; LL = log likelihood.

* p < .05 ** p < .01 [a] p = .07 [b] p = .09

TABLE 6.2.10. *Parameter estimates for model [2] in Spain* (equations [9] and [10])[†]

Ind. var.	SMA	SMA (w/o energy)	SR	SR (w/o energy)	SR (w/o inflation)
Constant	28.56	6.96	587.46	534.48	2164.95
	(.75)	(.17)	(.94)	(.57)	(2.41)*
IPI	−106.74	−92.24	−1004.62	−202.86	−565.10
	(−3.30)**	(−2.59)*	(−1.83)[b]	(−.21)	(−.46)
GAP	−121.55	−118.25	−3412.27	−5352.57	−6272.68
	(−1.96)[a]	(−1.56)	(−3.39)**	(−2.87)**	(−3.19)**
GDP	−4.79	−2.73	−188.08	−141.78	−171.57
	(−1.38)	(−.68)	(−3.18)**	(−1.70)	(−2.12)*
Inflation	1.89	5.67	−44.12	119.69	
	(.91)	(3.51)**	(1.28)	(2.54)*	
Energy	.55		36.93		
	(1.15)		(4.60)**		
AR	−.60	−.17	−.50	.44	.75
	(−2.49)*	(−.71)	(−2.04)[a]	(1.75)[c]	(3.55)**
Res.	19	21	18	20	20
DF	12	15	11	14	15
LL	−88.31	−98.61	−132.54	−153.83	−156.22

Note: Reported values are unstandardized coefficients; t-values appear in parentheses; Res. = number of residuals; DF = degrees of freedom; LL = log likelihood.

[†] IPI and CRI are highly correlated ($r = .93$). Since the regression results from equations with IPI and GAP or CRI and GAP do not differ much, only the IPI and GAP results are reported.

* $p < .05$ ** $p < .01$ [a] $p = .07$ [b] $p = .09$ [c] $p = .10$

years. Thus, the GAP itself stayed negative or close to zero, while labour mobilization built towards its massive peak years of 1975 and 1976. These 'concentrating' effects of the transition will be further explored in the following chapter.

Summary

In general, regression analysis confirms the conclusions drawn from the correlations (Tables 6.1.1–6.1.4), and so confirms the importance of the labour movement for the development of citizenship rights. But it also amplifies these conclusions, highlighting exceptions (and partial exceptions) and accentuating the differences between cases. Brazil is the paradigmatic case where labour's predominance cannot easily be contested. In Chile labour remains a central actor, but since it never succeeded in extending rights-in-practice (the real degrees of liberty within the society at large) its influence can only be measured by institutional changes over the longer term. The labour movement also appears preponderant in both Mexico and Spain, but in Mexico it mainly influences and responds to rights in consort with other social movements and forces, while in Spain it does not succeed in making any impact on citizenship rights, as such, before the moment of the democratic transition.

The regression analysis also makes clear that the relationship between social movements and citizenship rights is a two-way relationship. Once again, Brazil appears to provide the paradigmatic case in this regard, with both labour and other movements influencing rights-in-principle, just as rights-in-practice stimulates or elicits labour activity. In Chile both labour and other movements are also important to rights-in-principle, and, equally, appear to respond to institutional changes; but, differently to Brazil, the more unconventional protests by urban social movements appear at least as effective as labour in achieving regime change. In Mexico the same two-way effects are at work, but here it is the combination of labour with other movements that works to widen the gap between the rhetoric and reality of citizenship rights, just as this gap—and government initiatives—appear to call forth or provoke social movement protest. Only in Spain does this order of relationship remain opaque. In sum, the relationship between rights and movements can be said to be mutually conditioning but partial in Chile, mutually conditioning but weak in Mexico, and mutually constitutive and strong in Brazil.

The Spanish case is distinctive. There is no doubt that the principal opposition labour movement, the Workers' Commissions, grew massively during the latter years of the dictatorship, nor that it succeeded in colonizing the corporatist centrepiece of the regime, the Vertical Syndicate (Foweraker 1989). But the movement's ingenious combination of clandestine and open struggle achieved change in a piecemeal and informal fashion that did not alter rights-in-principle or rights-in-practice. On the contrary, the regime remained highly repressive until and through Franco's dying days. But even if labour's struggle was not reflected in the rights measures, it was effective in 'schooling the working class in "free" collective bargaining and in a sense of its democratic rights, so readying it for its massive mobilization at the moment of the formal and constitutional transition' (Foweraker 1989: 222). In Spain, therefore, the mutual effects of rights and movements are concentrated in the moment of transition; and in the following chapter different methods will attempt to capture the timing of these effects.

Non-recursive Modelling

The unidirectional modelling has explored the causal relationships between the social movement measures and the rights indices in each of the four cases, and has revealed the mutual effects of movements and rights in three of the cases (Brazil, Chile, and Mexico). It is clear that these mutual effects vary across the cases in at least two ways. First, the overall level or strength of the effects varies. In Brazil they are characterized as strong to the point of being 'mutually constitutive', whereas in Chile they condition each other only partially or inconsistently, while in Mexico their mutual conditioning appears relatively weak. Second, the specific effects of the distinct measures and indices one on the other also varies across cases, so creating a different profile of the mutual relationship between rights and movements in each case. The final stage of the regression analysis therefore sets out to complete the comparison of the relationship across cases by configuring this profile for each case. Its main aims are to distinguish the key measures and indices that shape the mutual effects, and to assess the relative strength of these effects both within and across cases. It does this by non-recursive modelling.

The unidirectional modelling looked at the relationship between rights and movements first from one direction, then from the other. In other words, models [1] and [2] separate the relationship between rights and movements into two distinct statistical expressions. Non-recursive modelling, on the other hand, seeks to explore the 'mutuality' of the effects operating in the relationship, and so conceives of the relationship between rights and movements *as occurring simultaneously*. It therefore requires the solution of two simultaneous equations. In formal terms the hypothetical relationship between rights and movements (as argued in Chapter 2) is as follows:

$$\text{Rights} \leftrightarrow \text{Social Movements} \qquad [12]$$

For the non-recursive model, individual rights and social movements are the endogenous variables. The other independent variables used in this chapter (GDP, Inflation, and Energy Consumption) are the exogenous variables. Testing the model requires parameters to be estimated for the two simultaneous equations, which are written as follows:

Rights (Y_1) = α_1 + β_1Social Movements (Y_2) + β_2GDP
$\qquad$ + β_3Inflation + β_4Energy + ε $\qquad$ [13]

Social Movements (Y_2) = α_2 + β_5Rights (Y_1) + β_6GDP
$\qquad$ + β_7Inflation + β_8Energy + ε $\qquad$ [14]

Where Y_1 and Y_2 are the endogenous variables in each of the two equations, and the three additional variables are exogenous. By placing individual rights and social movements on both sides of the equation, the strength of their mutual effects can be estimated. The technique used for this purpose is called two-staged least squares (2SLS), because two separate regression stages are needed,[19] which are written as follows:

Stage 1:

Rights (Y_1) = α_1 + β_2GDP + β_3Inflation
$\qquad$ + β_4Energy + ε; fit_1 $\qquad$ [15]

Social Movements (Y_2) = α_2 + β_5GDP + β_6Inflation
$\qquad$ + β_7Energy + ε; fit_2 $\qquad$ [16]

Stage 2

Rights (Y_1) = α_3 + $\beta_8$fit_2 + ε $\qquad$ [17]

Social Movements (Y_2) = α_4 + $\beta_9$fit_1 + ε $\qquad$ [18]

In the first stage [15–16], each endogenous variable is regressed separately on the exogenous variables and the predicted values (Fit_1 and Fit_2) are saved. Fit_1 is a proxy measure (also known as an instrument) for rights, which takes into account the effects of the exogenous variables. Fit_2 is a proxy measure for social movements which also takes into account the effects of the exogenous variables. In the second stage [17–18], each endogenous variable is separately regressed on these fitted values (or instruments), and the resulting parameter estimates in the second stage can then be compared to each other to assess the strength of the two original equations ([13] and [14]). 2SLS not only estimates a non-recursive model, but by comparing β_8 and β_9, it allows the relative strength of the two directions of the relationship to be tested.

---

[19] Technically, a system of simultaneous equations violates one of the assumptions of classic regression; however, two-staged least squares estimates parameters for the endogenous variables in the two equations separately (Kennedy 1992: 151–74).

Results

All possible combinations of rights indices and social movement measures were tested by 2SLS across the four cases. As expected, only the strongest relationships emerging from the unidirectional modelling produced significant results. Hence, there are two results for Brazil (IPI↔SR and CRI↔SR) and Chile (IPI↔SR and CRI↔SR), one for Mexico (GAP↔SMASR), and none for Spain.[20] These results are only reported for Stage 2 of the analysis (since Stage 1 is simply carried out to establish the proxy measures for the two endogenous variables). The parameter estimates for Fit_1 and Fit_2 (from Stage 2) are reported to assess the mutual strength of the non-recursive relationship between rights and movements. The 't' values of these estimates may serve as a gauge of this strength, and are included on the assumption that the higher the level of statistical significance the stronger the parameter. If the parameter for Fit_1 is stronger than the parameter for Fit_2, then the effect of rights on movements is stronger than the effect of movements on rights (model [2]). Alternatively, if the strength of the parameters is reversed, the effect of movements on rights is stronger than the effect of rights on movements (model [1]). If the strength of the parameters, or levels of statistical significance, are relatively equal, then the mutual effects are roughly the same.

Brazil

It was the correlations that first showed the importance of labour movement activity in Brazil, and the autoregression analysis confirmed that this activity had a positive and significant impact on both rights-in-principle (IPI) and rights-in-practice (CRI). Rights-in-practice, for their part, were seen to have a similar impact on labour mobilization. The non-recursive modelling again confirms the centrality of the relationship between labour activity and both rights-in-principle and rights-in-practice, but the test of the relative strength of their mutual effects modifies the autoregression results in some degree. On the one hand, labour mobilization is still effective in extending rights-in-principle (IPI), but these rights are as or more effective in stimulating labour mobilization. On the other, rights-in-practice are indeed effective in encouraging labour mobilization, but the corresponding influence of this mobilization on rights-in-practice is now much less certain (and statistically

---

[20] IPI↔SR and GAP↔SR were tested for Spain but revealed no mutual effects.

TABLE 6.3.1. *2SLS parameter estimates for Brazil* (second stage)

| | IPI↔SR | | CRI↔SR | |
	IPI	SR	CRI	SR
Constant	.58	−2464.18	.50	−1847.70
	(.112)	(−2.54)**	(8.21)**	(−1.29)
Fit_1		4879.78		5276.89
		(4.25)**		(2.16)*
Fit_2	.0001		.00005	
	(3.57)**		(.00004)	
AR	.81	.86	.62	.84
	(7.18)**	(6.49)**	(2.88)**	(6.08)**
Res.	25	23	25	23
DF	22	20	22	20
LL	32.99	−172.53	20.91	−177.72

Note: Reported values are unstandardized coefficients; t-values appear in parentheses; Res. = number of residuals; DF = degrees of freedom; LL = log likelihood.
* $p < .05$ ** $p < .01$

insignificant). The relationship between the formal rights of citizenship and labour activity remains 'mutually constitutive', therefore, but it is the gradual political liberalization of the regime itself (its policies of 'distension' and 'political opening') which actively encourages labour mobilization, and not vice versa.

Chile

The Chilean case is similar to that of Brazil insofar as the correlations revealed the strong associations between labour movement activity and the rights indices, while the autoregression results confirmed labour's positive and significant impact on rights-in-principle (IPI), and the similar impact of rights-in-principle and rights-in-practice (CRI) on labour activity. But autoregression also showed that labour's impact on rights-in-practice was rather weak (and that its impact on the GAP was actually negative). The non-recursive model confirms the strong mutual relationship between labour activity (SR) and rights-in-principle (IPI). It also demonstrates a similarly strong and mutual relationship between labour activity and rights-in-practice (CRI). In both instances the effect of labour on rights is very slightly stronger than the effect of rights on labour. This suggests that the mutual conditioning of rights

TABLE 6.3.2. *2SLS parameter estimates for Chile* (second stage)

| | IPI↔SR | | CRI↔SR | |
	IPI	SR	CRI	SR
Constant	.10	1.98	.12	−20.58
	(.841)	(.143)	(2.71)*	(−.941)
Fit_1		83.81		238.5
		(3.36)**		(3.14)**
Fit_2	.009		.003	
	(4.33)**		(3.93)**	
AR	.59	.25	.45	.46
	(2.71)*	(.914)	(1.53)	(1.81)
Res.	16	16	16	16
DF	13	13	13	12
LL	9.53	−71.31	21.72	−70.19

Note: Reported values are unstandardized coefficients; t-values appear in parentheses; Res. = number of residuals; DF = degrees of freedom; LL = log likelihood.
  * p < .05 ** p < .01

and movements in Chile is stronger than previously suspected, and that the Chilean labour movement was more effective in changing the behaviour of the regime than is usually allowed. However, it is salutary to recall the nature of the non-recursive model, which is designed to test the mutuality of this relationship. To the degree (it need not be a high degree) that labour mobilizes, and insofar (it need not be very far) that the regime varies rights-in-practice, these two activities appear to be mutually conditioning.

Mexico

Mexico is different. It was the combined term (SMASR) for social movement activity which was positively correlated with both rights-in-principle (IPI) and the GAP, and the regression analysis confirmed the positive impact of this combination on the GAP. Reversing the regression equations revealed that both IPI and the GAP have a similarly positive influence on SMASR. The discrete measures of social movement activity (SMA and SR), on the other hand, neither influenced nor were influenced by the rights indices. The non-recursive model clearly supports these findings by confirming both that the key element of the relationship between rights and movements is SMASR↔GAP, and that the mutual effects

TABLE 6.3.3. *2SLS parameter estimates for*
Mexico (second stage)

| | GAP↔SMASR | |
	GAP	SMASR
Constant	−.028	452.04
	(−1.75)	(3.60)**
Fit_1		8474.52
		(2.18)*
Fit_2	.00006	
	(2.18)*	
AR	−.04	.41
	(−.18)	(2.25)*
Res.	26	25
DF	23	22
LL	42.64	−182.49

Note: Reported values are unstandardized coefficients; t-values appear in parentheses; Res. = number of residuals; DF = degrees of freedom; LL = log likelihood.

within this relationship are equally strong. At the same time, these same effects operate much less strongly than between IPI↔SR in Brazil, or between IPI↔SR or CRI↔SR in Chile, which tends to vindicate the general conclusion that the rights-movements relationship in Mexico is mutually conditioning but relatively weak.[21]

[21] As a rule of thumb, all 't' values above 2.00 are considered to be statistically significant. The non-recursive model therefore produces a robust statistical relationship between SMASR and the GAP in Mexico. Nonetheless, the level of statistical significance is considerably lower than that of the analogous relationships in Chile and Brazil.

Relating Citizenship Rights and Social Movements through Time

The last chapter looked at the relationship between citizenship rights and social movements over time. For the periods under study in three of the four cases it was able to conclude that this relationship is mutually conditioning in different degrees and ways. In the fourth case, Spain, these interactive effects remained moot. The analysis now proceeds to examine how this relationship develops through time by searching for the key moments that do most to shape it. Since such moments may be precipitated either by changes in social movement activity or by changes in rights provision, the enquiry focuses on the critical years or turning points of both trends and calculates their mutual impact. Thus, similarly to the last chapter, the relationship is examined in both directions (using model [1] and model [2]), but, in this instance, multiple interrupted time-series regression analysis (MITS) is employed to distinguish the effects of the critical changes in social movement activity on citizenship rights, and vice versa. Later in the chapter Boolean 'truth tables' (Ragin 1987; Wickham-Crowley 1992) are constructed in order to establish the (necessary and sufficient) conditions for the impact of movements on rights, and vice versa, at particular moments in time, and to calculate the probabilities of this impact occurring at all.

MITS Regression

Brazil

Social Movements→Citizenship

The first step in examining the variable impact of social movement activity on citizenship rights is to select the years of most visible change in the social movement measures (as reported in Chapter

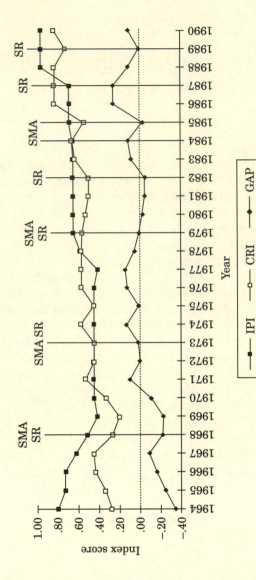

FIGURE 7.1.1: *Rights and critical years of mobilization in Brazil*

5) and superimpose them on the trends for the three rights measures (as reported in Chapter 4). Thus, Figure 7.1.1 shows the
trends for rights-in-principle (IPI), rights-in-practice (CRI), and
the GAP for Brazil, which are divided by vertical lines representing salient changes in labour (SR) and other (SMA) mobilization.
In years when both measures change together the vertical line is
marked by both symbols.

If the different rights measures are considered as trends which
are interrupted by changes in social mobilization, the objective of
the analysis is to estimate the effect of these interruptions. Multiple interrupted time-series analysis (MITS) serves this purpose
by regressing the dependent variable (in this instance a rights
measure) on the years of interruption. This method requires the
years of interruption to be coded as dichotomous dummy variables
(0 for the years preceding the change, and 1 for the years after the
change). In general, the parameter estimates that result from this
type of analysis reveal three things: the magnitude of the effect
that the particular year has on the dependent variable, the direction of that effect (either positive or negative), and whether this
effect is significant. But the present analysis is uniquely concerned
with the direction and significance of the estimates and not with
their magnitude. (If the trend of the dependent variable is conceived as a series of shorter lines, each with its own slope, then
the parameter estimates represent these shorter slopes that together compose the overall trend).[1] In formal terms MITS can be
stated as follows:

$$Y_t = \alpha + \beta_1 Year_1 + \beta_2 Year_2 + \beta_3 Year_3 + \ldots \beta_n Year_n + \varepsilon_t \quad [1]$$

In this equation, Y_t is the dependent variable over time (in this
instance IPI, CRI, or GAP), $\beta_{1\ldots n}$, are the parameter estimates,
$Year_{1\ldots n}$ are the individual years coded as dichotomous dummies,
and ε_t is the error term.

Past political science research has used MITS analysis to examine the effects of public policies, such as social security, coal mine
safety, and civil rights; the effects of specific laws, such as traffic
and gun control measures; the influence of major political shifts
like reform or revolution (Lewis-Beck 1986: 209); and the effects of
Latin American elections on macroeconomic performance (Remmer

---

[1] A second set of independent variables may be added to assess the effect of an
interruption on the intercept of the lines (to see whether the line jumps as a result
of the interruption). Since this study is uniquely concerned with changes in slope,
a simpler version of MITS analysis is employed. For a complete discussion of this
technique, see Lewis-Beck (1986).

TABLE 7.1.1. *Significant years of impact in Brazil*
(social movements→citizenship)

	IPI	CRI	GAP
SMA	1968 (−) 1979 (+)	1973 (+)	1973 (+)
SR	1968 (−) 1979 (+) 1987 (+)	1973 (+) 1987 (+)	1973 (+)

1993). However, whereas many of these studies have focused on the medium- or long-term effects of single events or occurrences of different kinds, the present analysis applies MITS reiteratively to successive critical years in the time-series trends of the different measures of rights and social movement activity. Finally, since auto-correlation remains a potential problem for MITS, just as it was for the regression analysis of Chapter 6, the autoregressive technique is again employed to estimate the parameters of the different equations.

Returning to Figure 7.1.1, the vertical lines represent the critical changes in social movement activity that are apparent from a visual examination of the trends in the social movement measures. But the results of the MITS analysis of the effects of these changes on citizenship rights (that is the results of model [1] as recorded in Table 7.1.1) only show the statistically significant years (or those very close to statistical significance, which are signalled as such). In other words, the figures for Brazil and the other cases may suggest more critical years than are in fact reported in the tables. Nonetheless, for each relationship in each case individual MITS regressions were run for all possible effects, and in this instance for the possible effects of the two social movement measures on the three rights measures, giving a three-by-two table with the dependent variables (IPI, CRI, GAP) along the top row and the independent variables (SMA, SR) in the first column. The sign in parentheses records the direction of the effect of that year on the dependent variable.[2]

It is clear from the table that labour mobilization (SR) provokes

---

[2] There are six regressions per case for the social movements–citizenship relationship, and a further six for the citizenship–social movements relationship, which, for the four cases, add up to 48 regressions in total. For this reason the regression results are presented in synoptic and tabular form throughout the chapter.

a reduction in rights-in-principle in 1968, but encourages improvements in rights-in-practice in 1973 (confirmed by its positive impact on the GAP in that year), in rights-in-principle in 1979, and in both orders of rights in 1987. Others forms of social movement activity (SMA) mirror and reinforce these effects for the 1968–79 period. In other words the MITS analysis tends to confirm the conclusion drawn from the standard regressions (see Chapter 6) that it is the labour movement that has the greatest long-term impact on citizenship rights in Brazil, but also reveals that labour's impact was bolstered by other social movements in both 1973 and 1979. It is probably no coincidence that both of these years were turning points in the political development of the military regime: 1973 marked the beginning of the military's political opening (*abertura*) or relaxation (*distensão*), while the reforms of 1979 ushered in a more liberal and plural party system.

Citizenship→Social Movements

The direction of the relationship is now reversed (as in model [2] of Chapter 6), so that Figure 7.1.2 depicts the trends in the social movement measures (SMA, SR) that are interrupted by the years of critical change in rights provision.

Since the MITS analysis now focuses on the impact of shifts in rights provision on social movement activity, the dependent variables (SMA, SR) are now placed along the top row of Table 7.1.2, with the independent variables (IPI, CRI, and GAP) aligned in the first column; and MITS again serves to elucidate the standard regression results. Whereas these results indicated that rights-in-practice had a negative impact on (non-labour) social movement activity (SMA) over time (see Chapter 6), MITS distinguishes the positive impact of all three rights measures in 1977–8 from the negative impacts in 1985, 1986, and (possibly) 1988, demonstrating that regime liberalization elicited more such activity in the later 1970s, but that the regime change of the mid-1980s tended to discourage it. Similarly, rights-in-practice were seen to stimulate labour mobilization, but MITS reveals that all three rights measures multiply these effects which themselves cluster around the years of democratic transition (1983, 1985, 1986, 1988). Thus, the massive response of labour to the implementation of a more liberal rights regime seems to make the influence of rights both more general and more concentrated than previously suspected. Nonetheless, it is equally evident that the significant years of rights influence on social movements overall (1977–8, 1983, 1985, 1986,

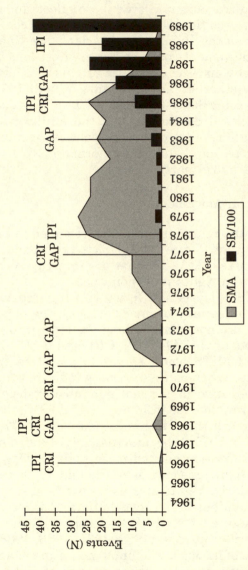

FIGURE 7.1.2: *Social movements and critical rights years in Brazil*

TABLE 7.1.2. *Significant years of impact in Brazil*
(citizenship→social movements)

	SMA	SR
IPI	1978 (+)	1985 (+)
	1988 (−)[a]	1988 (+)
CRI	1977 (+)	1985 (+)
	1985 (−)	
GAP	1977 (+)	1983 (+)
	1986 (−)	1986 (+)

[a] For 1988, $t = -1.86$ and $p = .08$

1988) are interleaved with the significant years of social movement impact on citizenship rights (1973, 1979, 1987), so reinforcing the finding (of Chapter 6) that the relationship between the two is mutually conditioning and constitutive.

Chile

Social Movements→Citizenship

The presentation of the MITS analysis for Chile and the sub-sequent cases follows the same pattern as for Brazil. It begins with the variable impact of social movement activity on the rights measures (according to model [1] of Chapter 6), and Figure 7.2.1 shows these rights trends divided by the critical years of social mobilization. Then the results of the MITS regressions on these key years are reported in Table 7.2.1.

The regression results (see Chapter 6) indicated that both labour and other social movement activity have a positive and significant effect on rights-in-principle in Chile, and MITS confirms this finding for 1980 and the transition years of the late 1980s. At the same time, labour's influence on rights-in-practice was weak, and MITS clarifies this finding by demonstrating that this influence (and that of other social movement activity) was confined to the last years of the regime (1987–90). Furthermore, MITS relates labour's negative influence on the GAP (perceived as a possibility in Chapter 6) to the major constitutional change of 1980. Finally, MITS pinpoints the positive impact of overall social movement activity on the GAP in 1984, indicating that the 'wave of protest' of 1983–4 temporarily extended the exercise of rights-in-practice despite the repressive disposition of the regime.

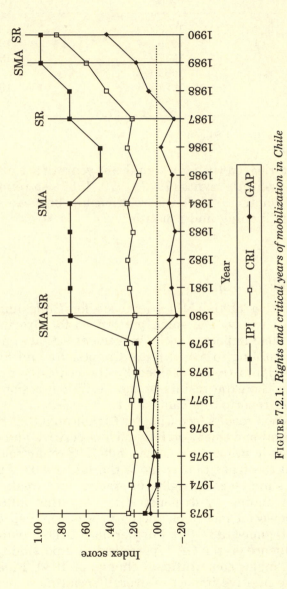

FIGURE 7.2.1: *Rights and critical years of mobilization in Chile*

TABLE 7.2.1. *Significant years of impact in Chile*
(social movements→citizenship)

	IPI	CRI	GAP
SMA	1980 (+)	1989 (+)	1980 (−)
	1989 (+)		1984 (+)
			1989 (+)
SR	1980 (+)	1987 (+)	1980 (−)
	1987 (+)	1990 (+)	1987 (+)
			1990 (+)

Citizenship→Social Movements

As in the Brazilian and subsequent cases, the relationship is now reversed to discover the variable impact of citizenship rights on social movement activity (as in model [2] of Chapter 6). Hence, Figure 7.2.2 shows the trends in the social movement measures divided by the critical years of rights changes, and Table 7.2.2 reports the results of the MITS regressions.

In the Chilean case MITS tends to qualify the regression results for model [2] in a similar way to model [1], insofar as the impact of rights-in-principle and rights-in-practice on labour is clearly stronger in the dying years of the regime (1987, 1988), and the impact of rights-in-principle on other social mobilization is largely owing to the constitutional change of 1980. Yet MITS adds a dimension to the analysis of this relationship by clearly bracketing the 'wave of protest' that occurred in 1983−4 with the *positive* impact of the GAP on non-labour mobilization in 1983 and its *negative* impact in 1985. The similarly negative impact of rights-in-practice in 1985 confirms that the temporary extension of these rights is now reversed, but the insertion of the positive influence of social movement activity on the GAP (1984) between the changing impact of the GAP itself (1983, 1985) must modify the conclusions of Chapter 6 by breaking the general rule that rights-in-practice are both insensitive to social movement activity and ineffective in evoking that activity. MITS demonstrates, to the contrary, that such mutual conditioning does indeed occur but that it is concentrated into the period of the 'wave of protest'. It will be seen that MITS modifies the regression results for Spain in analogous fashion by revealing the two-way effects at work in the mutual relationship between rights and social mobilization during the moment of democratic transition in that country.

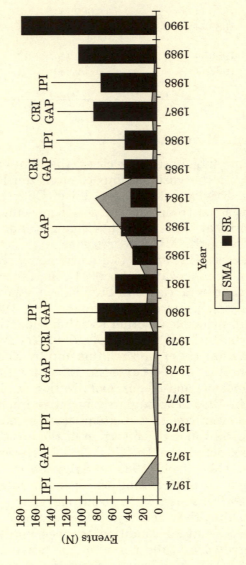

FIGURE 7.2.2: *Social movements and critical rights years in Chile*

TABLE 7.2.2. *Significant years of impact in Chile*
(citizenship→social movements)

	SMA	SR
IPI	1980 (+)[a]	1988 (+)[b]
CRI	1985 (−)	1987 (+)[c]
GAP	1983 (+)	1978 (+)[d]
	1985 (−)	

[a] For 1980, t = 2.06 and p = .07
[b] For 1988, t = 1.87 and p = .09
[c] For 1987, t = 2.04 and p = .06
[d] For 1978, t = 2.17 and p = .06

Mexico

Social Movements→Citizenship

As in the previous cases the variable impact of social movements on rights in Mexico, with the rights measures divided by key years of mobilization, is presented in Figure 7.3.1, and the results of the MITS regressions are reported in Table 7.3.1. But, differently from the previous cases, the MITS regressions now include the combined term SMASR, in deference to the (auto and non-recursive) regression results of Chapter 6. It will be recalled from that chapter that neither of the disaggregated measures of social movement activity had any impact on either rights-in-principle or rights-in-practice; whereas both labour activity (SR) and the combined term did have a positive and significant impact on the GAP, and the mutual effects of SMASR↔GAP proved to be the key element of the relationship between rights and movements in Mexico.

MITS tends to deny any labour impact on the different rights measures, but reveals that other forms of mobilization were occasionally influential, having a positive effect on rights-in-principle in the early 1970s, a negative effect on rights-in-practice in 1986, and a positive effect on the GAP in 1988. The combined term SMASR completes the picture with its negative impact on rights-in-practice in 1976 and 1986 (when it compounds the effects of SMA), and its positive impact on these same rights in 1980. It is plausible to infer that non-labour protest encouraged institutional improvement during Echeverría's 'political opening', but that the wave of broader-based protest towards the end of his administration in 1976 produced a deterioration in rights-in-practice. Similarly, it appears that the combination of social movement protest

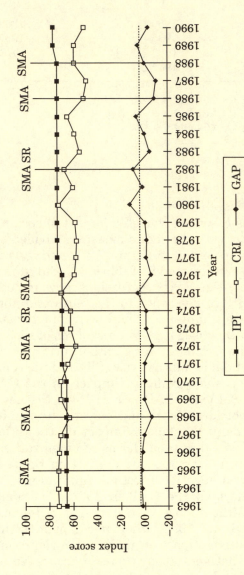

FIGURE 7.3.1: *Rights and critical years of mobilization in Mexico*

TABLE 7.3.1. *Significant years of impact in Mexico*
(social movements→citizenship)

	IPI	CRI	GAP
SMA	1972 (+)	1972 (−)[a]	1986 (−)
	1975 (+)	1986 (−)	1988 (+)
SR	None	1974 (−)	None
SMASR	None	1976 (−)[b]	1980 (+)
		1980 (+)[c]	
		1986 (−)	

[a] For 1972, t = −1.73 and p = .09
[b] For 1976, t = −1.98 and p = .06
[c] For 1980, t = 1.79 and p = .09

(SMASR) produced a momentary improvement in rights-in-practice at the beginning of the 1980s, but precipitated an accelerating decline in these rights following the 'electoral opening' of 1983–5. The latter effect was reversed by the mass mobilizations that both preceded and followed the presidential elections of 1988.

Citizenship→Social Movements

As in the previous cases, Figure 7.3.2 looks at the variable impact of the rights measures on social movement activity in Mexico, and the MITS regressions on the key years are reported in Table 7.3.2. Once again, the MITS regressions for Mexico include the combined term, SMASR.

Once the equation is reversed (as in model [2] of Chapter 6) a very different picture emerges, which diverges from the profile of the autoregression results. These results had indicated that both rights-in-principle (IPI) and the GAP had a significant and positive impact on combined social movement activity (SMASR). MITS tends to make rights-in-principle less salient, since their measure shifts its slope very little over the period. On the other hand, rights-in-practice proved recurrently effective in stimulating this combined activity (SMASR) until 1981, and equally effective in discouraging such activity after that date. These recurrent effects are reproduced on the disaggregated measures for labour and, to a lesser extent, non-labour mobilization. Furthermore the recurrent effects of the GAP mainly reproduce those of rights-in-practice, but the GAP has the additional and discrete effects of provoking more mobilization in 1976 (the year of the political clamp-down that followed the failure of Echeverría's 'political opening') and 1980

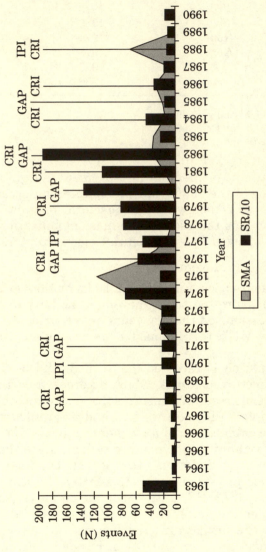

FIGURE 7.3.2: Social movements and critical rights years in Mexico

TABLE 7.3.2. *Significant years of impact in Mexico*
(citizenship→social movements)

	SMA	SR	SMASR
IPI	1970 (+)[a]	None	None
CRI	1972 (+)	1972 (+)	1972 (+)
	1976 (−)	1979 (+)	1979 (+)
	1988 (+)	1981 (+)	1981 (+)
		1982 (−)	1982 (−)
		1984 (−)	1984 (−)
GAP	1972 (+)	1976 (+)	1972 (+)[b]
	1976 (−)	1980 (+)	1976 (+)[c]
	1988 (+)	1982 (−)	1980 (+)
			1982 (−)

[a] For 1970, $t = 1.81$ and $p = .08$
[b] For 1972, $t = 1.84$ and $p = .08$
[c] For 1976, $t = 1.76$ and $p = .10$

(the same year that overall social movement activity had a positive impact on rights-in-practice).

Taking the significant years for both the GAP and rights-in-practice together, it is clear that social movement activity (both labour and other) is finely tuned to changes in regime behaviour, and that the accelerating decline in rights-in-practice (see Chapter 4), which accompanied the economic crisis and the austerity policies of the 1980s, was at least occasionally effective in discouraging that activity—until the resurgence of mobilization and protest in 1988. As a corollary, MITS adduces more circumstantial evidence in support of the dual proposition that institutional improvements in the 1970s (especially in the rights of participation) precipitated more protest in the electoral arena, and that this protest then provoked increasing repression and a decline of rights-in-practice —that were themselves challenged by the electoral mobilizations of 1988.

Spain

Social Movements→Citizenship

Citizenship→Social Movements

As in the previous cases, the trends in rights measures as divided by key years of mobilization are presented in Figure 7.4.1 (model [1]), and the trends in movement measures as divided by key

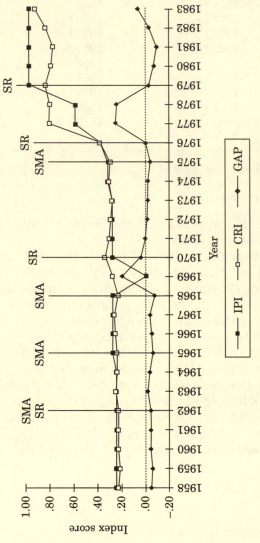

FIGURE 7.4.1: *Rights and critical years of mobilization in Spain*

TABLE 7.4.1. *Significant years of impact in Spain*
(social movements→citizenship)

	IPI	CRI	GAP
SMA	None	None	None
SR	1976 (+)	None	1976 (+)
	1979 (+)		1979 (−)

rights years are presented in Figure 7.4.2 (model [2]). Similarly, the results of the MITS regressions are reported in Tables 7.4.1 (model [1]) and 7.4.2 (model [2]).

The regression results revealed that the Spanish case is distinctive (see Chapter 6). In particular, the significant effects of social movement activity on rights (SR on the GAP, and SMA on IPI), and of rights on social movement activity (GAP on SR, and IPI on SMA) were seen to be mainly *negative*. It was subsequently argued that the difficulty of interpreting these results might be resolved by recognizing that the relationship between rights and movements in Spain is concentrated into, and in some sense distorted by the moment of democratic transition; and this argument is strongly supported by the MITS analysis. On the one hand, labour mobilization has a positive impact on rights-in-principle in both 1976, the year when both unions and parties became legal, and 1979, the first full year of the new democratic Constitution. (The negative impact on the GAP in the latter year simply reflects the huge institutional improvement implicit in the Constitution). On the other, all the rights measures have a positive impact on social mobilization in 1975 (the year of Franco's death and the beginning of the transition), while rights-in-principle has a negative effect on this mobilization (both labour and non-labour) in 1977, reflecting the closure of the political struggle for democracy once the legalization of unions and parties—including the Communist Party—had assured a dramatic decline in levels of protest. In other words, MITS succeeds in demonstrating the 'two-way' and mutually conditioning effects of social mobilization and citizenship rights in Spain by clearly bracketing the years of the democratic transition which delimit, concentrate, and intensify these effects.[3]

---

[3] The only year outside of the transition to appear as (barely) significant is 1969 (IPI on SR), when the lifting of the 'state of siege' precipitated further labour protest.

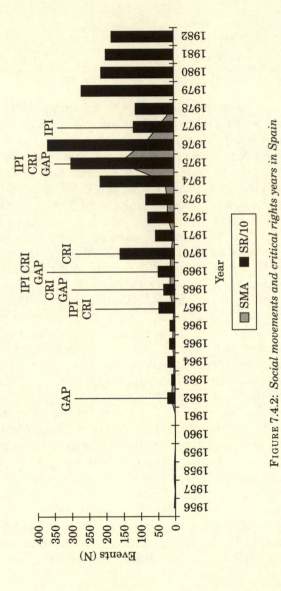

FIGURE 7.4.2: *Social movements and critical rights years in Spain*

TABLE 7.4.2. *Significant years of impact in Spain*
(citizenship→social movements)

	SMA	SR
IPI	1975 (+)	1969 (+)[a]
	1977 (−)	1975 (+)
		1977 (−)
CRI	1975 (+)	None
GAP	1975 (+)	1975 (+)[b]

[a] For 1969, t = 1.86 and p = .08
[b] For 1975, t = 1.93 and p = .08

Summary

By focusing on the changing slope of the dependent variable, MITS analysis sets out to discover the fluctuating impact of the independent variable through time. But since MITS regresses the dependent variable onto the critical years in the trend of the independent variable, it is inescapable that *any* exogenous event or circumstance occurring in those years may be the cause (partial or complete) of the shift in the dependent variable. Hence, MITS analysis might be suggestive of the fluctuating influence of rights on movements or movements on rights, but on its own it could not support strong causal statements. However, where MITS analysis is informed by the results of autoregressive modelling (of the kind that was conducted in Chapter 6), it can certainly create new insights into the causal relationships at work. For this reason, the exegesis of the MITS results has been argued throughout in terms of what it can add to the conclusions drawn from autoregressive modelling.

Modelling results for Brazil had shown labour to be preponderant in the struggle for citizenship rights, but the MITS analysis showed that labour mobilization was bolstered by other social movement activity during key political moments of the 1970s. At the same time, MITS modulated the impact of rights, and revealed the very different effects the rights measures had on non-labour social movement activity in the 1970s and 1980s, and their very strong impact on labour over the years of the democratic transition. In Mexico too, the MITS reshaped the modelling results by showing the sensitivity of labour and, in lesser degree, non-labour mobilization to changes in rights-in-practice, and the very different impact of the rights trends in the 1970s and 1980s. In Chile

MITS added a new dimension to the analysis by clearly bracketing the wave of protest of 1983–4 and demonstrating that rights-in-practice were both sensitive to and influential on social mobilization during this interlude (an insight that contradicted the general rules established by the modelling). Finally, in Spain MITS succeeds in solving the conundrum created by the modelling, and shows the strong two-way effects of rights and movements over the period of democratic transition.

Overall the MITS analysis both supports and modulates the proposition that there is a mutually conditioning relationship between social movement activity and citizenship rights over time. In Brazil the strongly 'constitutive' nature of this relationship is confirmed by the 'interleaving' of key rights years and key movement years. In Chile, where it had appeared that only rights-in-principle were effective in the relationship, rights-in-practice gain salience for 1983–4, and so reconfigure the profile of the struggle for citizenship in that country. In Mexico, MITS confirms the complexities of the mutual conditioning, with rights-in-principle and, it is now evident, rights-in-practice eliciting more social mobilization in the 1970s, before the secular decline in rights-in-practice and the consequent discouragement of social mobilization for much of the 1980s. Last but not least, in Spain MITS appears to rescue the proposition from unpropitious modelling results by revealing the powerful two-way effects at work during the democratic transition. Nonetheless, the Spanish case remains distinctive, and it is a matter for continuing debate whether citizenship rights were mainly won by social mobilization or were simply triggered by the death of Franco and the elite struggle for power which ensued in its wake.

Qualitative Comparative Analysis

In an original contribution to the debate over comparative methodology Charles Ragin (1987; 1994) has employed the logic of Boolean algebra to integrate the competing 'case-oriented' and 'variable-oriented' research strategies (Ragin 1994: 299). It will be recalled from Chapter 3 that comparative studies can be divided along three axes: quantitative versus qualitative, small-N versus large-N, or intensive versus extensive (Ragin 1994: 300–1). Ragin argues that these gulfs in comparative methodology can be bridged by what he calls 'qualitative comparative analysis', or QCA, which combines the strengths of both the case-oriented and variable-oriented research strategies, while maintaining the scientific rigour of comparative studies which employ quantitative methods

(Ragin 1994: 304). QCA considers cases 'holistically, as a configuration of conditions, not a collection of scores on variables,' where
the combination of variables takes precedence over individual
variables (Ragin 1994: 307–8). Consequently, QCA begins by constructing a 'truth table', where variables are coded dichotomously
to represent their presence or absence. The truth table 'lists the
different combinations of causal conditions and the value of the
outcome variable for the cases conforming to each combination'
(Ragin 1994: 309). By examining the presence or absence of independent variables, the truth table, when reduced through Boolean
algebra,[4] can reveal what combination of variables produces the
outcome of the dependent variable in question.

This comparative strategy has been employed by Wickham-
Crowley (1992) to isolate the necessary conditions for social revolution in Latin America. His truth table includes twenty-eight cases
that, since 1956, either had a guerrilla movement, or did not; and
either experienced social revolution led by this movement, or did
not. The table is then constructed by coding five conditions as present or absent: a guerrilla uprising; peasant and/or worker support; guerrilla military strength; an existing praetorian regime
as the target of the insurrection; and loss of US support by the
incumbent regime (Wickham-Crowley 1992: 312). He concludes
that only the combination of all five conditions leads to successful
revolution (Wickham-Crowley 1992: 313–26).

The Boolean method can be adapted for the purposes of the present study. Rather than examining what conditions are present
or absent across the four cases, a truth table can be constructed
for each case that identifies the presence or absence of conditions
in each year. In this way, the truth table can combine data from
Chapters 4 (rights), 5 (social movements and political demands),
and 6 (rights, social movements, and economic conditions) to reveal
the conditions for the impact of movements on rights, and vice
versa, as well as to calculate the probabilities of this impact occurring at all. There are therefore two primary questions which the
qualitative comparison seeks to address. First, under what conditions does social mobilization coincide with increased rights provision? Second, under what conditions does increased rights provision
coincide with social mobilization? The first question has three
possible outcomes, representing changes in IPI, CRI, and the GAP;
and the Boolean method will specify all the variables (including

---

[4] The method is called Boolean because Boolean algebra was developed for binary conditions, i.e. 1 = the condition is present, or 0 = the condition is not present.

independent rights variables) which contribute to the outcome. The second question has two possible outcomes, representing changes in SR and SMA (or more labour or other forms of social mobilization). Subsequently, the answers to these questions can be used to calculate the probability of such 'coincidences' by comparing the years of their occurrence to the total number of years under study in each case.

Boolean Truth Tables

The truth tables constructed for the four cases present the *annual* presence or absence of the same set of conditions, namely, favourable rights conditions (IPI, CRI, GAP), waves of social mobilization (SMA, SR), a high proportion of political demands (POLD), high inflation (INFL), economic crisis (ECON), peak energy consumption (ENERG), and defence spending as a proportion of total government expenditure (DEFEXP). The presence or absence of these conditions were decided by case-sensitive thresholds derived from their descriptive trends over time (and these thresholds are specified in the footnotes to each table). In addition to the data on rights (Chapter 4), social movements and political demands (Chapter 5) and economic performance (Chapter 6), defence expenditure was included as a proxy measure of the balance between spending on 'welfare' and spending on apparatuses of coercion and control.

The truth tables (Tables 7.5 through 7.8) are examined in the usual order (Brazil, Chile, Mexico, Spain). Quite apart from their algebraic reduction, each table can be read descriptively. Reading across the columns reveals the presence or absence of each condition in any one year. Reading down the columns reveals the years in which a particular condition is present or absent. It is also possible that a 'holistic' look at the table will discover clusters of conditions which are present over a number of years. But it is the algebraic reduction of the table which can best reveal the incidence and distribution of the various conditions, and so provide a proper account of their coincidences.[5]

Brazil

The algebraic reduction of the truth table reveals that social mobilization in Brazil tends to coincide with increases in rights

---

[5] The results of the Boolean algebraic analysis of the four truth tables are presented in raw form in Appendix C.

TABLE 7.5. *Boolean Truth Table for Brazil, 1964–1990*[†]

Year	IPI	CRI	GAP	SMA	SR	POLD	INFL	ECON	ENER	DEFEXP
1964	1	0	0	0	0	0	1	0	0	0
1965	1	0	0	0	0	0	1	1	0	0
1966	1	0	0	0	0	1	0	0	0	0
1967	1	1	0	0	0	1	0	0	0	0
1968	0	0	0	0	0	1	0	0	0	0
1969	0	0	0	0	0	0	0	0	1	0
1970	0	0	0	0	0	1	0	0	0	0
1971	0	0	1	0	0	0	0	0	0	0
1972	0	0	0	0	0	0	0	0	0	0
1973	0	0	0	0	0	0	0	0	0	0
1974	0	1	1	0	0	0	0	0	0	0
1975	0	0	0	0	0	0	0	0	0	0
1976	0	1	1	0	0	0	0	0	0	1
1977	0	1	1	0	0	0	0	0	0	1
1978	1	1	0	1	1	0	0	0	0	0
1979	1	1	0	1	1	0	1	0	1	1
1980	1	0	0	1	1	0	1	0	0	1
1981	1	0	0	1	1	0	1	1	0	1
1982	1	0	0	0	1	1	1	1	0	1
1983	1	1	1	1	1	0	1	1	0	1
1984	1	1	1	0	1	1	1	0	0	1
1985	1	0	0	1	1	0	1	0	0	1
1986	1	1	1	0	1	0	1	0	0	1
1987	1	1	1	0	1	0	1	0	0	1
1988	1	1	1	0	1	0	1	1	0	1
1989	1	1	0	0	1	0	1	0	1	1
1990	1	1	1	0	1	0	1	1	0	1

[†] Using the descriptive data from Chapter 4, the three rights measures were dichotomized. For IPI, if in any given year its value is greater than or equal to the value in 1978 (.59), it is coded as 1. For CRI, the threshold year is 1979 (.56). For the GAP, the threshold year is 1971 (.09). Using the descriptive data from Chapter 5 the two social movement measures were dichotomized. For SMA, any year that social mobilization is greater than or equal to the level in 1983 is coded as 1. For SR, any year that labour mobilization is greater than or equal to the level in 1978 is coded as 1. Political demands are coded as 1 in any year that the number of political demands exceeds material demands (i.e. DEMRAT > 1, see Chapter 5). For inflation in Brazil, any year where the rate is greater than or equal to 50 per cent is coded as 1. For economic crisis, any year where GDP growth is less than or equal to one per cent is coded as 1. For energy consumption, the peak years over the entire trend are coded as 1. For defence expenditure, any year where the value is less than the value in 1976 (10 per cent) is coded as 1.

provision, first, when the rights indices themselves coincide (IPI coinciding with CRI in ten of the twenty-seven years, and both coinciding with a positive increase in the GAP in six of the ten years); and, second, when rights provisions overall also coincide with high inflation and a low rate of defence expenditure (IPI coinciding with these variables in twelve, CRI in nine, and the GAP in six of the twenty-seven years). It does not appear that a rising proportion of political demands has any importance. The likelihood of social mobilization coinciding with increased rights is high, varying from thirteen of the twenty-seven years for IPI, to nine for CRI, and six for the GAP. It seems reasonable to suggest, therefore, that social mobilization coincides with increasing rights provision between one-third and one-half of the time. Moreover it is labour mobilization which is most important in this regard (nine out of thirteen for IPI, eight out of nine for CRI, and six out of six for the GAP), which goes some way to explain the strong degree of coincidence with high inflation, and with the tight budgetary constraints suggested by low levels of defence expenditure.

The truth table can then be interrogated in the reverse direction, to ascertain the conditions under which increasing rights provision coincides with high levels of social mobilization. In this case there is no indication that social movement measures must themselves coincide, but, once again, the rights indices tend to coincide with social mobilization when inflation is high and defence expenditure low (twelve out of twenty-seven years for SR and three for SMA). Political demands remain unimportant. Overall, increased rights provision coincides with high levels of mobilization in thirteen of the twenty-seven years, with labour mobilization accounting for most of these years (SR coincides with IPI and CRI together nine times, and with IPI alone a further four times, in contrast to SMA figures of one and four, respectively). In general, the results of the Boolean analysis provide strong support for the previous assessment (see Chapter 6) of the strong and 'mutually constitutive' nature of the rights-movements relationship in Brazil.

Chile

In Chile social mobilization again tends to coincide with increased rights provision when the rights indices themselves coincide (in four of the eighteen years for IPI and CRI together, and three for all three indices); and when defence expenditure is low (six out of eighteen years for IPI, four for CRI, and three for GAP) and political demands are increasing (three years for IPI and two for

TABLE 7.6. *Boolean Truth Table for Chile, 1973–1990*[†]

Year	IPI	CRI	GAP	SMA	SR	POLD	INFL	ECON	ENER	DEFEXP
1973	0	0	1	0	0	0	1	1	1	0
1974	0	0	1	1	0	0	1	1	0	0
1975	0	0	1	0	0	0	1	1	0	0
1976	0	0	1	0	0	0	1	0	0	0
1977	0	0	1	0	0	1	1	0	0	0
1978	0	0	1	0	0	1	1	0	0	0
1979	0	1	1	0	0	1	1	0	0	0
1980	1	0	0	0	0	1	1	0	1	0
1981	1	0	0	0	1	0	0	0	0	0
1982	1	0	0	1	0	0	0	1	0	0
1983	1	0	0	1	0	0	1	1	0	1
1984	1	1	0	1	0	1	0	0	0	1
1985	0	0	0	1	0	1	1	0	0	1
1986	0	1	0	0	0	0	0	0	0	1
1987	1	0	0	0	1	1	0	0	0	1
1988	1	1	1	0	1	1	0	0	0	1
1989	1	1	1	0	1	0	0	0	1	1
1990	1	1	1	0	1	0	0	1	0	1

[†] Descriptive data from Chapters 4, 5, and 6 were dichotomized using threshold years (in the case of citizenship rights and social movements), and critical values (in the case of the other conditions). The threshold year for IPI and CRI is 1984 (IPI = .72; CRI = .25), and for the GAP is 1970 (GAP = −.01). The threshold year for SMA is 1974, which captures both the social mobilization of the first year of the Pinochet regime and that of the 1980s. 1981 is used to capture the waves of labour mobilization in the early and late 1980s (see Chapter 5). Political demands are coded as in Brazil. For inflation, any year in which the rate is greater than or equal to 27 per cent is coded as 1. For economic crisis, any year in which the GDP grew less than 2 per cent is coded as 1. For energy consumption, peak years are coded as 1. For defence expenditure, any year in which the value is less than or equal to 12 per cent is coded as 1.

CRI), with the latter two measures themselves coinciding in two (CRI) or three (IPI) years. The likelihood of mobilization coinciding with increased rights varies from eight out of eighteen years for IPI, to four for CRI, and three for GAP. Labour again accounts for most of these associations (with SMA coinciding with the CRI, for instance, in just one year, 1984). As expected, given the intransigent nature of the regime, there is a lower probability that mobilization will alter rights-in-practice than in Brazil, with this impact occurring in less than a quarter of the relevant years.

Reversing the enquiry reveals that increases in the rights indices coincide with increasing mobilization when political demands increase (two out of eighteen years for both SMA and SR), when

TABLE 7.7. *Boolean Truth Table for Mexico, 1963–1990*[†]

Year	IPI	CRI	GAP	SMA	SR	SMASR	POLD	INFL	ECON	ENER	DEFEXP
1963	1	0	1	0	0	0	0	0	0	0	0
1964	1	0	1	0	0	0	0	0	0	0	0
1965	1	0	1	0	0	0	0	0	0	0	0
1966	1	0	1	0	0	0	0	0	0	0	0
1967	1	1	0	0	0	0	1	0	0	0	0
1968	1	1	0	0	0	0	1	0	0	0	0
1969	1	1	0	0	0	1	0	0	0	0	0
1970	1	1	0	0	0	1	0	0	0	0	0
1971	1	1	0	0	0	1	0	0	0	0	0
1972	1	0	0	1	0	1	0	0	0	0	0
1973	1	0	0	0	0	1	0	0	0	0	1
1974	1	0	0	1	1	1	0	0	0	0	0
1975	1	1	1	1	1	1	0	0	0	0	0
1976	1	1	0	1	1	1	0	0	0	0	0
1977	1	0	0	0	1	1	0	0	0	0	0
1978	1	0	0	0	1	1	0	0	0	0	0
1979	1	0	0	0	1	1	0	0	0	0	0
1980	1	1	1	0	1	1	0	0	0	0	0
1981	1	0	0	1	1	1	1	1	1	1	1
1982	1	1	1	1	0	1	1	1	1	0	0
1983	1	0	0	1	0	1	1	1	1	0	1
1984	1	0	0	0	1	0	0	1	0	1	0
1985	1	1	1	1	0	0	1	1	1	0	1
1986	1	0	0	0	1	1	0	1	1	0	0
1987	1	0	0	1	0	1	1	1	1	1	1
1988	1	0	0	0	0	0	1	1	0	0	0
1989	1	0	1	0	0	0	0	0	0	1	1
1990	1	0	0	0	0	0	0	0	0	0	0

[†] The threshold year for IPI and the GAP in Mexico is 1963 (IPI = .66; GAP = .02), and the threshold year for the CRI is 1968 (CRI = .69). Since the IPI is always present in the truth table, it is the modulation in the CRI and the GAP that is important here. The threshold year for SMA is 1972, for SR is 1975, and for SMASR is 1970. Political demands are coded as in Brazil and Chile. Years in which the inflation rate was greater than or equal to 50 per cent were coded as 1. For economic crisis, years in which the growth rate was less than or equal to 2 per cent were coded as 1. Peak years of energy consumption were coded as 1. For defence expenditure, any

defence expenditure declines (three years for both SMA and SR), and at moments of pronounced economic down-turn (1982 and 1983 to be precise). The probability that more rights will coincide with more mobilization varies from three over eighteen for SMA (1982, 1983, 1984) to five over eighteen for SR; and so it appears proper to suggest that an effective coincidence occurs about one-quarter of the time, at most. Since a descriptive reading of the table shows that the coincidences tend to cluster in the early 1980s, it is fair to say that the overall results confirm the 'partial' nature of the mutually conditioning effects of rights and movements in Chile, as reported in Chapter 6, as well as suggesting that specifically political demands may play an important role in catalysing these effects.

Mexico

The Boolean results for Mexico look different in at least three respects. First, according to our criteria the IPI conditions are always present, and cannot therefore be analysed by an algebra that assumes binary conditions. Second, for the reasons adduced in the exegesis of the MITS results, the truth table includes the combined social movement term, SMASR. Third, the Boolean reductions reveal the crucial importance of one year in particular, 1982, in a way that previous methods have not. In this year, and this year only, social mobilization coincides with increases in rights provisions (both CRI and GAP), as well as with economic crisis, high inflation, and a high level of political demands. Apart from this year it is rather unlikely that social mobilization will coincide with increased rights, since this occurs no more than roughly 10 per cent of the time (three out of twenty-eight years for both CRI and the GAP).

The key year of 1982 is again highlighted when the enquiry is reversed, with rights increases coinciding with a wave of mobilization in 1982 (SMA, SR, and SMASR), as well as with economic crisis, high inflation, and an increase in political demands. But, if the IPI is again discounted, there is little chance overall that rights increases will coincide with waves of mobilization, for this occurs only three times in twenty-eight years (CRI and the GAP with SMA, SR, and SMASR in 1975 and 1982, and with SR and SMASR in 1980).[6] Once again, therefore, these effects can only be expected to occur about 10 per cent of the time.

[6] It may be noted that the GAP coincides with SMASR as a dependent variable in the same years that SMASR coincides with the GAP as a dependent variable, i.e.

In general these low probabilities confirm the uncertainty and weakness of the mutual effects of rights and movements in Mexico revealed by the regression analysis of Chapter 6. Once again it appears that the mutual influence of rights and movements in Mexico is possibly more subtle than in the more overtly authoritarian contexts of military Brazil and military Chile, and is probably refracted through the state-chartered union corporations, on the one hand, and the electoral arena, on the other. Moreover the Boolean emphasis on the watershed year of 1982 tends to confirm the MITS findings which clearly distinguished between the period until 1981 (when SMA and SMASR had a generally positive impact on the IPI and the CRI, respectively, and both CRI and the GAP had positive effects on SMASR and the other social movement measures) and the period after 1981, but before 1988 (when SMA and SMASR had negative impacts on the CRI, and the CRI had a generally negative influence on SMASR and other social movement measures).

Spain

In Spain social mobilization tends to coincide with rights increases at times of high inflation (eleven out of twenty-six years for both IPI and CRI), and sometimes this effect is catalysed by an increased proportion of political demands (three years for both IPI and CRI). Similarly to Mexico, the results also highlight one single year, 1976, when this coincidence was associated with political demands, high inflation, economic crisis, and peak energy consumption. The importance of the labour movement to social protest in Spain explains the salience of high inflation, and the real surprise, therefore, is that social mobilization (either by the labour movement, other movements, or both together) coincides with rights increases in eleven (IPI) or twelve (CRI) of the twenty-six years. However, if the scope of the enquiry is confined to the authoritarian period (up to and including 1975) this high level of probability is dramatically reduced to one (IPI) or two (CRI) years out of eighteen. In this perspective the Boolean results confirm the findings of the autoregression and MITS analyses by focusing on the key years of the transition, and emphasizing the profound nature of that transition.

1975, 1980, and 1982; and this finding confirms the results of the non-recursive model of Chapter 6 which clearly revealed SMASR↔GAP to be the key element of the relationship between rights and movements in Mexico.

TABLE 7.8. *Boolean Truth Table for Spain, 1958–1983*[†]

Year	IPI	CRI	GAP	SMA	SR	POLD	INFL	ECON	ENER	DEFEXP
1958	0	0	0	0	0	0	0	0	0	0
1959	0	0	0	0	0	0	0	0	0	0
1960	0	0	0	0	0	0	0	0	0	0
1961	0	0	0	0	0	0	0	0	0	0
1962	0	0	0	0	0	0	0	0	0	0
1963	0	0	0	0	0	0	0	0	0	0
1964	0	0	0	0	0	0	0	0	0	0
1965	0	0	0	0	0	0	1	0	0	0
1966	0	0	0	0	0	0	0	0	0	0
1967	0	0	0	0	0	1	0	0	0	0
1968	0	0	0	0	0	1	0	0	0	0
1969	0	0	1	0	0	1	0	0	0	1
1970	0	1	1	0	1	1	0	0	0	1
1971	0	1	0	0	0	1	0	0	0	1
1972	0	1	0	0	0	1	0	0	0	1
1973	0	0	0	0	0	1	1	0	0	1
1974	1	1	0	1	1	1	1	0	0	1
1975	1	1	0	1	1	1	1	1	0	1
1976	1	1	0	1	1	1	1	1	1	0
1977	1	1	1	1	0	0	1	1	0	0
1978	1	1	1	0	0	0	1	0	1	0
1979	1	1	0	0	1	0	1	0	0	0
1980	1	1	0	0	1	0	1	0	0	0
1981	1	1	0	0	1	0	1	0	0	1
1982	1	1	0	0	1	0	1	0	0	1
1983	1	1	1	0	1	0	1	0	0	1

[†] The threshold year for IPI and CRI is 1975 (IPI= .31; CRI = .29), and for the GAP is 1970 (GAP = .04). The threshold year for SMA is 1974 and for SR is 1970. Since demands data were difficult to obtain for Spain (see Chapter 5), years were coded using the data from Maravall (1978), which show that from 1967 onwards 'solidarity and political claims' exceed all others (Maravall 1978: 37). Hence, years from 1967 onwards are coded as 1. Inflation remains relatively low in Spain throughout the Franco years, but rises in the mid-1960s and mid-1970s. The threshold for inflation in Spain is 10 per cent. Any year in which the growth rate was less than or equal to 3 per cent is coded as 1. Peaks in energy consumption were coded as 1, and years in which defence expenditures are less than or equal to 15 per cent are coded as 1.

Rights increases in Spain tend to coincide with social mobilization at moments of high inflation (eight out of twenty-six years for SR and four for SMA), which is sometimes associated with more political demands (three years for SMA and two for SR). Moreover, when the direction of the enquiry is reversed in this way, 1976 again emerges as a key year. The probability that rights increases will coincide with waves of mobilization varies widely between labour (nine years for SR) and other social protest (four for SMA); but the probability for the authoritarian period (up to and including 1975) is reduced to three and two years, respectively, so confirming the recurrent conclusions that the Francoist regime set out to restrict rights severely and was consistently successful in so doing.

Thus, the adaptation of QCA to time-series analysis can discover the particular combinations of conditions in which social movements have an impact on rights provision, and vice versa, and can gauge the likelihood of these combinations occurring at all. In this way it complements the MITS analysis, which reveals the critical years of social movement impact on rights provision, and vice versa, so that together QCA and MITS provide a sensitive reading of the mutual relationship between social movement activity and individual rights provision through time. This reading refines and sometimes modifies the perspective achieved through the standard regression analysis.

At the same time QCA has the capacity to integrate the diverse variables used at different stages in the analysis, namely the rights indicators from Chapter 4, the social movement measures from Chapter 5, and the economic variables from Chapter 6. In particular, QCA serves to draft the demands data into the analysis, using the DEMRAT ratio developed in Chapter 5. A preponderance of political demands proved unimportant in Brazil, but constituted a general condition for the mutual impact of social mobilization and rights provision in Chile, and was similarly important to the switch year of 1982 in Mexico, and to the transition years in Spain. By including this measure of a developing language of rights, QCA continues to develop the comparative analysis of the relationship between individual rights and social movements in these four countries.

8

Social Movements, Individual Rights, and Democratic Transitions

The main theme of the previous chapters has been the relationship between social movements and individual rights. The opening chapters explored the ways that this relationship is construed in theory and history. This initial review of the literature revealed a cluster of archetypal connections between movements and rights which appear and reappear across disciplines. These connections are often quite abstract, and cannot easily be translated into falsifiable hypotheses (Popper 1968). But they can be advanced as analytical propositions which serve as a guide to empirical research; and this was the strategy pursued here. Thus, the research design of the subsequent enquiry (Chapters 3, 4, and 5) translated these propositions into numerical statements that were available for statistical analysis (Chapters 6 and 7). In this way, the connections made in theory and history were tested in a contemporary context, and, by and large, were shown to be valid. But the propositions were not only demonstrated, but were demonstrated differently across cases; and it is these differential results that inform the construction of the comparative argument on individual rights and social movements. The making of an argument which is at once well modulated and authentically comparative is the main achievement of the present research.

This final chapter first reviews the principal propositions regarding the relationship between individual rights and social movements, and examines the evidence in their support by summarizing the results of the empirical enquiry and statistical analysis. The review considers the relationship in the separate perspectives of social movement activity and rights provision, before adopting a dual perspective which responds to the mutual influence of rights and movements. The objective is to describe the main contours of the integrated comparative argument, and so bring the research to completion. But the argument clearly has broader implications, and, in particular, may contribute to our understanding of democratic transition and consolidation in the contemporary period. Consequently, the chapter proceeds to explore this contribution by contrasting the principal research findings with the mainstream interpretations of recent democratic transitions. The aim is not to deliver a comprehensive critique of what is now a very large literature, but, more modestly, to indicate how the scope and power of the extant accounts might be improved by the inclusion of individual rights. In the interests of both continuity and economy, therefore, the discussion of democratic transitions is strictly disciplined by the struggle for rights.

The Social Movement Perspective

In this perspective, it is social struggle in the form of collective action which wins the individual rights of citizenship. Collective action finds expression in social movements, and specific social movements are able to win universal rights insofar as they engage in increasingly modular forms of action. The state is the primary focus of social movement activity, since it is only the state which can entrench individual rights by designing and supporting a legal system which protects rights and punishes infractions. Hence the rise of modern social movements and the growth of the modern state occur in tandem. But, since rights are both derived from and threatened by the state, they are won not only through but also against the state; and, in principle, many rights place limits on state power and prerogatives. Hence the historical expansion of citizenship rights also coincides with the growth of the modern state, and especially with its increasing administrative reach and its deployment of new forms of political control. Citizenship is therefore a political process, and its constitutional and procedural codes are constantly changing through contestation and negotiation. But it was argued that the core civil and political rights of modern citizenship are not negotiable.

Social movement activity under contemporary authoritarian regimes is taken to exemplify the historical process of citizenship struggle (and was described in Chapter 5). The regime provides the axis and context of the collective struggle for individual rights, and social movement activity rises and falls over time in a complex rhythm dictated by organizational, strategic, and discursive opportunities and constraints. In Brazil social mobilization takes off in the late 1970s and is sustained through the democratic transition of the mid-1980s. Labour mobilization continues throughout the 1980s, but other social movement activity declines after the transition. In Chile labour begins to mobilize at the beginning of the 1980s, and, with occasional downturns, continues to do so throughout the decade; whereas other social movement activity peaks in 1983–4. In Mexico labour mobilization in the mid-1970s is followed by other activity, and labour mobilization in the early 1980s is followed by peaks of combined activity (labour and other) in 1983, 1986, and 1988. In Spain the labour mobilization of the late 1960s and early 1970s is combined with other social movement activity during the peak years of the transition (1974–6), but labour sustains its mobilization later in the decade, while other social movement activity declines.

Overall it is clear that labour leads the process of social mobilization, insofar as the first wave of labour mobilization always precedes the first wave of mobilization by other social movements, and both the correlations and the autoregression analysis (Chapter 6) tend to confirm the primary place of labour in the struggle for citizenship rights. But autoregression also differentiated the impact of labour across cases, showing that it is important in Chile, but not apparently to rights-in-practice; it is important in Mexico, but mainly when acting in consort with other social movements; and that its importance is incontrovertible in Brazil but closely confined to the years of the democratic transition in Spain.

Social movements are also seen as schools of rights, with the processes of organization, mobilization, and strategic choice creating the means for a popular education in rights. An awareness of rights leads directly to the struggle to vindicate these rights, and so operationalizes the legal content of citizenship through public contestation and public demands for rights. In the terms of the research design these demands address both rights-in-principle and rights-in-practice, and Chapter 4 described the processes of regime liberalization that (in the social movement perspective) can be taken as circumstantial evidence of the success of social movements in this regard. This process is gradual and halting in Brazil, imperceptible in Chile until 1987 when it becomes very rapid, confined to the 1975–9 period in Spain, and at best uncertain in Mexico, where a declining record of rights-in-practice, especially during the 1980s, meant that Mexico appeared less democratic at the end of the period than it did at the beginning.

The qualitative comparative analysis, or QCA (Chapter 7), differentiated the probabilities of social mobilization making a difference to rights provision (and, by extension, to regime liberalization)

across the cases. Mobilization tends to make this difference between 35 to 50 per cent of the time in Brazil, less than 25 per cent
of the time in Chile, about 10 per cent of the time in Mexico, and
about 10 to 15 per cent of the time in Spain. This suggests that
the impact of mobilization is strong in Brazil, partial or inconsistent in Chile, and relatively weak in Mexico and Spain. But the
MITS analysis fills in this picture by focusing on specific waves of
mobilization through time, and shows that mobilization in Chile
had an especially strong impact, even on rights-in-practice, in 1983–
4, and that the main effects of mobilization in Spain were concentrated in the years of political transition (with QCA and MITS
together confirming the profound nature of this transition).

The Rights Perspective

In this perspective, rights can encourage or even elicit social struggle by providing social movements with a common language or
associational idiom, which is variously described as a set of tools,
a political resource, or a banner for action. As a common language,
rights serve to frame social movement activity and contribute to
make it more modular. In this way rights can both stimulate
social movement struggle by increasing its scope and catalysing
the spread of common demands across a variety of struggles,
and empower the movements by providing a political agenda and
creating a more proactive impetus. Especially important in this
regard is the role of rights in articulating the different sectoral,
communal, and regional struggles of the excluded for some form
of political inclusion. In the terms of the research design, social
movements may respond to the perceived GAP between rights-in-
principle and rights-in-practice. In broader analytical terms (see
Chapter 1), they may then act to resolve the tension between the
normative and descriptive content of citizenship through social
struggle.

The variation in rights-in-principle and rights-in-practice over
time was described in Chapter 4, which also demonstrates the
GAP that recurrently opens up between the two in all cases. This
GAP was largely negative in Chile, especially in the early and
middle 1980s, mainly negative in both Spain and Mexico, with
some positive peaks, and frequently switched sign but became
gradually more positive in Brazil. The probability of rights provision eliciting social movement activity varied widely across cases
(as suggested by the QCA of Chapter 7). Increasing provision is

associated with more mobilization about 50 per cent of the time in Brazil, about 25 per cent of the time (at most) in Chile, about 10 per cent of the time in Mexico, and some 10 to 15 per cent of the time in Spain. Similarly to the likelihood of mobilization effecting rights provision, these probabilities confirm the strength of the relationship between rights and movements in Brazil, contrasted to its relative inconsistency in Chile and its relative weakness in Mexico.

Once again, these observations are further modulated by the MITS analysis (Chapter 7) which reveals the specific effects of changes in rights provision as they occur through time. Thus, it is apparent that the impact of increased rights on non-labour social movement activity in Brazil was very different in the 1970s and 1980s, while the impact on labour mobilization was especially strong during the years of the democratic transition. Similarly in Mexico, rights trends had very different impacts on social mobilization in the 1970s and 1980s, with labour proving especially sensitive to increases in rights-in-practice. Moreover, QCA pinpoints 1982 as the critical switch year between the different patterns of these two decades in Mexico. Increases in rights-in-practice in Chile only have a perceptible impact in 1983–4, as expected, while in Spain rights increases were again most influential during the transition years of the mid-1970s.

As a result of the dissemination of rights demands, and of the role of rights in catalysing social mobilization, it is expected that the rights content of demand-making by social movements will increase over time, with rights demands becoming more generalized at the crest of major waves of mobilization. The evidence from Chapter 5 supports the proposition in all four cases, but the Brazilian case is complicated by the strong influence of conjunctures of record economic growth (early 1970s) and deep economic crisis (late 1970s and early 1980s). In Brazil, therefore, political demands predominate from 1964 to 1973, and material and economic demands take first place in subsequent years, with the composition of demands becoming more balanced from 1982 onwards. But political demands exceed all others not only in 1965–8 and 1970, but also in 1982 and 1984 (the year of the *diretas já* campaign). In Chile the big shift comes in 1983, with political demands predominating in 1983–4 and 1986–9, and closely accompanying the waves of protest of that decade. In 1984 the number of political and civil demands exceeded all others by a factor of ten. In Mexico political and civil demands begin to increase after 1978, while material demands decline after 1983, despite economic crisis and government austerity policies. Political demands are clearly predominant in 1967–8, 1981–4, and 1988. In Spain there is also a tendency for the proportion of political and civil demands to increase, with political demands clearly exceeding the rest in 1967, 1970, 1972, and 1974. In all cases, therefore, there is some tendency for rights demands to generalize as waves of mobilization reach their peak, but QCA suggests that possibly only in Chile did the peak of rights demands have a direct influence on rights provision. In general there seems good reason to accept that the discourse of rights achieves its political impact through the social movements which articulate it.

The Dual Perspective

It was proposed that the discourse of individual rights and social movements not only coexist in the public domain, but also condition each other's development and political trajectory. In its strongest form the proposition sees rights and movements as being mutually constitutive, which means, quite literally, that the one cannot develop without the other. The autoregression analysis (Chapter 6) supported the proposition by demonstrating a clear two-way relationship between rights and movements in three of the four cases. The relationship was characterized as strong to the point of being mutually constitutive in Brazil, as mutually conditioning but partial or inconsistent in Chile, and as mutually conditioning but relatively weak in Mexico. No such result was apparent for Spain, where it was hypothesized that these two-way effects were hidden by their extreme concentration in the moment of political transition.

The non-recursive modelling of the relationship bolstered these results by isolating the most significant elements and by showing the strength of the mutual effects in each case. The strongest mutual effects in Brazil were found between labour movement activity and rights-in-principle. Although rights-in-practice were effective in eliciting labour mobilization, the inverse effect was far less certain, suggesting that it was the gradual liberalization of the regime which encouraged this mobilization, and not vice versa. In Chile the model revealed strong mutual effects between labour mobilization and both orders of rights, whereas the autoregression results had suggested that labour's impact on rights-in-practice was rather weak. In Mexico the model confirmed that it is the combination of labour and other social movement activity, on the one hand, and the GAP, on the other, which are the key elements of the relationship, with their mutual effects being equally strong, but much weaker than the mutual effects evident in Brazil and Chile. This reinforces previous observations on the relative weakness of the relationship in Mexico. Not surprisingly the Spanish data remained unresponsive to this method of analysis.

Finally, the MITS analysis (Chapter 7) extended and modulated the different modes of regression results, and, in particular, revealed the way in which the strong mutual effects of rights and social mobilization in Spain were indeed concentrated in the moment of democratic transition. For Chile MITS uncovered the impact of rights-in-practice (just as the non-recursive model had done), while in Mexico it contributed new insights into the complexities of the mutual conditioning of rights and movements, and again revealed the clear distinction between the patterns of the 1970s and 1980s. QCA confirmed the complexities of the Mexican case, where the mutual effects of rights and movements are probably refracted through state-chartered labour corporations, on the one hand, and, on the other, through the increasingly important electoral arena. In Brazil MITS reinforced the mutually constitutive nature of the rights-movements relationship by revealing the dramatic interleaving of the key rights and key movement years.

Democratic Transition and Democratic Transformation

In his seminal article on democratic transitions, Rustow argued that most transitions are 'set off by a prolonged and inconclusive political struggle' (Rustow 1970: 352), and further suggested that one generation is usually the minimum period required to achieve such transitions. Since the subsequent literature on democratic transitions tends to see them as a critical moment in political time, it may be useful to distinguish between democratic *transition* per se and the period of democratic *transformation* which precedes it, and which 'creates the political conditions in which the transition takes place' (Foweraker 1989: 2). The study of democratic transitions might then properly focus on the 'changes of regime at government level, or on the legal-constitutional norms governing the operation of the democratic regime' (Foweraker 1989: 2), while research into democratic transformations would address the multiform struggles within civil society which prepare the political ground for these changes.

In this connection, the time-series analysis conducted in the present study serves to lengthen the perspective on democratic transitions and demonstrates the prolonged struggles of the periods of democratic transformation. It is clear that the waves of social mobilization that describe these periods are motivated increasingly by the struggle for rights, and it is the dissemination of a sense of individual rights through new forms of collective action that educates popular political actors and catalyses the creation of a new political culture, which is a rights culture (Foweraker 1995: chapter 5). The struggles of the labour movement, in particular, may play a key role both in creating this sense of democratic rights and in forging a tradition of free collective bargaining, which can underpin newly democratic arrangements (Foweraker 1989: 222 and passim). Nonetheless, there is no chiliastic vision which informs these struggles, and the evolution of the rights agenda is halting and contradictory. The trajectory of the labour movement itself often exemplifies these contradictions.

The longer perspective on democratic transitions provided by the time-series data amply illustrates the key role of the labour movement in the struggle for rights, and, by extension, the struggle for democracy. These findings confirm the conclusions of the major work of comparative historical sociology in the field, which sees the labour movement as the main democratic actor of the past one hundred years, even if this movement is rarely strong enough to achieve citizenship rights by itself, and must often depend on more powerful political allies or on splits in ruling-class coalitions (Rueschemeyer, Stephens, and Stephens 1992). But (as argued in Chapter 2) labour may often aspire to forms of corporate rights which are not universal, and, in both Spain and Latin America in particular, labour's citizenship rights are often restricted to a form of economic rights. In other words, the co-optation of the labour movement into a clientelistic and corporative framework may lead to a political trade-off between the political and social rights of citizenship for restricted and privileged sectors of the population (Malloy 1987). Such developments inevitably undercut any sense of universal rights and promote in their place a set of social benefits in the form of legal privileges and political prerogatives.

Nevertheless, such forms of 'regulated citizenship' (see Chapter 2) can precipitate wider struggles for civil and political rights; and even highly corporatized labour systems can create institutional contexts which are favourable to the emergence of combative labour movements. This was true of Spain, Brazil, and Mexico where the most effective labour movements arose from within the state-chartered union corporations of these authoritarian regimes

(Foweraker 1981, 1989, 1993). These movements (in Spain in the 1960s and 1970s and in Latin America in the 1970s and 1980s) put labour rights back on the political agenda. In the case of Brazil the new unionism of the late 1970s insisted that the workers themselves should decide their own forms of organization, while the strikes of 1979 seemed inspired by 'an assertion of rights rather than a demand for concessions' (Keck 1989: 289). And in all these cases direct bargaining between employers and authentic labour leaders bypassed the corporatist controls of the state, so securing the de facto right to strike and challenging the core of these exclusionary labour systems. State repression often accelerated the collapse of legal constraints and catalysed the liberation of labour for fuller citizenship.

The example of the labour movement in struggle is also an example of the process of democratic transformation. Social mobilization which is initially driven by demands which are immediate, material, and economic may catalyse broader demands for civil and political rights, especially in the restrictive political conditions of authoritarian regimes. The time-series data (Chapter 5) clearly demonstrate this shift in the pattern of demand-making, and so illustrate a crucial dimension of the struggle for rights. This slow and conflictual discovery and affirmation of universal rights is the lived experience of the citizenship process (Chapter 1). No discussion of democratic transition can be complete without a sense of this process and of its contribution to democratic transformation.

Elite and Popular Actors in Democratic Transitions

Most discussions of democratic transitions focus on elite actors and derive their typologies of transition from the *ex post* modelling of elite decision-making. Thus, Przeworski (1986, 1991) studies the choices made by different attitudinal groups of elite actors (liberalizers and hardliners) during the process of transition, while both Higley and Gunther (1992) and Hagopian (1990) consider elite pacts and settlements made at the moment of democratic transition. Colomer (1991) and Colomer and Pascual (1994) attempt to formalize these elite-centred studies through the application of game theory to the Spanish and Polish transitions. All these studies make useful and sometimes essential contributions to the analysis of democratic transition, but they tend to ignore the question of popular agency, and so miss an important aspect of the making of democracy. A focus on social movement activity, therefore, 'does not seek to deny so much as to complement those accounts which concentrate exclusively on elite actors and on centrist political forces' (Foweraker 1989: 1–2).

The first wide-ranging comparative study of democratic transition in southern Europe and Latin America noted that, while democracies may be brought down by conspiracies involving few actors, the liberalization and eventual fall of authoritarian regimes has the 'crucial component' of large-scale mobilization (O'Donnell and Schmitter 1986: 18). Moreover, it was argued that the process of liberalization might itself catalyse increasing opposition and a 'resurrection of civil society' (O'Donnell and Schmitter 1986: 26), which would then impel the transition forward. But despite these salutary observations it is the 'short-term manoeuvring' by elites (Levine 1988: 385) which remains central to the analysis, and the argument 'ignores the many ties that bind leaders to mass publics, for example, through political parties, trade unions, and secondary associations of all kinds', such as social movements (Levine 1988: 385). Hence, 'we are left with reified social forces moving at one level, and leaders interacting at another' (Levine 1988: 388).

Clearly it is important to pursue the political linkages between social movements and other forms of political associationalism, on the one hand, and the world of institutional politics, on the other. Studies of this kind may reveal the longer term impact of mobilization and demand-making on the broad contours of the legal and institutional terrain linking civil society to the state (Foweraker 1989: chapter 14; 1993: chapter 10). In this perspective it is apparent that social movements are capable of disputing state policies and catalysing institutional reforms (Scherer-Warren and Krischke 1987), as well as forcing the pace of democratic transitions. (There is little doubt that the direct elections campaign of 1984 in Brazil succeeded in bringing the transition forward if not in actually bringing it about.) And the partial co-optation or institutionalization of social movements may be a proper price to pay for the emergence of agile political actors that can negotiate with incumbent authoritarian regimes (J. Cohen and Arato 1992: 470).

The potential contribution of the present study is rather different. Without an institutionalist approach to popular agency, it clearly cannot pursue the question of political linkages. But it can and does unpack the catch-all notion of a 'resurrection of civil society', and it does succeed in measuring the development of the popular 'social forces' which are ignored in elite-centred accounts of democratic transition. Moreover, it sets out to address and measure the grand *incognitus* of social movement research, which is

usually referred to as the 'political impact' of social movements
(Lipsky 1968; Gamson 1975; Piven and Cloward 1977; Tarrow 1988;
Kitschelt 1990; Rucht 1990; J. Cohen and Arato 1992). Strange as
it may seem, this question is usually treated intransitively, as if it
were unimportant to know on what social movements are meant
to have an impact. Consequently, the question is only rarely operationalized to good effect. Although the impact of social movements
on individual rights is necessarily a partial account of their political impact overall, it does have the virtue of being relatively precise, and of having direct implications for the process of democratic
transition.

But with the transition to democracy it must be recognized that
the struggle for citizenship rights will move to the constitutional
sphere, and so social movements may lose their pre-eminent role
as defenders and promoters of civil and political rights. Every
state administration that is organized through bureaucratic power
relations will seek to institutionalize positive law and so create
'subjects capable of political obligation, and later the rights of
citizens' (J. Cohen and Arato 1992: 439); and a newly democratic
regime will seek to build legitimacy by insisting on these rights.
In other words, citizenship becomes an identity that is defended
and disseminated by the state against all class and regional differences, and against the specific identities and claims of social
movements (Touraine 1988: 75). During the period of democratic
transformation, it was social movements that had demanded citizenship rights and had challenged the regime to put these rights
into practice. Insofar as this occurs through democratic transition,
many of these demands are met, and the political impetus of the
movements begins to decline. 'Successful social movements inevitably lose their reason for being' (Jaquette 1989: 194).

Procedural Consensus and Political Benefits

The focus on elite decision-making, and the explicit exclusion of
popular agency, suggests that the literature on democratic transitions does not address the full set of conditions for democracy. In
effect, it explores the boundary conditions for procedural consensus among elite actors and seeks to establish the institutional
arrangements which will underpin elite pacts and settlements.
Broadly speaking this is the Lockean approach to the creation of
the civic culture of democracy, which, in the contemporary context, is imagined as a process of 'institutionalizing uncertainty'

(Przeworski 1986: 59). Once the process of transition is underway, the main concerns are the institutional constraints and opportunities which bind competing elites to the political outcome. In recent contributions both DiPalma (1990) and Sartori (1994) investigate the choice and construction of institutions, and their consequences, intended or otherwise.

The Lockean bias of this approach tends to ignore the equally important Humean emphasis on the delivery of tangible benefits, or, as Rustow puts it, on the 'wish to be rid of tangible evils' (Rustow 1970: 354). In other words, democracy is a matter of mass as well as elite, and the elite pacts which underpin democratic transition must be transmitted 'to the citizenry at large' (Rustow 1970: 357) in order to win its support for the newly minted democratic arrangements. But, as Moisés (1993) complained (Chapter 1), too little attention is paid to non-elite adherence to basic democratic values, and too little is made of equality before the law, the right to dissent, and government accountability. In short, the 'wish to be rid of tangible evils' is a wish to be rid of arbitrary government, oppression, insecurity, and authoritarian constraints; and the only way to achieve these freedoms is through universal rights and the rule of law. The most important tangible benefits are therefore *rights*, since it is rights which create the diffuse support for the emerging democratic system, which is very different from the specific and variable support for particular governments which will depend more on government performance, and the delivery of goods (Easton 1975). It is the guaranteed presence of particular liberties, immunities, and freedoms which operationalizes Sartori's key democratic principle of 'all power to nobody' (Sartori 1987: 72), and so delivers the substance of democracy to the individuals who compose the polity.

The distinction between rights and goods is critical to democratic transitions which take place in conditions of economic inequality, social exclusion, and scarcity. In Latin America, in particular, the transitions have been founded on covert and exclusionary pacts (Higley and Gunther 1992) between parties that are 'elitist, hierarchical and conservative' (Jaquette 1989: 206), and the result is the kind of 'restricted democracy' where social movements are 'isolated, repressed or marginalized' (Mainwaring and Viola 1984: 46). Consequently, there is little or no expectation that social movements will be able 'to radically transform large structures of domination or dramatically expand elite democracies' (Escobar and Alvarez 1992: 325). Economically, a strong adherence to neo-liberal policies precludes any gradual construction of social democracy. Politically, the new democracies remain 'unconnected with the lived experience of the mass of the population' (Whitehead 1992: 154), and this leads to 'a very partial form of democratic politics . . . in which the involvement of some bears a direct relation to the limited or non-participation of others' (Held 1992: 20). In these circumstances it is only rights, and the continuing struggle for rights, which will elicit popular support for democracy.

The danger is that these partial democracies will merely pay lip-service to liberal values and democratic rights, and continue to practice the politics of populism and clientelism. What will then remain constant is 'the inclination . . . to capture executive sources of benefits that flow more as patronage and privileges than as universal rights' (Malloy 1987: 252). The result will be a continuing gap 'between formal rights and actual rights, between commitments to treat citizens as free and equal and practices which do neither sufficiently' (Held 1992: 20). Since the transition to democracy may clearly not achieve an effective rule of law, with the rights writ running equally for all, it is clear that social mobilization will still have a vital role to play in securing democratic government. Whereas elite actors, party leaders and pressure groups tend to target the executive and 'operate through parties and legislatures only to defend achieved privileges' (Malloy 1987: 252), social movements will continue to press for more popular participation in decision-making and a more positive application of individual rights.

Rights and the New Political Agenda

Recent works on Latin American politics have attempted major historiographical revisions of its modern political history. They conclude that Latin American politics has entered a new era, but fail to specify the political content of this era. Alain Touraine's *Palavra e Sangue* (Touraine 1989) is a veritable tour de force which argues that the politics of the 1930–80 period is about participation and passion, and not about political representation and interests. He sees both participation (*palavra*) and passion or violence (*sangue*) coexisting within a 'dependent mode of development' which is the 'national popular model' (Touraine 1989: 185–92), where social actors are subordinated to political power and the state is not clearly differentiated from the political system (Munck 1993: 487). This model is the 'centre of reference' for understanding the political process (Touraine 1989: 189). As a corollary, social movements are absent from this process, since by his definition they would have to mount a frontal challenge to the basic rules of the model, rather than seeking various forms of participation within it (Foweraker 1995: chapter 2).

Similarly to Touraine, the Colliers' *Shaping the Political Arena* (Collier and Collier 1991) also see the politics of 1930–80 as a discrete period, but defined in their argument by the incorporation of the labour movement. The period is configured by populism and the top-down thrust of this incorporation, which subordinates the labour movement even while it confers a limited range of social, but not political rights (see Chapter 2). Although they insist on social agency, the Colliers do not grant much autonomy or initiative to the labour movement, but rather interpret agency 'through the choices of national political elites' (Munck 1993: 491).

Both of these works perceive that Latin American politics is no longer what it was, and suggest that some kind of sea-change is occurring in the 1970s and 1980s. The Colliers imply that labour now begins to insist on a more autonomous representation of its 'interests', while Touraine argues that the possibility of democracy turns on the rejection of populism and the formation of strong actors who can affirm and represent 'their interests at a political level' (Munck 1993: 494). But, on the evidence of the present study, the new era is not about *interests* but about *rights*, and the new political agenda is defined by the combination of a rights discourse with social mobilization by labour and other social movements. Moreover, since the key question of rights is absent from their analysis, these works fail to perceive a central element of the political process, which is the translation of demands for social rights into the struggle for political rights; and consequently miss the ways in which new forms of authoritarian regime in the continent catalysed this process, and threw the issue of rights into high political relief. Finally, the fact that analogous changes clearly took place in Spain in the 1960s and 1970s appears to suggest that the rights agenda is not confined to the new era of Latin American politics, but also characterizes new forms of democratic struggle elsewhere.

One caveat is in order. The sea-change to a new politics of rights is not a uniform or homogeneous process. On the contrary, it is uneven, fragmented, and contradictory. Very general interpretations of political change at continental or national level may see this change in terms of new templates that reorder the relationships between social movements and the state, or social movements and political society. There is little doubt that these relationships are changing, but the comparative argument developed here suggests that the changes can be either dramatically or subtly different across countries and regions, and from one period to the next. Such are the complexities of the changes that it is now suggested that the notion of democratic transition should be replaced by 'a set of transitions along the various key dimensions of democracy' (Fox 1994: 184), with democracy itself now being conceptualized 'not as a "regime" but as a composite of "partial regimes", each of which has been institutionalized around distinctive sites for the representation of social groups and the resolution of their ensuing conflicts' (Schmitter 1993: 4). The new modes of democratic composition are critically important to the question of rights, and will clearly influence both the depth and breadth of rights provision (see Chapter 2). The aggregate-level data compiled for this study cannot broach this question directly, and it begs further research. On the other hand, the struggle for rights must be seen as a universalizing process, and rights themselves as the cement which may finally bind the partial regimes together at national level. 'Constitutions . . . are an effort to establish a single, overarching set of "meta-rules" that would render these partial regimes coherent' (Schmitter 1993: 4).

Rights and the Making of Democracy

There is little doubt that civil society is important to democratic transition and consolidation, but there is considerable debate about the precise nature of civil society's contribution to the achievement of democracy. In the best enquiries, civil society is carefully theorized, as are its connections to political society and the state, and the social actors of civil society are differentiated according to their political agendas and political potential (J. Cohen and Arato 1992: chapter 11). Elsewhere, civil society is simply taken as the reference for cultural qualities called 'civicness', or some other equally anodyne neologism, and 'civicness' itself is assumed to be positive for democratic validity or performance. Thus, Schmitter argues that it is their greater 'civicness' that makes the democracies of southern Europe more resilient than those of Latin America (O'Donnell and Schmitter 1986: 6–8), while Putnam argues, in similar vein, that it is the greater 'civicness' of northern as opposed to southern Italy which determines both its higher level of economic development and its more effective democratic performance (Putnam 1994).

But the notion of 'civicness' does not include the effective presence of individual rights. In his critique of the political culture and 'amoral familism' of the Italian south Putnam (1994: 88) does not address the deeply patrimonial nature of this culture, or the consistent failure to distinguish the public from the private interest, which leaves the *res publica* (government and law) deeply enmeshed in private property, family relations, and political clans and clienteles. One consequence of the culture is that individual rights are vitiated by personal connections, political prerogatives, and clan loyalties and rivalries.[1] Since rights do not enter his definition of 'civicness', however, Putnam can look to the north and conclude that 'happiness is living in a civic community' (Putnam 1994: 113). More correctly, happiness is living without the mafia, and in the plain enjoyment and security of individual rights and equality before the law.

In this connection, it is important to note that Putnam's 'index of institutional performance' (Putnam 1994: 73–6, 80–1) is a measure of the delivery of goods, not of rights. In effect it is an amalgam of social policy outcomes, and a surrogate measure of social welfarism. In a recent review, Tarrow argues that it is this emphasis on 'effective policy performance' and the dismissal of the classical concern with 'popular sovereignty and individual rights' that lead Putnam to an 'elitist definition of democracy' (Tarrow 1996: 396). This may be true, if the concern with individual rights encompasses the political, and especially popular struggles required to achieve them.

After all, if 'civicness' is so good for democracy, it is important to understand its genesis. Putnam's thesis suggests that it is created by a long and slow process of historical accretion and sedimentation, which, in the case of northern Italy, took some nine hundred years. No doubt his argument will cause some dismay to those populations attempting to consolidate their democracies in a rather shorter time span. Indeed, his conclusions would seem to condemn large swathes of mankind to a savage and uncertain life in societies that fail to cohere, and to inept, disloyal, and capricious government. Putnam is forced inexorably into this reactionary stance because, despite Rustow's original strictures, he is committed to finding the 'functional requisites' of democracy (Rustow 1970: 361) rather than exploring the social agency that may achieve

[1] It is also a cultural context which is highly impervious to Putnam's research design, which aspires to measure government performance by the delivery of services from the (pristine) public to the (discrete) private realm.

it. As noted above, Rustow suggested that democratic transition might be achieved within a generation or two by a properly strategic agency with a proper sense of the autonomy of politics.[2]

Yet Putnam clearly recognizes the democratic value of social agency in the shape of civic associationalism. He asserts that 'Tocqueville was right: Democratic government is strengthened, not weakened, when it faces a vigorous civil society' (Putnam 1994: 181). But Putnam misreads de Tocqueville. On the one hand, he suggests that de Tocqueville understood the relationship between government and civil society as one of 'externality', which runs against the grain of de Tocqueville's account of democracy in America. On the other, he makes de Tocqueville out to be more Platonic than Aristotelian, and transforms civil society into a version of the good life, which is sustained by soccer clubs, campanology, and the Women's Institute. What is plainly missing from this account is an understanding of social movements and of their political struggles for individual rights. It is these struggles which are constitutive of the subjects of modern civil society, and constitutive of their sense of individual responsibility for the political community. 'He who cannot live in society is either a god or a beast.'

Social Movements and Individual Rights Revisited

The critique of Putnam is not gratuitous. In our view the connection between Putnam's notion of 'civicness' and democracy remains opaque precisely because it excludes the key elements required to make the connection in theory and history,[3] namely social movements, individual rights, and the state.[4] The state is a key analytical element because individual rights must be won through and often

---

[2] Rustow quotes Bernard Crick to the effect that 'the moral consensus of a free state is not something mysteriously prior to or above politics: it is the activity (the civilizing activity) of politics itself' (Crick 1962: 24).

[3] Putnam's enquiry seeks explanations for differences in 'civic competence' by transposing concepts derived from contemporary democratic politics to other periods of history and other political systems. As a consequence, Tarrow suggests, he commits an 'analogical error' (Tarrow 1996: 393), for Putnam's 'associations' may have different contents and functions in different periods. It is worth observing that this study adopts the inverse method of establishing the characteristic connections between social movements and individual rights as they recur in theory and in the historical record (Chapters 1 and 2), before proceeding to test these connections in the context of contemporary authoritarian regimes.

[4] For Tarrow, the missing link in Putnam's analysis is the process of state-building, and the historical impact of state strategies. He refers in particular to

against the state (Chapter 1), and this entails collective action, especially in the form of popular struggle by social movements. In this perspective, democracy is not so much about the delivery of goods as the achievement of rights.

This is the point of locating this study in the context of modern, authoritarian regimes, where government is arbitrary and often dangerous, and individuals are insecure and vulnerable. In contrast to Putnam's image of southern Italy, where the main threat comes from the 'uncivil' and prepotent actors of civil society, under these regimes it is the state itself which embodies authoritarian caprice and violence. Yet it is clear that 'civicness' can develop in these conditions, and that individual insecurity and civil disarray can be overcome through a collective struggle for individual and universal rights. This is therefore a proper context for testing the relationship between social movements and individual rights.

The results of the study suggest that the relationship between the associational capacity of civil society, or 'civicness', and democracy is indeterminate, since it must depend, *inter alia*, on the variable success of social movements in achieving citizenship rights. There is thus no possible linear relationship between 'civicness' and democracy. Partial struggles meet with partial and reversible success in winning universal rights. But it is possible to mark the rhythms of struggle and their variable impact on the provision of rights; and to trace the influence of the language and knowledge of rights on popular protest and democratic struggle. The conclusion is that social actors can make democracy, and not within the millenium but within a generation or two. It is not a democracy made in the image of a perfectly civic society, but it usually provides the political conditions for piecemeal social improvements and greater efficacy in the rule of law.

The lessons are clear. For Putnam democratic performance describes the content of democracy. Since this performance depends on the degree of 'civicness' of the civil society, and 'civicness' has

the 'semi-colonial status' of southern Italy following the Reunification of 1861, and its continuing subjection to 'patronage, paternalism and the power of money' (Tarrow 1996: 394). In his view, therefore, the lack of 'civicness' and the poor institutional performance of the contemporary south is at least partly owing to a 'political culture shaped by more than a century of political and administrative dependency' (Tarrow 1996: 395). Since this dependency included systematic corruption of the electoral process and the clientelistic control of prefects and judges, it clearly retarded the development of a rights culture. Furthermore, Tarrow sees significant links between 'progressive political traditions and civic capacity' in the north (Tarrow 1996: 394), so suggesting a comprehensively political explanation of the differential institutional performance of northern and southern Italy.

to do with cooperation and righteous conduct (the civic community), democracy is the result of good behaviour. The better we behave, the more democracy we get. But everything in the present study indicates the opposite, and, in particular, that the democratic qualities of civil society do not have to do with 'civicness' but with the associationalism which supports social mobilization and political contestation; that democracy is not the comfortable result of righteous conduct but the result of prolonged struggle in often difficult and dangerous circumstances; and that this struggle is not ultimately motivated by goods but by the individual rights which compose the popular substance of democracy. This study sets out to describe this struggle in a contemporary and comparative context, and to demonstrate the increasing relevance of individual rights to the social movements engaged in the struggle. It does so in the firm belief that the historical encounter between social movements and individual rights has only just begun.[5] Far from having run its course, the rights agenda has yet to realize the rudiments of its full political potential.

[5] This study has considered just four cases, one from southern Europe and three from Latin America. The rights agenda is likely to prove a powerful force for change in eastern and central Europe, southern and central Africa, and southeast Asia and China.

Appendix A

Case Synopses and Chronologies

This appendix provides a brief historical synopsis of each of the cases in this study, followed by a chronology of the most important historical events concerning citizenship rights and social movement activity over the four periods.

Brazil

For the years of this study, Brazil was ruled by a military authoritarian government that slowly returned power to civilians. The authoritarian period extends from 1964 to 1985, when the military lost control of its own electoral college, which then chose a civilian opposition leader as president. In 1989 Brazil held its first democratic election for the presidency since 1960. From 1966 to 1979, the regime maintained a two-party system with the ARENA party representing the military and conservative interests and the MDB representing what might be called the benign opposition. The bicameral Congress was closed only briefly during the period and the MDB won increasing representation in the Chamber of Deputies. In 1974 President Ernesto Geisel began gradually to liberalize the regime, which relaxed press censorship, encouraged the emergence of new political parties (1979), and allowed direct gubernatorial elections (1982). The process culminated in the promulgation of the 1988 Constitution. In the early years of the regime, political and civil rights were systematically denied. Most forms of civil unrest and social mobilization were severely curtailed until 1978, when industrial unions in the south began to mobilize against the regime. The 1980s saw a dramatic surge in social mobilization by urban and rural unions, urban neighbourhood associations, ecclesiastical base communities, and women's groups. The wave of protest in the 1980s featured the *diretas já* campaign for direct presidential elections in 1984, which mobilized millions of Brazilian citizens.

Year	Events Affecting Rights	Social Movement Activity
1964	President João Goulart is overthrown by the Brazilian military. Institutional Act #1 passed. General Humberto Castelo Branco president.	

1965	Institutional Act #2: existing parties abolished; indirect elections of president, vice-president, state governors; judiciary enlarged.	
1966	Institutional Act #3 and #4 passed.	Student and worker strikes.
1967	New Constitution. General Artur da Costa e Silva president.	
1968	Institutional Act #5: executive powers include suppression of political rights, suspension of habeas corpus; military tribunals established.	Worker strikes in Osasco and Contagem.
1969	New Constitution: more power to executive; Chamber of Deputies reduced; rights to assembly, association, and speech suppressed. General Emilio Garrastászu Médici president.	
1970	Elections timetable established for municipal elections (1972, 1976, 1980), and legislative elections (1974, 1978, 1982).	
1972	1969 Constitution Amended: gubernatorial elections indirect until 1974; direct elections postponed until 1978.	Strikes and protests at Villares Steel, Volkswagen, General Motors, and Ford.
1973		Strikes led by Metallurgical, Energy, and Textile unions.
1974	Open access to television. General Ernesto Geisel president. Beginning of *distensão* period of political liberalization.	Opposition party (MDB) wins majority in Chamber of Deputies.
1975		International Women's Day celebrations in Rio de Janeiro, São Paulo, and Belo Horizonte.
1976	Falcão Law forbids campaign use of television and radio.	Work stoppages, student demonstrations.
1977	Pacote de Abril: Congress closed, state governors and 1/3 of all senators indirectly elected, Falcão Law strengthened.	Student demonstrations; Cost of Living Movement.
1978	Institutional Act #5 abolished; habeas corpus reinstated for political	24 'ABC' strikes.

detainees; independent judiciary established.

1979	Political Amnesty Law; Party Reform Law brings end of two-party system; General João Baptista Figueiredo president.	113 'ABC' strikes; Cost of Living Movement activity; rural activity.
1980		60 'ABC' strikes; Movimento dos Sem Terra.
1981		96 'ABC' strikes.
1982	Direct gubernatorial elections	National Day of Protest.
1984		*Diretas Já* Campaign (January–April).
1985	Civilian President José Sarney. Illiterates given the vote.	
1988	New Constitution re-establishes all rights.	
1989	Direct presidential elections. Fernando Collor de Mello wins.	

Chile

On 11 September 1973 a military junta which included General Augusto Pinochet overthrew Popular Unity president Salvador Allende Gossens, ending Chile's long democratic tradition. After the coup, the military quickly consolidated its authority. General Pinochet emerged as the undisputed leader, declaring himself president of the republic in 1974, and promulgating a new Constitution in 1980. In a bid to remain in power Pinochet held a plebiscite in 1988, but only won 45 per cent support. This defeat precipitated a rapid transition to democracy and the victory of Christian Democrat Patrício Aylwin in the 1989 elections. In the early years of the military regime, dissidents and suspected subversives were routinely detained, tortured, exiled, or executed. This pattern of repression continued into the early 1980s, when it was replaced by a strategy of forceful intimidation of civil society through the use of arbitrary arrest, detention, and torture. Social mobilization hardly got off the ground in the 1970s, but started to build in 1980, reaching its peak during the 1983–84 'days of national protest'. At the end of the decade, mobilization was encouraged by the plebiscite of 1988 and the elections of 1989.

Year	Events Affecting Rights	Social Movement Activity
1973	Military overthrows Popular Unity government of Salvador Allende Gossens. 1925 Constitution suspended: Congress dissolved;	Worker and middle-class demonstrations precede military coup.

Decree-Law #1 vests all power in junta; Popular Unity outlawed; all other party activity suspended; denial of habeas corpus.

1974	Decree-Law 527: junta has constitutional and legislative authority; executive power exercised by leader of junta who is Supreme Chief of the Nation (later amended to President of Republic).	Worker and student strikes and demonstrations.
1975		Coal miners strikes.
1976	Constitutional Acts: Council of State (1), Essential Bases of Chilean Institutionality (2), Rights and Duties of Citizens (3), States of Emergency (4).	Copper workers strike.
1977	Official suppression of all parties; internal security force (DINA) replaced by CNI.	
1978	Constitutional Act #4 amended to allow habeas corpus suspensions in emergency; plebiscite to approve new institutional order (January); general amnesty for military (April).	Worker strikes led by *Coordinadora Nacional Sindical* (CNS).
1979	Labour Plan regulating union membership and activity.	CNS strikes.
1980	New Constitution guarantees political and civil rights, which can nonetheless be suspended under 29 transitory articles.	
1981		First National Congress of *Pobladores*; strikes for right to put wage demands, and for union freedoms.
1983		11 May: first Day of National Protest; protests continue in May, June, July, August, September, October, and into 1984.
1985	State of Siege: all rights suspended.	
1987	Political parties legalized; eligible voters registered.	
1988	Pinochet loses national plebiscite on continued rule.	Massive demonstration of Campaign for the NO!
1989	Patrício Aylwin wins democratic election	

Mexico

Mexico is a one-party dominant political system, and the Institutional Revolutionary Party (PRI) has been in power for 65 years. During the period 1963–90, the PRI dominated the political system through co-optation or repression of political opponents, and manipulation of electoral results. Since elections have never been free or fair, and political and civil rights have always been fragile and subject to reversal, Mexico has remained an authoritarian regime. In the years following the massacre of student protesters in the Plaza de Tlatelolco, in 1968, the regime attempted to liberalize the system, and modified the electoral rules to encourage opposition parties to contest elections. But the provision of political and civil rights continued to be patchy and imperfect, and actually appeared to deteriorate during the 1980s. The most intensive moments of social mobilization occurred in 1965, 1968, 1972, 1975, 1979–82, 1985, and 1988.

Year	Events Affecting Rights	Social Movement Activity
1963	Party Deputy reform.	
1965		Doctors' strikes.
1968		Student demonstrations culminate in October massacre of students in Plaza de Tlatelolco.
1970	Voting age lowered from 21 to 18; Luis Echeverría elected president.	
1972		Rural mobilization: peasant and student solidarity.
1973	Article 123 of Constitution amended to increase government control over labour.	Strikes led by university and rail workers.
1975		Rural mobilization and struggle for land.
1976	López Portillo elected president. No candidate runs from main opposition party (PAN).	
1977	Federal Law on Political Organisations and Electoral Processes (LOPPE) loosens restrictions on party activity.	
1978	General amnesty for those convicted of political crimes.	
1981		Urban mobilizations led by National Coordinating Committee of the

Year	Events Affecting Rights	Social Movement Activity
		Urban Popular Movement (CONAMUP).
1982	Election of Miguel de la Madrid who promises Moral Renovation; financial crisis.	Worker strikes; urban, rural, and teacher mobilization increases.
1985	Earthquake in Mexico City destroys urban infrastructure, especially in poorer areas.	Coordinating Committee for Earthquake Victims (CUD) mobilizes around urban reconstruction.
1986		CUD, CONAMUP mobilizations joined by women's groups.
1987		CUD marks First Day of Unity of the Urban Popular Movement (19 September).
1988	Hotly contested elections. National electoral computer goes down. PRI candidate, Carlos Salinas de Gortari, declared the winner.	Cárdenas leads mobilization by Frente Democrática Nacional.
1989	Electoral Code reformed.	

Spain

Franco's authoritarian regime retained all power in the executive until the moment of his death in 1975. The legal structure of the state was founded on a series of Organic Laws, culminating in the Constitution of 1967. Although these laws established the rights and duties of all Spanish citizens, Franco was always able to suppress both civil and political rights through their emergency clauses (as he did during the state of siege in 1969). Political controls were exercised primarily through the massive corporatist apparatus of the Vertical Syndicate, and the popular opposition to the regime was spearheaded by the illegal labour movement, and by student organizations. Social mobilization increased throughout the 1960s and early 1970s, and then exploded during the years of democratic transition following Franco's death. A new democratic Constitution was promulgated in 1978.

Year	Events Affecting Rights	Social Movement Activity
1958	Law of Collective Contracts designed to achieve regulated collective bargaining.	Strikes led by Workers' Commissions.
1961		Student strikes in Barcelona.

1962		First wave of workers' strikes (n = 425).
1963		Worker, miner, student strikes and protests.
1966	Succession referendum. Press Law attempts to liberalize press censorship.	Worker strikes and student demonstrations.
1967	Organic Law approved by 85% in national referendum: consolidates Organic Laws.	
1968		Students, workers, women, and church demonstrate.
1969	Juan Carlos sworn as successor. Carrero Blanco is vice-president. State of Exception declared: constitutional guarantees suspended, and planned Statute of Associations suppressed.	
1973	Carrero Blanco made president, but is assassinated. Navarro takes over.	
1975	Franco dies.	Massive demonstrations led by workers and students.
1976	Law of Political Reform: Francoist Assembly dissolved; bicameral system set up with universal suffrage. Political Associations Bill (March): all parties except totalitarian parties legalized.	Peak of non-labour mobilization.
1977	Communist Party and unions legalized.	Peak of labour mobilization.
1978	New Constitution: parliamentary monarchy established with full liberal democratic rights. King is head of state, but power resides in two houses of parliament.	

....

Appendix B

....

Banks Legal Institutional Index
(BANKSLII) Components

The following six variables from A. S. Banks' (1971, 1994) *Cross-Polity Times Series Data Archive* were used to construct a legal institutional index, which is used in Chapter 4 as a baseline for the scores produced by the Institutional Procedural Index (IPI). Summing the six variables produces an index with a range of 1–17, where a score of one (1) shows the absence of all six institutional variables and a seventeen (17) shows the presence of all six institutional variables.

V114   Legislative Effectiveness (Upper Chamber)
     (0) No Legislature
     (1) Largely Ineffective
     (2) Partially Effective
     (3) Effective[1]

V115   Competitiveness of the Nomination Process
     (0) No Legislature
     (1) Largely Non-competitive
     (2) Partially Competitive
     (3) Competitive

V117   Party Legitimacy
     (0) No parties, or all but dominant party and satellites excluded
     (1) Significant exclusion of parties
     (2) Extreme parties excluded
     (3) No parties excluded

V131   Executive Effectiveness (Selection)
     (1) Non Elected
     (2) Indirectly Elected
     (3) Directly Elected[2]

V136   Legislative Effectiveness (Lower House)
     (0) No Legislature

[1] See A. S. Banks (1971: pp. xvi–xvii) for a further explanation of the institutional variables.
[2] Banks's original variable was recoded inversely for the purposes of constructing the Legal Institutional Index. This coding rewards a nation for having a directly elected executive.

    (1) Largely Ineffective
    (2) Partially Effective
    (3) Effective

V137 Legislative Selection
    (0) No Legislature
    (1) Non-elected
    (2) Elected

....

Appendix C

....

Boolean Results

The Boolean algebraic solutions for the two models of citizenship rights and social movements (tested in Chapter 7) are shown here. Under each case, the dependent or *outcome* variable is to the left of the equals sign (=) in the line marked Model. Upper-case letters signify the presence of a variable and lower-case letters signify the absence of a variable. Following each solution are the years in which that solution occurs. An asterisk (*) marks those solutions where a *combination* of the principal citizenship rights and social movement variables are present (i.e. IPI, CRI, GAP; SMA, SR). The *probability* is calculated by counting the years that have an asterisk and dividing them by the total years in the period.

Brazil

Minimized Truth Table #1
Model: IPI = CRI + GAP + SMA + SR + POLD + INFL + ECON + ENER + DEFEXP
Outputs Minimized: 1
Method: Akers (Fast)

*CRI gap SMA SR pold infl econ ener defexp +	[1978]
CRI gap sma sr POLD infl econ ener defexp +	[1967]
cri gap sma sr pold INFL ener defexp +	[1964, 1965]
*cri gap SMA SR pold INFL ener DEFEXP +	[1980, 1981, 1985]
*CRI GAP sma SR INFL econ ener DEFEXP +	[1984, 1986, 1987]
*CRI GAP SR pold INFL ECON ener DEFEXP +	[1983, 1988, 1990]
*cri gap sma SR POLD INFL ECON ener DEFEXP +	[1982]
*CRI gap SR pold INFL econ ENER DEFEXP	[1979, 1989]

Probability = 13:27 (48%)

Minimized Truth Table #2
Model: CRI = IPI + GAP + SMA + SR + POLD + INFL + ECON + ENER
+ DEFEXP
Outputs Minimized: 1
Method: Akers (Fast)

*IPI gap SMA SR pold infl econ ener
  defexp +   [1978]
ipi GAP sma sr pold infl econ ener
  DEFEXP +   [1976, 1977]
*IPI GAP sma SR INFL econ ener
  DEFEXP +   [1984, 1986, 1987]
*IPI GAP SR pold INFL ECON ener
  DEFEXP +   [1983, 1988, 1990]
*IPI gap SR pold INFL econ ENER
  DEFEXP   [1979, 1989]

Probability = 9:27 (33%)

Minimized Truth Table #3
Model: GAP = IPI + CRI + SMA + SR + POLD + INFL + ECON + ENER
+ DEFEXP
Outputs Minimized: 1
Method: Akers (Fast)

ipi CRI sma sr pold infl econ ener +   [1974, 1976, 1977]
*IPI CRI sma SR INFL econ ener
  DEFEXP +   [1984, 1986, 1987]
*IPI CRI SR pold INFL ECON ener
  DEFEXP   [1983, 1988, 1990]

Probability = 6:27 (22%)

Minimized Truth Table #4
Model: SMA = IPI + CRI + GAP + SR + POLD + INFL + ECON + ENER
+ DEFEXP
Outputs Minimized: 1
Method: Akers (Fast)

*IPI CRI gap SR pold infl econ ener
  defexp +   [1978]
*IPI cri gap SR pold INFL ener DEFEXP   [1980, 1981, 1985]

Probability = 4:27 (15%)

Minimized Truth Table #5
Model: SR = IPI + CRI + GAP + SMA + POLD + INFL + ECON + ENER
+ DEFEXP
Outputs Minimized: 1
Method: Akers (Fast)

*IPI CRI gap SMA pold infl econ ener
  defexp +   [1978]

*IPI cri gap SMA pold INFL ener
  DEFEXP +   [1980, 1981, 1985]
*IPI CRI GAP sma INFL econ ener
  DEFEXP +   [1984, 1986, 1987]
*IPI CRI GAP pold INFL ECON ener
  DEFEXP +   [1983, 1988, 1989]
*IPI cri gap sma POLD INFL ECON
  ener DEFEXP +   [1982]
*IPI CRI gap pold INFL econ ENER
  DEFEXP   [1979, 1989]

Probability = 13:27 (48%)

Chile

Minimized Truth Table #1
Model: IPI = CRI + GAP + SMA + SR + POLD + INFL + ECON + ENER
  + DEFEXP
Outputs Minimized: 1
Method: Akers (Fast)

*cri gap sma SR pold infl econ ener
  defexp +   [1981]
*cri gap SMA sr pold infl ECON ener
  defexp +   [1982]
cri gap sma sr POLD INFL econ ENER
  defexp +   [1980]
*CRI gap SMA sr POLD infl econ ener
  DEFEXP +   [1984]
*cri gap sma SR POLD infl econ ener
  DEFEXP +   [1987]
*CRI GAP sma SR POLD infl econ ener
  DEFEXP +   [1988]
*CRI GAP sma SR pold infl ECON ener
  DEFEXP +   [1990]
*cri gap SMA sr pold INFL ECON ener
  DEFEXP +   [1983]
*CRI GAP sma SR pold infl econ
  ENER DEFEXP   [1989]

Probability = 8:18 (44%)

Minimized Truth Table #2
Model: CRI = IPI + GAP + SMA + SR + POLD + INFL + ECON + ENER
  + DEFEXP
Outputs Minimized: 1
Method: Akers (Fast)

ipi gap sma sr pold infl econ ener
   DEFEXP +   [1986]
*IPI gap SMA sr POLD infl econ ener
   DEFEXP +   [1984]
*IPI GAP sma SR POLD infl econ ener
   DEFEXP +   [1988]
*IPI GAP sma SR pold infl ECON ener
   DEFEXP +   [1990]
*IPI GAP sma SR pold infl econ
   ENER DEFEXP   [1989]

Probability = 4:18 (22%)

Minimized Truth Table #3
Model: GAP = IPI + CRI + SMA + SR + POLD + INFL + ECON + ENER
   + DEFEXP
Outputs Minimized: 1
Method: Akers (Fast)

ipi sma sr POLD INFL econ ener
   defexp +   [1977, 1978, 1979]
ipi cri sr pold INFL ECON ener defexp +   [1974, 1975]
ipi cri sma sr pold INFL ECON defexp +   [1973, 1975]
*IPI CRI sma SR POLD infl econ ener
   DEFEXP +   [1988]
*IPI CRI sma SR pold infl ECON ener
   DEFEXP +   [1990]
*IPI CRI sma SR pold infl econ ENER
   DEFEXP +   [1989]
ipi cri sma sr pold INFL ener defexp   [1975, 1976]

Probability = 3:18 (17%)

Minimized Truth Table #4
Model: SMA = IPI + CRI + GAP + SR + POLD + INFL + ECON + ENER
   + DEFEXP
Outputs Minimized: 1
Method: Akers (Fast)

*IPI cri gap sr pold infl ECON ener
   defexp +   [1982]
*IPI CRI gap sr POLD infl econ ener
   DEFEXP +   [1984]
ipi cri gap sr POLD INFL econ ener
   DEFEXP +   [1985]
*IPI cri gap sr pold INFL ECON ener
   DEFEXP   [1983]

Probability = 3:18 (17%)

Minimized Truth Table #5
Model: SR = IPI + CRI + GAP + SMA + POLD + INFL + ECON + ENER
 + DEFEXP
Outputs Minimized: 1
Method: Akers (Fast)

*IPI cri gap sma pold infl econ ener
 defexp +   [1981]
*IPI cri gap sma POLD infl econ ener
 DEFEXP +   [1987]
*IPI CRI GAP sma POLD infl econ ener
 DEFEXP +   [1988]
*IPI CRI GAP sma pold infl ECON ener
 DEFEXP +   [1990]
*IPI CRI GAP sma pold infl econ ENER
 DEFEXP   [1989]

Probability = 5:18 (28%)

Mexico

Model: IPI = CRI + GAP + SMA + SR + POLD + INFL + ECON + ENER
 + DEFEXP

Note: Since IPI is *always present* in Mexico during the pertinent years,
it is not available for Boolean solutions, which require conditions which
are sometimes present and sometimes absent.

Minimized Truth Table #1
Model: CRI = IPI + GAP + SMA + SR + POLD + INFL + ECON + ENER
 + DEFEXP
Outputs Minimized: 1
Method: Akers (Fast)

*IPI GAP sma SR pold infl econ ener
 defexp +   [1980]
IPI gap sma sr POLD infl econ ener
 defexp +   [1967, 1968]
*IPI GAP SMA SR POLD INFL ECON
 ener defexp +   [1982]
IPI GAP sma sr pold INFL econ ENER
 defexp +   [1985]
*IPI GAP SMA SR pold infl econ ener
 DEFEXP   [1975]

Probability = 3:28 (11%)

Minimized Truth Table #2
Model: GAP = IPI + CRI + SMA + SR + POLD + INFL + ECON + ENER
 + DEFEXP

Outputs Minimized: 1
Method: Akers (Fast)

*IPI CRI sma SR pold infl econ ener
  defexp +   [1980]
*IPI CRI SMA SR POLD INFL ECON
  ener defexp +   [1982]
IPI CRI sma sr pold INFL econ
  ENER defexp +   [1985]
*IPI CRI SMA SR pold infl econ ener
  DEFEXP +   [1975]
IPI cri sma sr pold infl econ ENER
  DEFEXP   [1989]

Probability = 3:28 (11%)

Minimized Truth Table #3
Model: SMA = IPI + CRI + GAP + SR + POLD + INFL + ECON + ENER
  + DEFEXP
Outputs Minimized: 1
Method: Akers (Fast)

*IPI cri gap sr POLD INFL ECON ener +   [1983, 1988]
*IPI CRI GAP SR POLD INFL ECON
  ener defexp +   [1982]
*IPI CRI GAP SR pold infl econ ener
  DEFEXP +   [1975]
*IPI cri gap POLD INFL ECON ener
  DEFEXP   [1983, 1986]

Probability = 6:28 (21%)

Minimized Truth Table #4
Model: SR = IPI + CRI + GAP + SMA + POLD + INFL + ECON + ENER
  + DEFEXP
Outputs Minimized: 1
Method: Akers (Fast)

*IPI CRI GAP sma pold infl econ ener
  defexp +   [1980]
*IPI cri gap sma POLD INFL econ ener
  defexp +   [1984]
*IPI CRI GAP SMA POLD INFL ECON
  ener defexp +   [1982]
*IPI CRI GAP SMA pold infl econ ener
  DEFEXP +   [1976]
*IPI cri gap sma POLD infl econ ENER
  DEFEXP   [1981]

Probability = 5:28 (18%)

Note: Since SMASR in Mexico figures so prominently in the regression analysis of Chapter 6, and in the MITS analysis of Chapter 7, it is included in the Boolean tables. The following results are for SMASR in Mexico.

Minimized Truth Table #5
Model: CRI = IPI + GAP + SMA + SR + SMASR + POLD + INFL
  + ECON + ENER + DEFEXP
Outputs Minimized: 1
Method: Akers (Fast)

*IPI GAP sma SR SMASR pold infl econ	
ener defexp +	[1980]
IPI gap sma sr smasr POLD infl econ	
ener defexp +	[1967, 1968]
*IPI GAP SMA SR SMASR POLD INFL	
ECON ener defexp	[1982]
IPI GAP sma sr smasr pold INFL econ	
ENER defexp +	[1985]
*IPI GAP SMA SR SMASR pold infl econ	
ener DEFEXP	[1975]

Probability = 3:28 (11%)

Minimized Truth Table #6
Model: GAP = IPI + CRI + SMA + SR + SMASR + POLD + INFL
  + ECON + ENER + DEFEXP
Outputs Minimized: 1
Method: Akers (Fast)

*IPI CRI sma SR SMASR pold infl econ	
ener defexp +	[1980]
*IPI CRI SMA SR SMASR POLD INFL	
ECON ener defexp+	[1982]
IPI CRI sma sr smasr pold INFL econ	
ENER defexp +	[1985]
*IPI CRI SMA SR SMASR pold infl econ	
ener DEFEXP +	[1975]
IPI cri sma sr smasr pold infl econ	
ENER DEFEXP	[1989]

Probability = 3:28 (11%)

Minimized Truth Table #9
Model: SMASR = IPI + CRI + GAP + SMA + SR + POLD + INFL
  + ECON + ENER + DEFEXP
Outputs Minimized: 1
Method: Akers (Fast)

*IPI cri gap SMA pold infl econ ener	
defexp +	[1972, 1974, 1976]

*IPI cri gap SR pold infl econ ener
   defexp +   [1976, 1977, 1978, 1979]
*IPI CRI GAP sma SR pold infl econ ener
   defexp +   [1980]
*IPI cri gap sma SR POLD INFL econ
   ener defexp +   [1984]
*IPI cri gap SMA sr POLD INFL ECON
   ener +   [1983, 1988]
*IPI CRI GAP SMA SR POLD INFL
   ECON ener defexp +   [1982]
*IPI CRI GAP SMA SR pold infl econ
   ener DEFEXP +   [1975]
*IPI cri gap SMA POLD INFL ECON
   ener DEFEXP +   [1983, 1986]
*IPI cri gap sma SR POLD infl econ
   ENER DEFEXP   [1981]

Probability = 16:28 (57%) with IPI; 3:28 (11%) without IPI

Spain

Minimized Truth Table #1
Model: IPI = CRI + GAP + SMA + SR + POLD + INFL + ECON + ENER
  + DEFEXP
Outputs Minimized: 1
Method: Akers (Fast)

*CRI gap sma SR pold INFL econ ener +   [1979, 1980, 1981, 1982]
*CRI GAP SMA sr pold INFL ECON ener
   defexp +   [1977]
CRI GAP sma sr pold INFL econ ENER
   defexp +   [1978]
*CRI gap SMA SR POLD INFL ECON
   ENER defexp +   [1976]
*CRI sma SR pold INFL econ ener
   DEFEXP +   [1981, 1982, 1983]
*CRI gap SMA SR POLD INFL ener
   DEFEXP   [1974, 1975]

Probability = 11:26 (42%) for 1958–1983; 1:18 (6%) for 1958–1975.

Minimized Truth Table #2
Model: CRI = IPI + GAP + SMA + SR + POLD + INFL + ECON + ENER
  + DEFEXP
Outputs Minimized: 1
Method: Akers (Fast)

*IPI gap sma SR pold INFL econ ener +   [1979, 1980, 1981, 1982]
*IPI GAP SMA sr pold INFL ECON ener
  defexp +   [1977]
IPI GAP sma sr pold INFL econ ENER
  defexp +   [1978]
*IPI gap SMA SR POLD INFL ECON
  ENER defexp +   [1976]
ipi gap sma sr POLD infl econ ener
  DEFEXP +   [1971, 1972]
*ipi GAP sma SR POLD infl econ ener
  DEFEXP +   [1970]
*IPI sma SR pold INFL econ ener
  DEFEXP +   [1981, 1982, 1983]
*IPI gap SMA SR POLD INFL ener
  DEFEXP   [1974, 1975]

Probability = 11:26 (42%) for 1958–1983; 2:18 (11%) for 1958–1975.

Minimized Truth Table #3
Model: GAP = IPI + CRI + SMA + SR + POLD + INFL + ECON + ENER
  + DEFEXP
Outputs Minimized: 1
Method: Akers (Fast)

*IPI CRI SMA sr pold INFL ECON ener
  defexp +   [1977]
IPI CRI sma sr pold INFL econ ENER
  defexp +   [1979]
ipi cri sma sr POLD infl econ ener
  DEFEXP +   [1969]
*ipi CRI sma SR POLD infl econ ener
  DEFEXP   [1970]

Probability = 2:26 (8%) for 1958–1983; 1:18 (6%) for 1958–1975.

Minimized Truth Table #3
Model: SMA = IPI + CRI + GAP + SR + POLD + INFL + ECON + ENER
  + DEFEXP
Outputs Minimized: 1
Method: Akers (Fast)

*IPI CRI GAP sr pold INFL ECON ener
  defexp +   [1977]
*IPI CRI gap SR POLD INFL ECON
  ENER defexp +   [1976]
*IPI CRI gap SR POLD INFL ener
  DEFEXP   [1974, 1975]

Probability = 4:26 (15%) for 1958–1983; 2:18 (11%) for 1958–1975.

Minimized Truth Table #4

Model: SR = IPI + CRI + GAP + SMA + POLD + INFL + ECON + ENER
+ DEFEXP

Outputs Minimized: 1

Method: Akers (Fast)

*IPI CRI gap sma pold INFL econ ener +   [1979, 1980, 1981, 1982]
*IPI CRI gap SMA POLD INFL ECON
  ENER defexp +   [1976]
*ipi CRI GAP sma POLD infl econ ener
  DEFEXP +   [1970]
*IPI CRI sma pold INFL econ ener
  DEFEXP +   [1981, 1982, 1983]
*IPI CRI gap SMA POLD INFL ener
  DEFEXP   [1974, 1975]

Probability = 11:26 (42%) for 1958–1983; 3:18 (17%) for 1958–1975.

References

Almeida, A. M., and Lowry, M. (1976), 'Union Structure in the Recent History of Brazil', *Latin American Perspectives*, 3 (Winter): 98–119.

Alonso, J. (1988), *Los Movimientos Sociales en el Valle de México (II)* (México, DF: Ediciones de la Casa Chata).

Alvarez, F. (1988), 'Peasant Movements in Chiapas', *Bulletin of Latin American Research*, 7 (2): 277–98.

Alvarez, S. E. (1990), *Engendering Democracy in Brazil: Women's Movements in Transition Politics* (Princeton: Princeton University Press).

Alves, M. H. M. (1984), 'Grassroots Organizations, Trade Unions and the Church: A Challenge to the Controlled Abertura in Brazil', *Latin American Perspectives*, 11 (1): 73–102.

—— (1985), *State and Opposition in Military Brazil* (Austin: University of Texas Press).

AME (Associação dos Moradores) (1982), *Movimento Comunitário em Sête Barras, Vale do Ribeira, Estado de São Paulo, 1978–1982*, Caderno No. 1 (São Paulo: FASE).

Americas' Watch (1988), *Chile: Human Rights and the Plebiscite* (Washington, DC).

—— (1991a), *Human Rights in Mexico: A Policy of Impunity* (Washington, DC).

—— (1991b), *Prison Conditions in Mexico* (New York).

—— (1991c), *Rural Violence in Brazil* (Washington, DC).

Amnesty International (1986), *Mexico: Human Rights in Rural Areas* (London).

—— (1991), *Mexico: Torture with Impunity* (New York).

Anderson, B. (1983), *Imagined Communities* (London: Verso).

Anderson, P. (1974), *Lineages of the Absolutist State* (London: New Left Books).

Andrain, C. F., and Apter, D. E. (1995), *Political Protest and Social Change* (London: Macmillan).

Andrews, G. (1991) (ed.), *Citizenship* (London: Lawrence and Wishart).

Andrews, R. (1992), 'Black Political Protest in São Paulo, 1888–1988', *Journal of Latin American Studies*, 24 (February): 147–73.

Angell, A. (1991), 'Chile Since 1958', in *Cambridge History of Latin America*, xiii (Cambridge: Cambridge University Press), 311–82.

Anglade, C. (1986), *Sources of Legitimacy in Latin America: The Mechanisms of Consensus in Exclusionary Societies*, XI World Conference of Sociology, New Delhi.

—— (1994), 'Democracy in Latin America', in I. Budge and D. McKay (eds.), *Developing Democracy* (London: Sage Publications), 233–52.

Anuario Estadístico de España (1952–1987), Años 27–62 (Madrid: Instituto Nacional De Estadístico).

Antunes, R. (1994), 'Recent Strikes in Brazil', *Latin American Perspectives*, 21 (1): 24–37.

Arat, Z. F. (1991), *Democracy and Human Rights in Developing Countries* (Boulder, Colo. and London: Lynne Rienner Publishers).

Arriagada, G. (1988), *Pinochet: The Politics of Power* (Boston: Unwin Hyman).

Article 19 (1988), *Information, Freedom and Censorship: A World Report 1988* (Harlow: Longman).

—— (1991), *Information, Freedom and Censorship: World Report 1991* (London: Library Association Publishing).

Assies, W. (1992), *To Get out of the Mud: Neighborhood Associativism in Recife, 1964–1988* (Amsterdam: CEDLA).

—— (1993), 'Urban Social Movements and Local Democracy in Brazil', *European Review of Latin American and Caribbean Studies*, 55 (December): 39–58.

Bailey, J. (1988), *Governing Mexico: The Statecraft of Crisis Management* (London: Macmillan Press).

Baldemar, R., Hirata, J. F., Meza, H., Palacios, R., and Ponce, Y. (1978), *Las Invasiones de Tierra en Sinaloa* (Sinaloa, Mexico: Universidad Autónoma de Sinaloa).

Ballantyne, L. M. (1988), 'Documenting Brazil's Political and Social Movements, 1966–1986: The Library of Congress Experience', *SALALM*, 33 (3): 375–83.

Baloyra, E. A. (1987) (ed.), *Comparing New Democracies: Transition and Consolidation in Mediterranean Europe and the Southern Cone* (Boulder, Colo.: Westview Press).

Banks, A. S. (1971), *Cross-Polity Time Series Data Archive* (Cambridge, Mass.: MIT Press).

—— (1979), *Cross-Polity Time Series Data Archive* (Binghamton, NY: State University of New York at Binghamton).

—— (1994), *Cross-Polity Time Series Data Archive* (Binghamton, NY: State University of New York at Binghamton).

Banks, D. L. (1992), 'New Patterns of Oppression: An Updated Analysis of Human Rights Data', in T. B. Jabine and R. P. Claude (eds.), *Human Rights and Statistics: Getting the Record Straight* (Philadelphia: University of Pennsylvania Press), 364–91.

Barbalet, J. M. (1988), *Citizenship: Rights, Struggle and Class Inequality* (Milton Keynes: Open University Press).

Barber, B. (1986), *Strong Democracy: Participatory Politics for a New Age* (Berkeley: University of California Press).

Barnes, J. (1983), 'Appendix: Human Rights and the Pinochet Decade', in P. J. O'Brien and J. Roddick (eds.), *Chile, the Pinochet Decade: The Rise and Fall of the Chicago Boys* (London: Latin American Bureau), 110–18.

Barrera, M., and Valenzuela, J. S. (1986), 'The Development of Labor

Movement Opposition to the Military Regime', in J. S. Valenzuela and A. Valenzuela (eds.), *Military Rule in Chile* (Baltimore: Johns Hopkins University Press), 230–69.

Barsh, R. L. (1993), 'Measuring Human Rights: Problems of Methodology and Purpose', *Human Rights Quarterly*, 15 (1): 87–121.

Bartra, A. (1977), 'Seis Años de Lucha Campesina', Mexico, DF: Facultad de Economía de la Universidad Nacional Autónoma de México.

Bellamy, R. (1993), 'Citizenship and Rights', in R. Bellamy (ed.), *Theories and Concepts of Politics* (Manchester: Manchester University Press), 43–76.

Bendix, R. (1964), *Nation-Building and Citizenship: Studies of our Changing Social Order* (New York: Wiley).

—— (1978), *Kings or People: Power and the Mandate to Rule* (Berkeley: University of California Press).

Bennett, V. (1992), 'Urban Popular Movements in Mexico, 1968–1988', in A. Escobar and S. E. Alvarez (eds.), *The Making of Social Movements in Latin America* (Boulder, Colo.: Westview), 240–59.

Berg-Schlosser, D., and De Meur, G. (1994), 'Conditions of Democracy in Interwar Europe: A Boolean Test of Major Hypotheses', *Comparative Politics*, 26 (3): 253–80.

Blanc, J. (1966), 'Las Huelgas en el Movimiento Obrero Español', *Horizonte Español*.

Bock, G., and James, S. (1992), *Beyond Equality and Difference: Citizenship, Feminist Politics, Female Subjectivity* (London and New York: Routledge).

Boli-Bennett, J. (1981), 'Human Rights or State Expansion? Cross-National Definitions of Constitutional Rights, 1870–1970', in V. P. Nanda, J. R. Scarritt, and G. W. Shepherd (eds.), *Global Human Rights: Public Policies, Comparative Measures, and NGO Strategies* (Boulder, Colo.: Westview), 173–93.

Bollen, K. A. (1979), 'Political Democracy and the Timing of Development', *American Sociological Review*, 44: 572–87.

—— (1992), 'Political Rights and Political Liberties in Nations: An Evaluation of Rights Measures, 1950 to 1984', in T. B. Jabine and R. P. Claude (eds.), *Human Rights and Statistics: Getting the Record Straight* (Philadelphia: University of Pennsylvania Press), 188–215.

—— (1993), 'Liberal Democracy: Validity and Method Factors in Cross-National Measures', *American Journal of Political Science*, 37 (4): 1207–30.

—— and Jackman, R. (1985), 'Political Democracy and the Size and Distribution of Income', *American Sociological Review*, 50: 438–57.

Boran, A. (1989), 'Popular Movements in Brazil: A Case Study of the Movement for the Defence of *Favelados* in São Paulo', *Bulletin of Latin American Research*, 8 (1): 83–109.

Bordogna, L., Primo Cella, G., and Provasi, G. (1989), 'Labour Conflicts in Italy before the Rise of Fascism, 1881–1923: A Quantitative Analysis', in L. Haimson and C. Tilly (eds.), *Strikes, Wars and Revolutions in International Perspective* (Cambridge: Cambridge University Press), 217–46.

Boschi, R. (1987a), *A Arte da Associação: Política de Base e Democracia no Brasil* (IUPERJ: Vertice).

—— (1987b), 'Social Movements and the New Political Order in Brazil', in J. D. Wirth, E. de Oliveira Nunes, and T. E. Bogenschild (eds.), *State and Society in Brazil* (Boulder, Colo.: Westview Press), 179–212.

Bowles, S., and Gintis, H. (1987), *Democracy and Capitalism: Property, Community and the Contradictions of Modern Social Thought* (New York: Basic Books).

Brand, K. W. (1990), 'Cyclical Aspects of New Social Movements: Waves of Cultural Criticism and Mobilization Cycles of New Middle Class Radicalism', in R. Dalton and M. Kuechler (eds.), *Challenging the Political Order: New Social and Political Movements in Western Democracies* (Cambridge: Polity Press), 23–42.

Brockett, C. D. (1991), 'The Structure of Political Opportunities and Peasant Mobilization in Central America', *Comparative Politics*, 23 (April): 253–74.

Bruce, N. F. (1972a), 'A New Approach to Spanish Labour Problems', *Iberian Studies*, 1 (2): 75–81.

—— (1972b), 'A New Approach to Spanish Labour Problems (continued)', *Iberian Studies*, 2 (1): 53–4.

Brysk, A. (1994), *The Politics of Human Rights in Argentina: Protest, Change and Democratization* (Stanford, Calif.: Stanford University Press).

Burkhart, R. E., and Lewis-Beck, M. (1994), 'Comparative Democracy: The Economic Development Thesis', *American Political Science Review*, 88 (4): 903–10.

Burros, E. (1985) (ed.), *Movimientos Sociales en el Noroeste de México* (Sinaloa, Mexico: Universidad Autónoma de Sinaloa).

Caistor, N. (1984), 'Spread the Word in Chile: The Struggle for an Independent Press', *Index on Censorship*, 13 (5): 16–18.

Campbell, H. (1993), 'Tradition and the New Social Movements: The Politics of Isthmus Zapotec Culture', *Latin American Perspectives*, 20 (3): 83–97.

Campero, G. (1986) (ed.), *Los Movimientos Sociales y la Lucha Democrática en Chile* (Santiago: CLACSO-ILET).

—— (1987), *Entre la Sobrevivencia y la Acción Política: Las Organizaciones de Pobladores en Santiago* (Santiago: Estudios ILET).

—— and Valenzuela, J. A. (1984), *El Movimiento Sindical en el Régimen Militar Chileno, 1973–1981* (Santiago: Estudios ILET).

Cañadell, R. M. (1993), 'Chilean Woman's Organizations: Their Potential for Change', *Latin American Perspectives*, 20 (4): 43–60.

Cardney, M. (1980), 'Chile's Working Class Women: A Smouldering Cauldron', *World Student Christian Federation Journal*, 11 (4): 21–3.

Cardoso, R. C. L. (1983), 'Movimentos Sociais Urbanos: Balanço Crítico', in B. Sorj and M. H. Tavares de Almeida (eds.), *Sociedade e Política no Brasil Pós-64* (São Paulo: Editora Brasilense), 215–39.

Carr, R., and Fusi, J. P. (1981), *Spain: Dictatorship to Democracy*, 2nd edn. (London: Allen and Unwin).

Casanova, P. G., and Camín, H. A. (1987), *México ante la Crisis* (México, DF: Siglo Veintiuno Editores).

Castanho, D. A. (1988), *Caminhos das CEBs no Brasil* (Rio de Janeiro: Marques Saraiva Gráficos Editores).

Castells, M. (1982), 'Squatters and Politics in Latin America: A Comparative Analysis of Urban Social Movements in Chile, Peru and Mexico', in H. Safa (ed.), *Toward a Political Economy of Urbanization in Third World Countries* (New Delhi: Oxford University Press), 249–82.

—— (1983), *The City and the Grassroots* (London: Edward Arnold).

Castillo, C. (1975), 'Women in the Chilean Resistance', *NACLA Report on the Americas*, 9 (6): 26–9.

Castro, A. C. (1989), *La Historia Oculta del Régimen Militar, Chile: 1973–1988* (Santiago: Editorial Antárctica, SA).

CBB (Comissão dos Bairros de Belém) (1982a), *Da Luta pela Terra para Organização Comunitária, 1981–1982* (Belém: FASE).

—— (1982b), *Uma Experiencia de Organização Popular e a Contribuição da FASE nesse Processo* (Belém: FASE).

Chilean Human Rights Commission (1992), *Summary of the Truth and Reconciliation Commission Report* (Santiago).

Chuchryk, P. (1984), 'Protest Politics and Personal Life: The Emergence of Feminism in a Military Dictatorship, Chile 1973–1983', Ph.D. dissertation (York University).

Cingranelli, D. L. (1988), *Human Rights: Theory and Measurement* (London: MacMillan Press).

Clarke, B. (1993), 'Citizen Human', in *Citizenship* (London: Pluto Press), 4–30.

CMS (Centro de Memória Sindical) and CNDM (Conselho Nacional dos Direitos da Mulher) (1986), 'Estas Somos Nós', Brasília.

CNTI (Congresso Nacional dos Trabalhadores na Indústria) (1979), 'Carta de Princípios', *Revista de Cultura Contemporânea*, 2: 101–2.

Coad, M. (1982), 'New Protests in Chile', *Index on Censorship*, 11 (6): 17–18.

Cohen, J., and Arato, A. (1992), *Civil Society and Political Theory* (Cambridge, Mass.: MIT Press).

Cohen, Y. (1989), *The Manipulation of Consent: The State and Working Class Consciousness in Brazil* (Pittsburgh: University of Pittsburgh Press).

—— (1994), *Radicals, Reformers, and Reactionaries: The Prisoner's Dilemma and the Collapse of Democracy in Latin America* (Chicago: University of Chicago Press).

Collier, D. S. (1979), *The New Authoritarianism in Latin America* (Princeton: Princeton University Press).

Collier, D. S., and Collier, R. B. (1991), *Shaping the Political Arena: Critical Junctures, the Labor Movement, and Regime Dynamics* (Princeton: Princeton University Press).

Colomer, J. M. (1991), 'Transitions by Agreement: Modelling the Spanish Way', *American Political Science Review*, 85 (4): 1283–1302.

—— and Pascual, M. (1994), 'The Polish Games of Transition', *Communist and Post-Communist Studies*, 27 (3): 275–94.

Comisión Nacional de Verdad y Reconciliación (1991), *Informe de la Comisión Nacional de Verdad y Reconciliación*, vols. 1–3 (Santiago: La Nación).

Concha Malo, Miguel (1988), 'La Violación a los Derechos Humanos Individuales en México (período: 1971–1986)', in P. G. Casanova and J. Cadena (eds.), *Primer Informe sobre la Democracia: México 1988* (México: Siglo Veintiuno Editores).

Constable, P., and Valenzuela, A. (1991), *A Nation of Enemies: Chile under Pinochet* (New York: W. W. Norton and Company).

Cook, M. L., Middlebrook, K. J., and Horcasitas, J. M. (1994) (eds.), *The Politics of Economic Restructuring: State–Society Relations and Regime Change in Mexico* (San Diego: Center for US–Mexican Studies).

Cooper, M. (1984), 'Pinochet, Your Days are Numbered', *Mother Jones*, 9 (1): 28–30.

Coordenadoría de Conflitos Agrários (1986), 'Violência contra Mulheres e Menores Trabalhadores Rurais', Brasília.

Coordinadora Unica de Damnificados (Mexico City) (1986), 'Pliego de Demandas Presentado por la Coordinadora Unica de Damnificados al Presidente de la República', *Revista Mexicana de Sociología*, 48 (2): 293–7.

Coppedge, M. (1990), 'Measuring Polyarchy', *Studies in Comparative International Development*, 25 (1): 51–72.

—— and Reinicke, W. (1988), 'A Scale of Polyarchy', in R. D. Gastil (ed.), *Freedom in the World: Political Rights and Civil Liberties, 1987–1988* (New York: Freedom House), 101–21.

Cornelius, W. A. (1987), 'Political Liberalization in an Authoritarian Regime: Mexico, 1976–1985', in J. Gentleman (ed.), *Mexican Politics in Transition* (Boulder, Colo. and London: Westview Press), 15–40.

—— (1996), *Mexican Politics in Transition: The Breakdown of a One-Party-Dominant Regime* (Monograph Series 41; San Diego: Center for US–Mexican Studies, University of California).

—— and Craig, A. L. (1991), *The Mexican Political System in Transition* (Monograph Series 35; San Diego: Center for US–Mexican Studies, University of California).

—— Gentleman, J., and Smith, P. H. (1989) (eds.), *Mexico's Alternative Political Futures* (Monograph Series 30; San Diego: Center for US–Mexican Studies, University of California).

Corrêa, H. (1980), *O ABC de 1980* (Rio de Janeiro: Civilização Brasileira).

Costain, A. N. (1992), *Inviting Women's Rebellion: A Political Process Interpretation of the Women's Movement* (Baltimore: Johns Hopkins University Press).

—— and Majstorovic, S. (1994), 'Congress, Social Movements and Public Opinion: Multiple Origins of Women's Rights Legislation', *Political Research Quarterly*, 47 (1): 111–35.

Covarrubias, P., and Franco, R. (1978) (eds.), *Chile: Mujer y Sociedad* (Santiago: UNICEF).

CPT (Comissão Pastoral da Terra) (1977), 'Fazenda Primavera: A Luta Contínua é de Todo o Brasil' (São Paulo: Andradina).

Crick, B. (1962), *In Defense of Politics* (Harmondsworth: Penguin).

Cutright, P., and Wiley J. A. (1969), 'Modernization and Political Representation: 1927–1966', *Studies in Comparative International Development*, 5: 23–44.

Da Silva, J. V. R. (1985), 'A escola é nossa', in *De olho na Cidade* (Porto Alegre: Núcleo Miguel Dias).

Dahl, R. A. (1971), *Polyarchy: Participation and Opposition* (New Haven: Yale University Press).

—— (1989), *Democracy and its Critics* (New Haven: Yale University Press).

Dassin, J. (1986) (ed.), *Torture in Brazil: A Report by the Archdiocese of São Paulo* (New York: Vintage Books).

Davis, D. E. (1988), 'Protesta social y cambio político en México', *Revista Mexicana de Sociología*, 50 (2): 89–122.

—— (1992), 'The Sociology of Mexico: Stalking the Path Not Taken', *Annual Review of Sociology*, 18: 395–417.

—— (1994), 'Failed Democratic Reform in Contemporary Mexico: From Social Movements to the State and Back Again', *Journal of Latin American Studies*, 26: 375–408.

de Albuquerque, C. M. C. P. (1984), 'Algumas Experiências do Movimento de Mulheres do PMDB/Santa Catarina', Florianópolis.

de la Maza, G., and Garcés, M. (1985), *La Explosión de las Mayorías: Protesta Nacional 1983–1984* (Santiago: Educación y Comunicaciones).

del Campo, S. (1994), *Tendencias Sociales en España (1960–1990)*, i (Bilbao: Fundación BBV).

de Souza, A. (1981), 'Governo e Sindicatos no Brasil: a Perspectiva dos Anos 80', *Dados*, 24 (2): 139–59.

de Tocqueville, A. (1961), *Democracy in America* (New York: Schocken).

Delarbre, R. T. (1976), 'Lucha Sindical y Política: el Movimiento Spicer', *Cuadernos Políticos*, 8: 75–90.

Diamond, L., Linz, J. J., and Lipset, S. M. (1989) (eds.), *Democracy in Developing Countries*, iv. *Latin America* (Boulder, Colo.: Lynne Rienner Publishers).

Dinges, J. (1983), 'The Rise of the Opposition', *NACLA Report on the Americas*, 17 (5): 15–26.

DiPalma, G. (1990), *To Craft Democracies: An Essay on Democratic Transitions* (Berkeley: University of California Press).

Dobb, M. (1963), *Studies in the Development of Capitalism* (New York: International Publishers).

Dogan, M., and Pelassy, D. (1990), *How to Compare Nations* (Chatham, NJ: Chatham House).

dos Santos, W. G. (1979), *Cidadania e Justiça* (Rio de Janeiro: Editora Campus).

—— (1990), *Que Brasil é Este? Manual de Indicadores Políticos e Sociais* (IUPERJ: Vertice).

Drake, P., and Jaksic, I. (1991) (eds.), *The Struggle for Democracy in Chile, 1982–1990* (Lincoln and London: University of Nebraska Press).

Drass, K. A., and Ragin, C. C. (1989), *QCA: Qualitative Comparative Analysis* (Evanston, III.: Center for Urban Affairs and Policy Research, Northwestern University).

Duff, E. A., and McCamant, J. (1976), *Violence and Repression in Latin America: A Quantitative and Historical Analysis* (New York: Free Press).

Durkheim, E. (1960), *The Division of Labor in Society* (New York: Free Press).

—— (1992), *Professional Ethics and Civic Morals* (London: Routledge).

Duvall, R., and Shamir, M. (1980), 'Indicators from Errors: Cross-National, Time Serial Measures of the Repressive Disposition of Government', in Charles Lewis Taylor (ed.), *Indicator Systems for Political, Economic, and Social Analysis* (Cambridge, Mass.: Oelgeschlager, Gunn and Hain, Publishers, Inc.), 155–82.

Easton, D. (1975), 'A Reassessment of the Concept of Political Support', *British Journal of Political Science*, 5 (4): 435–58.

Eckstein, S. (1989), *Power and Popular Protest: Latin American Social Movements* (Berkeley: University of California Press).

Eisinger, P. K. (1973), 'The Conditions of Protest Behavior in American Cities', *American Political Science Review*, 67: 11–28.

Ellwood, S. (1976), 'The Working Class under the Franco Regime', in P. Preston (ed.), *Spain in Crisis* (Sussex: Harvester Press), 157–82.

Erickson, K. P. (1977), *The Brazilian Corporative State and Working Class Politics* (Berkeley: University of California Press).

Escobar, A., and Alvarez, S. E. (1992), *The Making of Social Movements in Latin America* (Boulder, Colo.: Westview).

Esping-Andersen, G. (1985), 'Power and Distributional Regimes', *Politics and Society,* 14 (2): 223–56.

—— (1989), *Three Worlds of Welfare Capitalism* (Cambridge: Polity Press).

Espinoza, V. (1986), 'Los Pobladores en La Política', in G. Campero (ed.), *Los Movimientos Sociales y la Lucha Democrática en Chile* (Santiago: CLACSO-ILET).

Evans, P. B. (1979), *Dependent Development: The Alliance of Multinational, State and Local Capital in Brazil* (Princeton; Princeton University Press).

Fagen, R. R., and Cornelius, W. A. (1970), *Political Power in Latin America: Seven Confrontations* (Englewood Cliffs, NJ: Prentice Hall, Inc.), 297–340.

Falabella, G. (1980), 'Labour under Authoritarian Regimes: The Chilean Union Movement, 1973–1979', Ph.D. dissertation (University of Sussex).

Falcoff, M. (1982), 'The Timerman Case', in H. Wiarda (ed.), *Human*

Rights and US Human Rights Policy (Washington, DC: American Enterprise Institute), 60–78.

Faria, J. E. (1989), 'Ordem Legal e Mudança Social: a Crise do Judiciário e a Formação do Magistrado', in J. E. Faria (ed.), *Direito e Justiça* (São Paulo: Atica).

Faure, A. M. (1994), 'Some Methodological Problems in Comparative Politics', *Journal of Theoretical Politics*, 6 (3): 307–22.

Federação de Mulheres Fluminenses (1982), 'As Mulheres do Rio de Janeiro e Suas Lutas', *Cadernos do CEAC (Centro de Estudos e Ação Comunitária)*, 9.

Fernández, J. A. E. (1987), 'Colección de Documentos para la Historia de la Oposición Política en Chile (1973–1981)' (Amsterdam: CEDLA), Microfiche.

Fernández de Castro, I., and Martínez, J. (1963), *España Hoy* (Paris: Ruedo Ibérico).

Feyerabend, P. (1975), *Against Method* (London: Verso).

Fiechter G. A. (1975), *Brazil Since 1964: Modernisation under a Military Régime* (London: Macmillan).

Fishman, R. M. (1990), *Working-Class Organization and the Return to Democracy in Spain* (Ithaca, NY: Cornell University Press).

Fitzgibbon, R. H. (1967), 'Measuring Democratic Change in Latin America', *Journal of Politics*, 29: 129–66.

Foley, M. W. (1991), 'Agenda for Mobilization: The Agrarian Question and Popular Mobilization in Contemporary Mexico', *Latin American Research Review*, 26 (2): 39–74.

Foucault, M. (1977a) *Discipline and Punish: The Birth of the Prison* (New York: Pantheon Books).

—— (1977b), *Language, Counter-Memory, Practice*, ed. D. Bouchard (Ithaca, NY: Cornell University Press).

Foweraker, J. (1981), *The Struggle for Land: A Political Economy of the Pioneer Frontier in Brazil, from 1930 to the Present Day* (Cambridge: Cambridge University Press).

—— (1982), 'Accumulation and Authoritarianism on the Pioneer Frontier of Brazil', *Journal of Peasant Studies*, 10 (1): 95–117.

—— (1989), *Making Democracy in Spain: Grass-Roots Struggle in the South, 1955–1975* (Cambridge: Cambridge University Press).

—— (1993), *Popular Mobilization in Mexico: The Teacher's Movement 1977–1987* (Cambridge: Cambridge University Press).

—— (1995), *Theorizing Social Movements* (London: Pluto Press).

—— (1996), 'Measuring Citizenship in Mexico', in M. Serrano and V. Bulmer-Thomas (eds.), *Rebuilding the State: Mexico after Salinas* (London: Institute of Latin American Studies), 79–98.

—— and Craig, A. (1990) (eds.), *Popular Movements and Political Change in Mexico* (Boulder, Colo.: Lynne Reinner).

Fox, J. (1994), 'The Difficult Transition from Clientelism to Citizenship', *World Politics*, 46: 151–84.

Fraser, R. (1976), 'Spain on the Brink', *New Left Review*, March–April: 3–33.

Frederico, C. (1987), 'A Resistência à Ditadura', *A Esquerda e o Movimento Operário 1964–1984*, i (São Paulo: Editores Nôvos Rumos).

—— (1990), 'A Crise do "Milagre Brasileiro"', *A Esquerda e o Movimento Operário 1964–1984*, ii (Belo Horizonte: Nossa Terra).

Freedom House (1990), *Freedom in the World: Political and Civil Liberties, 1989–1990* (New York: Freedom House).

—— (1995), *Freedom in the World: Political and Civil Liberties, 1994–1995* (New York: Freedom House).

Freeman, J. R. (1983), 'Granger Causality and the Time Series Analysis of Political Relationships', *American Journal of Political Science*, 27: 327–58.

Frias, P. (1989), *El Movimiento Sindical Chileno en la Lucha por la Democracia, 1973–1988* (Santiago).

Fundamental Laws of the State: The Spanish Constitution (1972), (Madrid: Ministry of Information and Tourism).

Galván, E. T. (1966), 'Students' Opposition in Spain', *Government and Opposition*, 1 (4): 467–86.

Gamson, W. A. (1975), *The Strategy of Social Protest* (Homewood, Ill: Dorsey Press).

Gardy, A. (1994), 'Mexico: A Grassroots Challenge', *NACLA Report on the Americas*, 26 (3): 8–11.

Garretón, M. A. (1986), 'Political Processes in an Authoritarian Regime: The Dynamics of Institutionalization and Opposition in Chile, 1973–1980', in J. S. Valenzuela and A. Valenzuela (eds.) *Military Rule in Chile* (Baltimore: Johns Hopkins University Press), 144–83.

—— (1989*a*) 'Popular Mobilization and the Military Regime in Chile: The Complexities of the Invisible Transition', in S. Eckstein (ed.), *Power and Popular Protest* (Berkeley: University of California Press), 259–77.

—— (1989*b*), *The Chilean Political Process* (London: Unwin Hyman).

—— (1994), 'Human Rights and Processes of Democratisation', *Journal of Latin American Studies*, 26: 221–34.

Garrido, L. J. (1989) 'The Crisis of *Presidencialismo*', in W. A. Cornelius, J. Gentleman, and P. H. Smith (eds.), *Mexico's Alternative Political Futures* (Monograph Series 30; San Diego: Center for US–Mexican Studies, University of California), 417–34.

Gasiorowski, M. J. (1995), 'Economic Crisis and Regime Change: An Event History Analysis', *American Political Science Review*, 89 (4): 882–97.

Gastil, R. D. (1987), *Freedom in the World: Political and Civil Liberties, 1986–1987* (New York: Freedom House).

—— (1989), *Freedom in the World: Political and Civil Liberties, 1988–1989* (New York: Freedom House).

—— (1990), 'The Comparative Survey of Freedom: Experiences and Suggestions', *Studies in Comparative International Development*, 25: 25–50.

Gay, R. (1990), 'Neighborhood Associations and Political Change in Rio de Janeiro', *Latin American Research Review*, 25 (1): 102–8.

Geertz, C. (1983), *Local Knowledge: Further Essays in Interpretative Anthropology*, (New York: Basic Books).

Geraldo de Sousa Junior, J. (1988), 'A Nôva Constituição e os Direitos de Cidadão', *Vozes*, 82 (2): 28–34.

Giddens, A. (1982), *Profiles and Critiques in Social Theory* (London: Macmillan).

—— (1985), *The Nation-State and Violence* (London: Macmillan).

Gilbert, A. (1994), *The Latin American City* (London: Latin American Bureau).

Giner, S. (1976), 'Power, Freedom and Social Change in the Spanish University, 1939–1975', in P. Preston (ed.), *Spain in Crisis* (Sussex: Harvester Press), 183–211.

Gohn, M. d. G. (1982), *Reivindicações Populares Urbanos* (São Paulo: Cortez Editora).

Goldstone, J. A. (1980), 'The Weakness of Organization: A New Look at Gamson's *The Strategy of Social Protest*', *American Journal of Sociology*, 85 (5): 1017–42.

Gómez, S. (1982), *Instituciones y Procesos Agrários en Chile* (Santiago: FLACSO).

Gorender, J. (1987), *Combate nas Trevas: a Esquerda Brasileira das Ilusões Perdidas à Luta Armada* (São Paulo: Atica).

Gramsci, A. (1973), *Selections from the Prison Notebooks*, ed. Q. Hoare and G. N. Smith (London: Lawrence and Wishart).

Greenfield, G. M., and Maram, S. L. (1987), *Latin American Labor Organizations* (New York: Greenwood Press).

Grzybowski, C. (1987), *Caminhos e Descaminhos dos Movimentos Sociais no Campo* FASE (Rio de Janeiro: Vozes).

—— (1990), 'Rural Workers' Movements and Democratization in Brazil', *Journal of Development Studies*, 26: 18–43.

Gujarati, D. N. (1988), *Basic Econometrics*, 2nd edn. (London: McGraw-Hill).

Gunther, R., Sani, G., and Shabad, G. (1988), *Spain after Franco: The Making of a Competitive Party System* (Los Angeles: University of California Press).

Gupta, D. K., Jongman, A. J., and Schmid, A. P. (1994), 'Creating a Composite Index for Assessing Country Performance in the Field of Human Rights: Proposal for a New Methodology', *Human Rights Quarterly*, 16 (1): 131–62.

Gurr, T. R. (1970), *Why Men Rebel* (Princeton: Princeton University Press).

Gutiérrez, R. (1981), 'Juchitán, municipio comunista', *Revista de Ciencias Sociales y Humanidades*, 2: 251–80.

Guzmán, M. G. (1982), 'Afectaciones Petróleas en Tabasco: el Movimiento del Pacto Ribereño', *Revista Mexicana de Sociología*, 44 (1): 167–89.

Haber, P. L. (1992), 'Collective Dissent in Mexico: The Politics of Contemporary Urban Movements', Ph.D. dissertation (Columbia University).

Haber, P. L. (1994), 'The Art and Implications of Political Restructuring in Mexico: The Case of Urban Popular Movements', in M. L. Cook, K. J. Middlebrook, and J. M. Horcasitas (eds.), *The Politics of Economic Restructuring: State–Society Relations and Regime Change in Mexico* (San Diego: Center for US–Mexican Studies), 277–303.

Habermas, J. (1973), *Legitimation Crisis* (London: Heinemann).

—— (1987), *The Philosophical Discourse of Modernity* (Cambridge, Mass.: MIT Press).

—— (1989), *The Structural Transformation of the Public Sphere* (Cambridge: Polity Press).

Hagopian, F. (1990), 'Democracy by Undemocratic Means? Elites, Political Pacts and Regime Transition in Brazil', *Comparative Political Studies*, 23 (2): 147–70.

Haimson, L., and Tilly, C. (1989), *Strikes, Wars and Revolutions in an International Perspective* (Cambridge: Cambridge University Press).

Hall, S., and Held, D. (1989), 'Citizens and Citizenship', in S. Hall and M. Jacques (eds.), *New Times: The Changing Face of Politics in the 1990s* (London: Lawrence and Wishart), 189–213.

Harvey, N. (1988), 'Personal Networks and Strategic Choices in the Formation of an Independent Peasant Organization: The OCEZ of Chiapas, Mexico', *Bulletin of Latin American Research*, 7 (2): 299–312.

—— (1990), 'Corporatist Strategies and Popular Responses in Rural Mexico: State and Opposition in Chiapas, 1970–1988', Ph.D. dissertation (University of Essex).

Heater, D. (1990), *Citizenship: The Civic Ideal in World History, Politics, and Education* (London: Longman).

Held, D. (1989), 'Citizenship and Autonomy', in *Political Theory and the Modern State* (Cambridge: Polity Press), 189–213.

—— (1991a), 'Editor's Introduction', in D. Held (ed.), *Political Theory Today* (Cambridge: Polity Press).

—— (1991b) (ed.), *Political Theory Today* (Cambridge: Polity Press).

—— (1992), 'Democracy: From City-States to a Cosmopolitan Order?', *Political Studies*, 40, Special Edition on 'Prospects for Democracy': 10–39.

Helliwell, J. F. (1994), 'Empirical Linkages between Democracy and Economic Growth', *British Journal of Political Science*, 24: 225–48.

Hellman, J. A. (1983), *Mexico in Crisis*, 2nd edn. (London: Holmes and Meier).

—— (1994), 'Mexican Popular Movements, Clientelism, and the Process of Democratization', *Latin American Perspectives*, 21 (2): 124.

Hernández, R. (1987), *La Coordinadora Nacional del Movimiento Urbano Popular, CONAMUP: Su Historia 1980–1986* (Equipo Pueblo).

Hewitt, W. E. (1990), 'Religion and the Consolidation of Democracy in Brazil: The Role of the Communidades Eclesiais de Base (CEBS)', *Sociological Analysis*, 50 (2): 139–52.

Hibbs, D. A. (1973), *Mass Political Violence: A Cross-National Causal Analysis* (New York: John Wiley and Sons).

—— (1976), 'Industrial Conflict in Advanced Industrial Societies', *American Political Science Review*, 70: 1033–58.

Higley, J., and Gunther, R. (1992), *Elites and Democratic Consolidation in Latin America and Southern Europe* (Cambridge: Cambridge University Press).

Hill, C. (1958), *Puritanism and Revolution: Studies in the Interpretation of the English Revolution of the 17th Century* (London: Secker and Warburg).

Hilton, R. (1976) (ed.), *The Transition from Feudalism to Capitalism* (London: New Left Books).

Hobsbawm, E. J. (1968), *Labouring Men: Studies in the History of Labour* (London: Wiedenfeld and Nicolson).

—— (1977), *The Age of Revolution: Europe 1789–1848* (London: Sphere Books).

Hollyman, J. L. L. (1974), 'The Press and Censorship in Franco Spain', *Iberian Studies*, 3 (2): 60–9.

Horcasitas, J. M. (1989), 'The Future of the Electoral System', in W. A. Cornelius, J. Gentleman, and P. H. Smith (eds.), *Mexico's Alternative Political Futures* (Monograph Series 30; San Diego: Center for US–Mexican Studies, University of California), 265–90.

—— (1993), *El Tiempo de la Legitimidad: Elecciones, Autoritarismo y Democracia en México* (México, DF: Cal y Arena).

Hottinger, A. (1974), 'Spain in Transition: Prospects and Policies', *The Washington Papers*, 19 (Washington: Center for Strategic International Studies).

Humana, C. (1983), *World Human Rights Guide* (London: Hutchinson).

—— (1986), *World Human Rights Guide* (New York: Facts on File Publications).

—— (1992), *World Human Rights Guide* (New York: Facts on File Publications).

Humphrey, J. (1979), 'Auto Workers and the Working Class in Brazil', *Latin American Perspectives*, 6 (4): 71–89.

—— (1982), *Capitalist Control and the Worker's Struggle in the Brazilian Auto Industry* (Princeton: Princeton University Press).

ILO (International Labour Office) (1969), 'Report of the Study Group to Examine the Labour and Trade Union Situation in Spain', *Official Bulletin, Second Special Supplement*, 52 (4), Geneva.

—— (1950–90), *Statistical Yearbook*.

Inkeles, A. (1991) (ed.), *On Measuring Democracy* (New Brunswick: Transaction Publishers).

Inter-American Commission on Human Rights (1984), *25 Years of Struggle for Human Rights in the Americas* (Washington, DC: Organization of American States).

International Commission of Jurists (1992), *Chile: A Time of Reckoning, Human Rights and the Judiciary* (Geneva: Centre for the Independence of Judges and Lawyers).

Jabine, T. B., and Claude, R. P. (1992), *Human Rights and Statistics: Getting the Record Straight* (Philadelphia: University of Pennsylvania Press).

Jacobi, P. R. (1980), 'Movimentos Sociais Urbanos no Brasil', *Boletim Informativo e Bibliográfico de Ciências Sociais*, 9: 22–30.

—— (1984), 'São Paulo: las Luchas de los Excluidos de la Ciudad por el Derecho a la Ciudadanía, 1970–1982', *Revista Mexicana de Sociología*, 46 (4): 191–209.

Jaquette, J. (1989) (ed.), *The Women's Movement in Latin America: Feminism and the Transition to Democracy* (Winchester, Mass.: Unwin Hyman).

Jáuregui, F., and Vega, P. (1983), *Crónica del Anti-franquismo, 1939–1962: Los Hombres que Lucharon por Devolver la Democracia a España* (Editorial Argos Vergara).

Jelin, E. (1993), 'Como Construir Ciudadanía? Una Visión desde Abajo', *European Review of Latin American and Caribbean Studies*, 55: 21–37.

Jenkins, J. C., and Klandermans, B. (1995) (eds.), *The Politics of Social Protest: Comparative Perspectives on States and Social Movements* (London: UCL Press).

—— and Perrow, C. (1977), 'Insurgency of the Powerless: Farm Worker Movements (1946–1972)', *American Sociological Review*, 42: 249–68.

Johnson, K. F. (1976), 'Scholarly Images of Latin American Political Democracy in 1975', *Latin American Research Review*, 11 (2): 129–41.

—— (1977), 'Research Perspectives on the Revised Fitzgibbon-Johnson Index of the Image of Political Democracy in Latin America, 1945–1979', J. A. Wilkie and K. Ruddle (eds.), *Quantitative Latin American Studies* (Statistical Abstract of Latin America; Los Angeles: UCLA).

—— (1981), 'The 1980 Image-Index Survey of Latin American Political Democracy', *Latin American Research Review*, 16: 193–201.

Kant de Lima, R. (1990), 'Constituição, Direitos Humanos e Processo Penal Inquisitorial: Quem Cala, Consente?', *Dados*, 33 (3): 471–88.

Kaufman, E. (1988), *Crisis in Allende's Chile: New Perspectives* (New York: Praeger Press).

Keane, J. (1988), *Democracy and Civil Society* (London: Verso).

Keck, M. (1989), 'The "New Unionism" in the Brazilian Transition', in A. Stepan (ed.), *Democratizing Brazil* (New York: Oxford University Press), 252–98.

—— (1992), *The Worker's Party and Democratization in Brazil* (New Haven: Yale University Press).

Kennedy, P. (1992), *A Guide to Econometrics*, 3rd edn. (Cambridge, Mass.: MIT Press).

Kimmel, M. S. (1990), *Revolution: A Sociological Interpretation* (Philadelphia: Temple University Press).

King, D. (1987), *The New Right: Politics, Markets, and Citizenship* (London: Macmillan).

King, P. J. (1989), 'Comparative Analysis of Human Rights Violations under Military Rule in Argentina, Brazil, Chile, and Uruguay', in J. W. Wilkie and E. Ochoa (eds.), *Statistical Abstract of Latin America*, 27 (Los Angeles: University of California), 1043–65.

Kinzo, M. (1988), *Legal Opposition Politics under Authoritarian Rule in Brazil* (London: Macmillan Press in Association with St Antony's College, Oxford).

Kitschelt, H. (1986), 'Political Opportunity Structures and Political Protest: Anti-Nuclear Movements in Four Democracies', *British Journal of Political Science*, 16: 58–95.

—— (1990), 'New Social Movements and the Decline of Party Organization', in R. Dalton and M. Kuechler (eds.), *Challenging the Political Order: New Social Movements in Western Democracies* (Cambridge: Polity Press), 179–208.

Klandermans, B. (1992), 'The Case for Longitudinal Research on Movement Participation', in M. Diani and R. Eyerman (eds.), *Studying Collective Action* (London: Sage), 55–75.

Klein, E. (1984), *Gender Politics: From Consciousness to Mass Politics* (Cambridge, Mass.: Harvard University Press).

Köppen, E. (1985), 'Bibliografía de Movimientos Sociales en México: Selección de Estudios de Caso por Entidad Federativa', *Revista Mexicana de Sociología*, 47 (4): 261–98.

Koss, E. S. (1980), *Ordenamiento Constitucional* (Santiago: Editorial Jurídica de Chile).

Krane, D. (1983), 'Opposition Strategy and Survival in Praetorian Brazil, 1964–1979', *Journal of Politics*, 45 (1): 22–63.

Kriesi, H. (1988), 'Local Mobilization for the People's Petition of the Dutch Peace Movement', in B. Klandermans, H. Kriesi, and S. Tarrow (eds.), *From Structure to Action: Comparing Movements across Cultures* (International Social Movements Research, 1; Greenwich, Conn.: JAI Press).

—— Koopmans, R., Dyvendak, I. W., and Giugni, M. G. (1995), *Social Movements in Western Europe: A Comparative Analysis* (London: UCL Press).

Krischke, P. (1991), 'Church Base Communities and Democratic Change in Brazilian Society', *Comparative Political Studies*, 24: 186–210.

Kucinski, B. (1982), *Brazil: State and Struggle* (London: Latin American Bureau).

Küppers, G. (1994), *Compañeras: Voices from the Latin American Women's Movement* (London: Latin American Bureau).

Kymlicka, W., and Norman, W. (1994), 'Return of the Citizen: A Survey of Recent Work on Citizenship Theory', *Ethics*, 104: 352–81.

Laraña, E. (1994), 'Social Movements in Spain', *La Revue Tocqueville*, 15 (1): 119–40.

LASA (Latin American Studies Association) (1989), 'The Chilean Plebiscite: A First Step Toward Democratization', Report by the International Commission of the Latin American Studies Association to Observe the Chilean Plebiscite.

Leiva, F. I. (1988), 'Chile's Poor and the Struggle for Democracy', in G. Rojo and J. J. Hassett (eds.), *Chile: Dictatorship and the Struggle for Democracy* (Gaithersburg, Md.: Ediciones Hispanoamerica), 75–98.

——— and Petras, J. (1987), 'Chile: New Urban Movements and the Transition to Democracy', *Monthly Review*, July–August: 109–24.

Lenin, V. I. (1967), *The Development of Capitalism in Russia* (Moscow: Progress Publishers).

Lerner, D. (1963), *The Passing of Traditional Society* (New York: Free Press).

Levine, D. (1988), 'Paradigm Lost: Dependency to Democracy', *World Politics*, 40 (3): 377–94.

Levy, D. (1986), 'Chilean Universities under the Junta: Regime and Policy', *Latin American Research Review*, 21 (3): 95–128.

Lewis-Beck, M. (1986), 'Interrupted Time Series', in W. D. Berry and M. Lewis-Beck (eds.), *New Tools for Social Scientists* (Beverly Hills, Calif.: Sage Publications), 209–40.

Library of Congress (1988), *Brazil's Popular Groups: 1966–1986*, collection of pamphlets, serials, and ephemera on 27 reels of microfilm.

Lieberman, S. (1985), *The Contemporary Spanish Economy: Historical Perspective* (London: Allen and Unwin).

Lijphart, A. (1971), 'Comparative Politics and the Comparative Method', *American Political Science Review*, 65 (3): 682–93.

——— (1984), *Democracies: Patterns of Majoritarian Consensus Government in Twenty-One Countries* (New Haven: Yale University Press).

Limongi, F., and Przeworski, A. (1994), *Democracy and Development in South America, 1946–1988* (Madrid: Juan March Institute).

Linz, J. J. (1964), 'An Authoritarian Regime: Spain', in E. Allardt and S. Rokkan (eds.), *Mass Politics* (New York: Free Press), 251–83.

——— (1973) 'Opposition in and under an Authoritarian Regime: The Case of Spain', in R. A. Dahl (ed.), *Regimes and Oppositions* (New Haven: Yale University Press), 171–260.

——— and Stepan. A. (1978) (eds.), *The Breakdown of Democratic Regimes: Latin America* (Baltimore: Johns Hopkins University Press).

Lipset, S. M. (1959), 'Some Social Requisites for Democracy', *American Political Science Review*, 53: 69–105.

——— (1960), *Political Man* (London: Heinemann).

——— (1994), 'Social Requisites for Democracy Revisited', *American Sociological Review*, 59 (1): 1–22.

Lipsky, M. (1968), 'Protest as a Political Resource', *American Political Science Review*, 62 (4): 1144–58.

Loaeza, S. (1994), 'Political Liberalization and Uncertainty in Mexico', in M. L. Cook, K. J. Middlebrook, and J. M. Horcasitas (eds.), *The Politics of Economic Restructuring: State–Society Relations and Regime Change in Mexico* (San Diego: Center for US–Mexican Studies), 105–20.

Locke, J. (1975), *An Essay Concerning Human Understanding*, ed. P. H. Nidditch (Oxford: Clarendon Press).

López, A. L. (1988), *El Movimiento Campesino en los Llanos de Victoria, Durango, 1970–1980* (Mexico, DF: Siglo Veintiuno Editores).

López-Pintor, R. (1987), 'Mass and Elite Perspectives in the Process of Transition to Democracy', in E. A. Baloyra (ed.), *Comparing New Democracies: Transition and Consolidation in Mediterranean Europe and the Southern Cone* (Boulder, Colo. and London: Westview Press), 79–108.

Loveman, B. (1986), 'Military Dictatorship and Political Opposition in Chile, 1973–1986', *Journal of Inter-American Studies and World Affairs*, 28 (4): 1–38.

—— (1991), '¿Misión Cumplida? Civil Military Relations and the Chilean Political Process', *Journal of Interamerican Studies and World Affairs*, 33 (4): 35–74.

—— (1993), *The Constitution of Tyranny: Regimes of Exception in Spanish America* (Pittsburgh: University of Pittsburgh Press).

—— (1994), ' "Protected Democracies" and Military Guardianship: Political Transitions in Latin America, 1978–1993', *Journal of Interamerican Studies and World Affairs*, 36 (2): 105.

Lowenstein, R. L. (1967), 'Measuring World Press Freedom as a Political Indicator', Ph.D. dissertation (University of Missouri).

Lowry, M. (1979), 'Students and Class Struggle in Brazil', *Latin American Perspectives*, 6 (4): 101–7.

McAdam, D., McCarthy, J. D., and Zald, M. N. (1996) (eds.), *Comparative Perspectives on Social Movements: Political Opportunities, Mobilizing Structures, and Cultural Framings* (Cambridge: Cambridge University Press).

McDowall, D., McCleary, R., Meidinger, E. E., and Hay, R. A. (1980), *Interrupted Time Series* (Sage University Paper, 21; Beverly Hills, Calif.: Sage Publications).

Macpherson, C. B. (1966), *The Real World of Democracy* (Oxford: Clarendon Press).

—— (1972), *The Political Theory of Possessive Individualism: Hobbes to Locke* (London: Oxford University Press).

Mainwaring, S. (1986), 'The Transition to Democracy in Brazil', *Journal of Interamerican Studies and World Affairs*, 28: 149–79.

—— (1987), 'Urban Popular Movements, Identity, and Democratization in Brazil', *Comparative Political Studies*, 20 (2): 131–59.

—— (1989), 'Grass-Roots Catholic Groups and Politics in Brazil', in S. Mainwaring and A. Wilde (eds.), *The Progressive Church in Latin America* (South Bend, Ind.: University of Notre Dame Press), 151–92.

—— and Viola, E. (1984), 'New Social Movements, Political Culture and Democracy: Brazil and Argentina in the 1980s', *Telos*, 61 (Fall): 17–52.

—— and Wilde, A. (1989), *The Progressive Church in Latin America* (South Bend, Ind.: University of Notre Dame Press).

—— O'Donnell, G., and Valenzuela, J. S. (1992) (eds.), *Issues in Democratic Consolidation: The New South American Democracies in Comparative Perspective* (South Bend, Ind.: University of Notre Dame Press).

Malloy, J. (1987), 'The Politics of Transition in Latin America', in J. M.

Malloy and M. A. Seligson (eds.), *Authoritarians and Democrats: Regime Transition in Latin America* (Pittsburgh: University of Pittsburgh Press), 235–58.

Mann, M. (1987), 'Ruling Class Strategies and Citizenship', *Sociology*, 21 (3): 339–54.

—— (1993*a*), *The Sources of Social Power*, ii. *The Rise of Classes and Nation-States 1760–1914* (Cambridge: Cambridge University Press).

—— (1993*b*), *The Struggle between Authoritarian Rightism and Democracy, 1920–1975* (Madrid: Juan March Institute).

Maravall, J. (1978), *Dictatorship and Political Dissent: Workers and Students in Franco's Spain* (London: Tavistock Publications).

Maricato, E. (1988), 'The Urban Reform Movement in Brazil', *International Journal of Urban and Regional Research*, 12 (1): 137–8.

Marshall, T. H. (1963), 'Citizenship and Social Class', in *Sociology at the Crossroads and Other Essays* (London: Heinemann), 67–127.

—— (1965), *Class, Citizenship and Social Development* (Garden City, NY: Anchor Books).

Martinez, C. F. (1985), 'La Lucha por la Tierra en el Sur de Sonora y el Frente Campesino Independiente (1975–1976)', in E. Burros (ed.), *Movimientos Sociales en el Noroeste de México* (Sinaloa: Universidad Autónoma de Sinaloa), 85–101.

Marugán, R. P. (1992), 'Cronología de la Transición y la Consolidación Democrática', in R. Cotarelo (ed.), *Transición Política y Consolidación Demócrata, España (1975–1986)* (Madrid: Centro de Investigaciones Sociológicas), 547–616.

Marx, G. T., and Wood, J. L. (1975), 'Strands of Theory and Research in Collective Behavior', *Annual Review of Sociology*, 1: 363–428.

Marx, K. (1976), *Preface and Introduction to A Contribution to the Critique of Political Economy* (Peking: Foreign Languages Press).

—— (1981), *On the Jewish Question (1843)*, in *Karl Marx: Early Writings* (Harmondsworth: Penguin Books).

Maybury-Lewis, B. (1991), 'The Politics of the Possible: The Growth and Development of the Brazilian Rural Workers' Trade Union Movement, 1964–85', Ph.D. dissertation (Columbia University).

Maxwell, K. (1983), *The Press and the Rebirth of Iberian Democracy* (Westport, Conn.: Greenwood Press).

Medina, C. A. (1991), 'Social Action and Development: The Case of Brazil', *Community Development Journal*, 26 (3): 172–7.

Melucci, A. (1988), 'Getting Involved: Identity and Mobilization in Social Movements', in B. Klandermans, H. Kriesi, and S. Tarrow (eds.), *From Structure to Action: Comparing Movements across Cultures* (International Social Movements Research, 1; Greenwich, Conn.: JAI Press), 329–48.

—— (1989), *Nomads of the Present*, ed. J. Keane and P. Mier (Philadelphia: Temple University Press).

Mendes, A. (1982), *Movimento Estudantil no Brasil* (São Paulo: Brasilense).

Menéndez, I. (1982), 'El Sindicalismo Independiente en Yucatán', *Revista Mexicana de Sociología*, 44 (1): 189–214.

Meyer, D. S. (1993), 'Protest Cycles and Political Process: American Peace Movements in the Nuclear Age', *Political Research Quarterly*, 47: 451–79.

Middlebrook, K. J. (1982), 'The Political Economy of Mexican Organized Labor, 1940–1978', Ph.D. dissertation (Ann Arbor: University of Michigan).

—— (1989), 'Sounds of Silence: Organized Labor's Response to Economic Crisis in Mexico', *Journal of Latin American Studies*, 21 (2): 195–220.

Mill, J. S. (1843/1970), *A System of Logic* (London: Longman).

Moisés, J. A. (1979), 'Current Issues in the Labor Movement in Brazil', *Latin American Perspectives*, 6 (4): 51–70.

—— (1982), 'What's the Strategy of the "New Syndicalism"?', *Latin American Perspectives*, 9 (4): 55–73.

—— (1993), *Democratization, Mass Political Culture and Political Legitimacy in Brazil* (Madrid: Juan March Institute).

Mommsen, W. J. (1990), 'The Varieties of Nation State in Modern History: Liberal, Imperial, Fascist and Contemporary Notions of Nation and Nationality', in M. Mann (ed.), *The Rise and Decline of the Nation State* (Oxford: Blackwell), 210–26.

Montero, J. R. (1992), *Sobre la Democracia en España: Legitimidad, Apoyos Institucionales y Significados* (Madrid: Juan March Institute).

Moore, B., Jr. (1973), *Social Origins of Dictatorship and Democracy: Landlord and Peasant in the Making of the Modern World* (Harmondsworth: Penguin University Books).

Mouffe, C. (1992) (ed.), *Dimensions of Radical Democracy* (London: Verso).

Muller, E. N., and Seligson, M. A. (1987), 'Inequality and Insurgency', *American Political Science Review*, 81 (2): 425–51.

Munck, G. L. (1993), 'Between Theory and History and Beyond Traditional Area Studies: A New Comparative Perspective on Latin America', *Comparative Politics*, 25 (4): 475–98.

—— (1994), 'Democratic Transitions in Comparative Perspective', *Comparative Politics*, 26 (3): 355–75.

Murilo de Carvalho, J. (1985), 'República e Cidadanias', *Dados*, 28 (2): 142–61.

Nagengast, C., Stavenhagen, R., and Kearney, M. (1992), *Human Rights and Indigenous Workers: The Mixtecs in Mexico and the United States* (Current Issue Brief No. 4; San Diego: Centre for US–Mexican Studies, University of California).

Nanda, V. P., Scarritt, J. R., and Shepherd, G. W. (1981), *Global Human Rights: Public Policies, Comparative Measures, and NGO Strategies* (Boulder, Colo.: Westview).

Navarro, Z. (1994), 'Democracy, Citizenship and Representation: Rural Social Movements in Southern Brazil, 1978–1990', *Bulletin of Latin American Research*, 13 (2): 129–54.

Nixon, R. B. (1960), 'Factors Related to Freedom in National Press Systems', *Journalism Quarterly*, 37 (Winter): 13–28.

—— (1965), 'Freedom in the World's Press: A Fresh Appraisal with New Data', *Journalism Quarterly*, 42 (Winter): 3–5, 118–19.

Nunes, E. (1986), 'Movimientos y Prácticas Urbanas en el Brasil', *Revista Mexicana de Sociología*, 48 (4): 73–86.

O'Brien, P. J. (1986), 'Chile: Protest and Repression', *Third World Affairs*, 113–24.

—— and Roddick, J. (1983) (eds.), *Chile, the Pinochet Decade: The Rise and Fall of the Chicago Boys* (London: Latin American Bureau).

O'Donnell, G. (1973), *Modernization and Bureaucratic Authoritarianism* (Berkeley: Institute of International Studies).

—— (1988), 'Challenges to Democratization in Brazil', *World Policy Journal*, 5 (2): 281–300.

—— (1992), 'Delegative Democracy?', *Working Paper*, 172, Helen Kellogg Institute (South Bend, Ind.: University of Notre Dame).

—— (1993), 'Sobre o Estado, a Democratização e Alguns Problemas Conceituais', *Nôvos Estudos CEBRAP*, 36.

—— and Schmitter, P. C. (1986), *Transitions from Authoritarian Rule: Tentative Conclusions about Uncertain Democracies* (Baltimore: Johns Hopkins University Press).

—— —— and Whitehead, L. (1986) (eds.), *Transitions from Authoritarian Rule: Comparative Perspectives* (Baltimore: Johns Hopkins University Press).

Offe, C. (1985), 'New Social Movements: Challenging the Boundaries of Institutional Politics', *Social Research*, 52 (4): 817–68.

—— and Preuss, U. K. (1991), 'Democratic Institutions and Moral Resources', in D. Held (ed.), *Political Theory Today* (Cambridge: Polity Press), 143–71.

Oppenheim, L. H. (1993), *Politics in Chile: Democracy, Authoritarianism, and the Search for Development* (Boulder, Colo.: Westview Press).

Organization of American States (1985), *Report on the Situation of Human Rights in Chile* (Washington, DC).

Orozco, V. (1976), 'Las Luchas Populares en Chihuahua', *Cuadernos Políticos*, 9: 49–66.

Oszlak, O. (1987), 'Privatización Autoritária y Recreación de la Escena Pública', in O. Oszlak (ed.), *Proceso, Crisis y Transición Democrática* (Buenos Aires: Centro Editor de América Latina), 31–48.

Otero, G. (1989), 'The New Agrarian Movement: Self-Managed, Democratic Production', *Latin American Perspectives*, 16 (4): 28–59.

Oxhorn, P. D. (1988), 'Organizaciones Poblacionales y Constitución Actual de la Sociedad Civil', *Revista Mexicana de Sociología*, 50 (2): 221–38.

—— (1994), 'Where Did All the Protesters Go? Popular Mobilization and the Transition to Democracy in Chile', *Latin American Perspectives*, 21 (3): 49–68.

—— (1995), *Organizing Civil Society: The Popular Sectors and the Struggle for Democracy in Chile* (University Park: Pennsylvania State University Press).

Paige, J. (1975), *Agrarian Revolution: Social Movements and Export Agriculture in the Underdeveloped World* (New York: Free Press).

Panizza, F. (1993), 'Human Rights: Global Culture and Social Fragmentation', *Bulletin of Latin American Research*, 12 (2): 205–14.

Pansters, W. (1990), *Politics and Power in Puebla: The Political History of a Mexican State, 1937–1987* (Amsterdam: CEDLA).

Paoli, M. C. (1992), 'Citizenship, Inequalities, Democracy and Rights: The Making of a Public Space in Brazil', *Social and Legal Studies*, 1: 143–59.

Payne, L. (1991), 'Working Class Strategies in the Transition to Democracy in Brazil', *Comparative Politics*, 23: 221–38.

Pérez-Díaz, V. (1991), *La Emergencia de la España Democrática: la 'Invención' de una Tradición y la Dudosa Institucionalización de una Democracia* (Madrid: Juan March Institute).

—— (1992), *Civil Society and the State: The Rise and the Fall of the State as the Bearer of a Moral Project* (Madrid: Juan March Institute), January.

Perlo, M., and Schteingart, M. (1985–6), 'Movimientos Sociales Urbanos en México: Algunos Reflexiones en Torno a la Relación: Processos Sociales Urbanos—Respuesta de los Sectores Populares', *Revista Mexicana de Sociología*, 46 (4): 105–25.

Petras, J., and Cañadell, R. (1992), 'Social Movements in Chile Today', *Labour, Capital and Society*, 25 (2): 198–217.

—— and Leiva, F. I. (1988), 'Chile: The Authoritarian Transition to Electoral Politics', *Latin American Perspectives*, 15 (3): 97–114.

Phillips, A. (1991), 'Citizenship and Feminist Theory', in G. Andrews (ed.), *Citizenship* (London: Lawrence and Wishart), 76–90.

Piauí Alternativa, 2 (May 1986): 5.

—— 7 (May 1986): 1; 6.

—— 9 (May 1987): 3.

Piven, F. F., and Cloward, R. A. (1977), *Poor People's Movements: Why They Succeed, How They Fail* (New York: Pantheon Press).

Poe, S., Pilatovcky, S., Miller, B., and Ogundele, A. (1994), 'Human Rights and US Foreign Aid Revisited: The Latin American Region', *Human Rights Quarterly*, 16: 539–58.

Poe, S. C., and Tate, C. N. (1994), 'Repression of Human Rights to Personal Integrity in the 1980s: A Global Analysis', *American Political Science Review*, 88 (4): 853–72.

Polanyi, K. (1957), *The Great Transformation: The Political and Economic Origins of our Time* (Boston: Beacon Press).

Pompermayer, M. (1987) (ed.), *Movimentos Sociais em Minas Gerais: Emergência e Perspectivas* (Belo Horizonte: UFMG).

Popper, K. A. (1968), *The Logic of Scientific Discovery* (London: Hutchinson).

Posadas, F., and García, B. (1985), 'Movimiento de los Obreros Agrícolas en Sinaloa (1977–1983)', in E. Burros (ed.), *Movimientos Sociales en el*

Noroeste de México (Sinaloa: Universidad Autónoma de Sinaloa), 17–43.

Poulantzas, N. (1973*a*), *Political Power and Social Classes* (London: New Left Books).

—— (1973*b*), 'Marxism and Social Classes', *New Left Review*, 78: 27–55.

Powell, G. B. (1982), *Contemporary Democracies: Participation, Stability, and Violence* (Cambridge, Mass.: Harvard University Press).

Power, T. (1991), 'Politicized Democracy: Competition, Institutions, and "Civic Fatigue" in Brazil', *Journal of Interamerican Studies and World Affairs*, 33 (4): 75–112.

Preston, P. (1974), 'Spain in Crisis: The Assassination of Carrero Blanco and the Aftermath', *Iberian Studies*, 3 (1): 33–8.

—— (1976) (ed.), *Spain in Crisis* (Sussex: Harvester Press).

—— (1986), *The Triumph of Democracy in Spain* (New York: Metheun).

Princeton University (1985), *Chile, Protesta Nacional (1983–1984)*, Princeton, New Jersey, micofilm collection of pamphlets and ephemera from the major political actors of the 1983–4 protests.

Pritchard, K. (1986), 'Comparative Human Rights: An Integrative Explanation', Ph.D. dissertation (University of Wisconsin–Milwaukee).

Przeworski, A. (1986), 'Some Problems in the Study of the Transition to Democracy', in G. O'Donnell, P. C. Schmitter, and L. Whitehead (eds.), *Transitions from Authoritarian Rule: Comparative Perspectives* (Baltimore: Johns Hopkins University Press), 47–63.

—— (1991), *Democracy and the Market* (Cambridge: Cambridge University Press).

—— and Teune, H. (1970), *The Logic of Comparative Social Inquiry* (New York: John Wiley).

Putnam, R. (1994), *Making Democracy Work: Civic Traditions in Modern Italy* (Princeton: Princeton University Press).

Pye, L. W. (1990), 'Political Science and the Crisis of Authoritarianism', *American Political Science Review*, 84 (1): 3–19.

Ragin, C. C. (1987), *The Comparative Method: Moving Beyond Qualitative and Quantitative Strategies* (Berkeley: University of California Press).

—— (1994), 'Introduction to Qualitative Comparative Analysis', in T. Janoski and A. Hicks (eds.), *The Comparative Political Economy of the Welfare State* (Cambridge: Cambridge University Press), 299–320.

Ramírez Saiz, J. M. (1986), *El Movimiento Urbano Popular en México* (México, DF: Siglo Vientiuno Editores).

Razeto, L., Klenner, A., Ramírez, A., and Urmeneta, R. (1986), *Las Organizaciones Económicas Populares* (Santiago: VAN, SA).

Reiter, R. B., Zunzunegui, M. V., and Quiroga, J. (1992), 'Guidelines for Field Reporting of Basic Human Rights Violations', in T. B. Jabine and R. P. Claude (eds.), *Human Rights and Statistics: Getting the Record Straight* (Philadelphia: University of Pennsylvania Press), 90–126.

Relatório do 1° Encontro da Mulher Servidura Pública do Paraná (1985).

Rello, F. (1986), *Bourgeoisie, Peasants and the State in Mexico: The Agrarian Conflict of 1976* (Geneva: UNRISD Participation Programme).

Remmer, K. L. (1980), 'Political Demobilization in Chile, 1973–1978', *Comparative Politics*, 12: 275–301.

—— (1993), 'The Political Economy of Elections in Latin America, 1980–1991', *American Political Science Review*, 87 (2): 393–407.

Rocha, J. (1994), 'Acting on Faith', *NACLA Report on the Americas*, 23 (4): 36–40.

Roddick, J. (1984), 'Chile 1924 and 1979: Labour Policy and Industrial Relations through Two Revolutions', Occasional Papers (Glasgow: Institute for Latin American Studies, University of Glasgow).

—— (1989), 'Chile', in J. Carrière, N. Haworth, and J. Roddick (eds.), *The State, Industrial Relations and the Labour Movement in Latin America*, i (London: MacMillan), 178–262.

Rodríguez-Velásquez, D. (1989), 'Mexico: From Neighborhood to Nation', *NACLA Report on the Americas*, 23 (4): 22–8.

Roett, R. (1984), *Brazil: Politics in a Patrimonial Society* (New York: Praeger Press).

Rojas, T. D. (1993), 'The Use of Nonviolent Sanctions by the Frente Democrático Nacional (FDN)', Ph.D. dissertation (Medford, Mass: Tufts University).

Roxborough, I., and Bizberg, I. (1983), 'Union Locals in Mexico: The "New Unionism" in Steel and Automobiles', *Journal of Latin American Studies*, 15 (1): 117–35.

Rubin, B. R., and Newberg, P. R. (1980), 'Statistical Analysis for Implementing Human Rights Policy', in P. R. Newberg (ed.), *The Politics of Human Rights* (New York: New York University Press), 268–84.

Rubin, J. W. (1987), 'State Policies, Leftist Oppositions, and Municipal Elections: The Case of the COCEI in Juchitán', in Arturo Alvarado Mendoza (ed.), *Electoral Patterns and Perspectives in Mexico* (San Diego: Center for US–Mexican Studies, University of California), 127–60.

Rucht, D. (1990), 'The Strategies and Action Repertoires of New Movements', in R. Dalton and M. Kuechler (eds.), *Challenging the Political Order: New Social Movements in Western Democracies* (Cambridge: Polity Press), 156–75.

—— and Ohlemacher, T. (1992), 'Protest Event Data: Collection, Uses and Perspectives', in M. Diani and R. Eyerman (eds.), *Studying Collective Action* (London: Sage), 76–106.

Ruelas, B. R., and Hirata Galindo, J. F. (1985), 'El Movimiento Campesino y las Invasiones de Tierras en Sinaloa durante 1976', in E. Burros (ed.), *Movimientos Sociales en el Noroeste de México* (Sinaloa: Universidad Autónoma de Sinaloa), 67–83.

Rueschemeyer, D., Stephens, E. H., and Stephens, J. (1992), *Capitalist Development and Democracy* (Cambridge: Polity Press).

Ruiz-Tagle, J. (1986), 'El Movimiento Sindical y la Crisis del Capitalismo Autoritário', in G. Campero (ed.), *Los Movimientos Sociales y la Lucha Democrática en Chile* (Santiago: CLACSO-ILET).

Rustow, D. A. (1970), 'Transitions to Democracy: Toward a Dynamic Model', *Comparative Politics*, 2: 337–63.

Ryan, J. (1994), 'Survey Methodology', *Freedom Review*, January–February: 9–15.

Sader, E. (n.d.), *Movimento Popular Urbano* (São Paulo: FASE).

Safran, W. (1981), 'Civil Liberties in Democracies: Constitutional Norms, Practices, and Problems of Comparison', in V. P. Nanda, J. R. Scarritt, and G. W. Shepherd (eds.), *Global Human Rights: Public Policies, Comparative Measures, and NGO Strategies* (Boulder, Colo.: Westview), 195–210.

Sanders, D., and Ward, H. (1994), Time-Series Techniques for Repeated Cross-Section Data', in R. Davies and A. Dale, (eds.), *Analysing Social and Political Change: A Casebook of Methods* (London: Sage), 201–23.

Sanderson, S. (1979), 'La Lucha Agrária en Sonora, 1970–1976: Manipulación, Reforma y la Derrota del Populismo', *Revista Mexicana de Sociología*, 41 (4): 1181–1232.

—— (1981), *Agrarian Populism and the Mexican State: The Struggle for Land in Sonora* (Berkeley: University of California Press).

Santos, R. (1984), 'Una Historia Obrera de Brasil: 1888–1979', in P. G. Casanova (ed.), *Historia del Movimiento Obrero en América Latina* (México, DF: Siglo Veintiuno Editores).

Sartori, G. (1987), *The Theory of Democracy Revisited* (Chatham, NJ: Chatham House Publishers).

—— (1994), *Comparative Constitutional Engineering* (London: Macmillan).

Scherer-Warren, I. (1988), 'Los Trabajadores Rurales en el Sur de Brasil y la Democratización de la Sociedad', *Revista Mexicana de Sociología*, 50 (1): 243–58.

—— and Krischke, P. (1987), *Uma Revolução no Cotidiano? Os Nôvos Movimentos Sociais na America do Sul* (São Paulo: Brasilense).

Schmitter, P. C. (1992), 'The Consolidation of Democracy and Representation of Social Groups', *American Behavioural Scientist*, 35 (4): 422.

—— (1993), *Some Propositions about Civil Society and the Consolidation of Democracy* (Vienna: Institute of Advanced Studies).

—— and Karl, T. L. (1991), 'What Democracy Is . . . and Is Not', *Journal of Democracy*, 2 (Summer): 73.

Schneider, C. (1992), 'Radical Opposition Parties and Squatters Movements in Pinochet's Chile', in A. Escobar and S. E. Alvarez (eds.), *The Making of Social Movements in Latin America* (Boulder, Colo.: Westview), 260–75.

Schneider, R. M. (1971), *The Political System of Brazil: Emergence of a Modernizing Authoritarian Regime, 1964–1970* (New York: Columbia University Press).

Schuurman, F. J., and Heer, E. (1992), *Social Movements and NGOs in Latin America: A Case Study of the Women's Movement in Chile* (Nijmegen Studies in Development and Cultural Change, 11; Fort Lauderdale, Fla.: Verlag Breitenbach Publishers).

Schwartz, B. (1987), 'Chile: The Cost of Failure', *Race and Class*, 28 (Winter): 55–61.

Scott, J. C. (1985), *Weapons of the Weak: Everyday Forms of Peasant Resistance* (New Haven: Yale University Press).

Sheahan, J. (1987), *Patterns of Development in Latin America: Poverty, Repression, and Economic Strategy* (Princeton: Princeton University Press).

Shorter, E., and Tilly, C. (1971), 'The Shape of Strikes in France, 1830–1960', *Comparative Studies in Society and History*, 13 (January): 60–86.

Sigaud, L. (1980), *Greve nos Engenhos* (Rio de Janerio: Paz e Terra).

Skidmore, T. E. (1988), *The Politics of Military Rule in Brazil, 1964–1985* (New York and Oxford: Oxford University Press).

Skocpol, T. (1979), *States and Social Revolutions* (Cambridge: Cambridge University Press).

Smith, D. (1991), *The Rise of Historical Sociology* (Philadelphia: Temple University Press).

Snow, D. A., and Benford, R. D. (1992), 'Master Frames and Cycles of Protest', in A. D. Morris and C. Mueller (eds.), *Frontiers in Social Movement Theory* (New Haven: Yale University Press).

Snow, D. A., Rochford, B., Worden, S. K., and Benford, R. D. (1986), 'Frame Alignment Processes, Micromobilization and Movement Participation', *American Sociological Review*, 51: 464–81.

Snyder, D., and Tilly, C. (1972), 'Hardship and Collective Violence in France: 1830–1960', *American Sociological Review*, 37: 520–32.

Soko, G. T., and Grossi, G. V. (1986), 'El Problema de la Recomposición de los Actores Campesinos en una Perspectiva Redemocratizadora: Algunos Elementos de Análisis', G. Campero (ed.), *Los Movimientos Sociales y la Lucha Democrática en Chile* (Santiago: CLACSO-ILET).

Somarriba, M. M. G., Valadares, M. G., and Afonso, M. R. (1984), *Lutas Urbanas em Belo Horizonte* (Petrópolis: Vozes).

Spector, P. E. (1993), *SAS® Programming for Researchers and Social Scientists* (London: Sage).

Stepan, A. (1971), *The Military in Politics: Changing Patterns in Brazil* (Princeton: Princeton University Press).

—— (1989), *Democratizing Brazil: Problems of Transition and Consolidation* (New York: Oxford University Press).

—— and Skach, C. (1993), 'Constitutional Frameworks and Democratic Consolidation: Parliamentarism versus Presidentialism', *World Politics*, 46 (October): 1–22.

Stephen, L. (1992), 'Women in Mexico's Popular Movements: Survival Strategies Against Ecological and Economic Impoverishment', *Latin American Perspectives*, 19 (1): 78–96.

Stones, R. (1991), 'Strategic Context Analysis: A New Research Strategy for Structuration Theory', *Sociology*, 25 (4): 673–95.

Szulc, T. (1967), 'Stirrings in Spain', *The Progressive*, March: 25–8.

Tabak, F. (1987), *Mulher e Democracia no Brasil* (Rio de Janeiro: PUC).

Tarrow, S. (1988), 'National Politics and Collective Action: Recent Theory and Research in Western Europe and the United States', *Annual Review of Sociology*, 14: 421–40.

Tarrow, S. (1989), *Democracy and Disorder: Protest and Politics in Italy 1965–75* (Oxford: Clarendon Press).

—— (1990), *Struggle, Politics and Reform: Collective Action, Social Movements, and Cycles of Protest* (Ithaca, NY: Cornell Studies in International Affairs, Western Societies Program).

—— (1993*a*), 'Modular Collective Action and the Rise of the Social Movement: Why the French Revolution was Not Enough', *Politics and Society*, 21 (1): 69–90.

—— (1993*b*), 'Cycles of Collective Action: Between Moments of Madness and the Repertoire of Contention', *Social Science History*, 17 (2): 281–308.

—— (1993*c*), 'Social Protest and Policy Reform: May 1968 and the *Loi d'Orientation* in France', *Comparative Political Studies*, 25 (4): 579–607.

—— (1994*a*), 'Social Movements in Europe: Movement Society or Europeanization of Conflict?', Seminar on Politics in Western Europe, Oxford: Nuffield College, 9 February.

—— (1994*b*), *Power in Movement: Social Movements, Collective Action and Politics* (Cambridge: Cambridge University Press).

—— (1995), 'Social Movements and Democratic Development', in S. M. Lipset, *et al.*, *The Encyclopedia of Democracy*, i (Washington, DC: Congressional Quarterly Press), 1142–7.

—— (1996), 'Making Social Science Work across Space and Time: A Critical Reflection on Robert Putnam's *Making Democracy Work*', *American Political Science Review*: 90 (2) (June): 389–97.

Tavares de Almeida, M. H. (1983), 'O Sindicalismo Brasileiro entre a Conservação e a Mudança', in B. Sorj and M. H. Tavares de Almeida (eds.), *Sociedade e Política no Brasil Pós-64* (Editora Brasilense), 191–214.

Taylor, C. L., and Hudson, M. (1972) (eds.), *World Handbook of Political and Social Indicators*, 2nd edn. (New Haven: Yale University Press).

—— and Jodice, D. A. (1983) (eds.), *World Handbook of Political and Social Indicators: Political Protest and Government Change*, ii, 3rd edn. (New Haven: Yale University Press).

Terán, L., and Melchor, I. (1985), 'Consideraciones Sobre el Movimiento Estudantil en Sinaloa', in E. Burros (ed.), *Movimientos Sociales en el Noroeste de México* (Sinaloa: Universidad Autónoma de Sinaloa), 243–63.

Therborn, G. (1976), *Science, Class and Society* (London: New Left Books).

—— (1977), 'The Rule of Capital and the Rise of Democracy', *New Left Review*, 103: 3–42.

Thomas, H. (1962), 'The Balance of Forces in Spain', *Foreign Affairs*, 41 (October): 208–21.

Thompson, E. P. (1974), *The Making of the English Working Class* (Harmondsworth: Penguin Books).

Tilly, C. (1978), *From Mobilization to Revolution* (Reading Mass.: Addison-Wesley).

—— (1979), 'Repertoires of Contention in America and Britain', in M. Zald and J. McCarthy (eds.), *Social Movements in an Organizational Society* (New Brunswick, NJ: Transaction Books), 126–55.

—— (1984), 'Social Movements and National Politics', in W. Bright and S. Harding (eds.), *State Building and Social Movements* (Ann Arbor: University of Michigan Press), 297–317.

—— (1990), *Coercion, Capital and the European States, AD 990–1990* (Oxford: Blackwell).

—— (1993), *European Revolutions, 1492–1992* (Oxford: Blackwell).

—— Tilly, L., and Tilly, R. (1975), *The Rebellious Century* (Cambridge, Mass.: Harvard University Press).

Tironi, E. (1989), 'Ação coletiva e autoritarismo no Chile', *Dados*, 32 (2): 187–202.

Torton, M. (1984), 'Diretas Já Yields to Negotiations', *NACLA Report on the Americas*, July/August: 17–19.

Touraine, A. (1988), *The Return of the Actor: Social Theory in Post-Industrial Society* (Minneapolis: University of Minnesota Press).

—— (1989), *Palavra e Sangue: Política e Sociedade na América Latina* (São Paulo: Editora da Universidade Estadual de Campinas).

Turner, B. S. (1986), *Citizenship and Capitalism: The Debate over Reformism* (London: Allen and Unwin).

—— (1991), 'Prolegomena to a General Theory of Social Order', *Citizenship, Civil Society and Social Cohesion*, London: ESRC Workshop, 23 February.

—— (1992), 'Preface', in E. Durkheim, *Professional Ethics and Civic Morals*, 2nd edn. (London: Routledge), xiii–xlii.

United Nations Development Programme (1991), *Human Development Report 1991* (New York: Oxford University Press), 13–21.

United States State Department (1981), *Country Reports on Human Rights Practices* (Washington, DC: US Government Printing Office).

—— (1983), *Country Reports on Human Rights Practices* (Washington, DC: US Government Printing Office).

—— (1985), *Country Reports on Human Rights Practices* (Washington, DC: US Government Printing Office).

—— (1987), *Country Reports on Human Rights Practices* (Washington, DC: US Government Printing Office).

Valenzuela, A. (1991), 'The Military in Power: The Consolidation of One Man Rule', in P. Drake and I. Jaksic (eds.) (1991), *The Struggle for Democracy in Chile, 1982–1990* (Lincoln and London: University of Nebraska Press), 21–72.

Valenzuela, E. (1986), 'Los Jóvenes y la Crisis de la Modernización', in G. Campero (ed.), *Los Movimientos Sociales y la Lucha Democrática en Chile* (Santiago: CLACSO-ILET).

Valenzuela, J. S., and Valenzuela, A. (1986), *Military Rule in Chile: Dictatorship and Opposition* (Baltimore: Johns Hopkins University Press).

Vanhanen, T. (1990), *The Process of Democratization: A Comparative Study of 147 States, 1980–1988* (New York: Crane Russak).

Vásquez, M. C. (1981), 'Chile: "3,500 Women Took to the Streets . . ." Women and Unions in Chile', *Resources for Feminist Research*, 10 (1): 7–8.

Vicaría de la Solidaridad (1988), *Derechos Humanos en Chile, 1987* (Santiago).

Vilar, S. (1976), *La Oposición a la Dictadura: Protagonistas de la España Democrática* (Barcelona: Ayma).

'Waiting for Franco', *The Economist*, 11 April 1964.

Walzer, M. (1989), 'Citizenship', in T. Ball and J. Farr (eds.), *Political Innovation and Conceptual Change* (Cambridge: Cambridge University Press), 211–19.

—— (1992), 'The Civil Society Argument', in C. Mouffe (ed.), *Dimensions of Radical Democracy* (London: Verso), 89–107.

Waylen, G. (1992), 'Rethinking Women's Political Participation and Protest: Chile 1970–1990', *Political Studies*, 40: 299–314.

Weffort, F. C. (1972), 'Participação e Conflito Industrial: Contagem e Osasco 1968', *Cadernos CEBRAP*, 5 (São Paulo).

Welch, S. (1975), 'The Impact of Urban Riots on Urban Expenditures', *American Journal of Political Science*, 19 (4): 741–60.

Werneck, V. L. (1983), 'O Problema da Cidadania na Hora da Transição Democrática', *Revista de Ciencias Sociais*, 26 (3): 243–64.

Whitehead, L. (1992), 'The Alternatives to Liberal Democracy: A Latin American Perspective', in D. Held (ed.), *Political Studies*, 40. Special Edition on 'Prospects for Democracy'.

—— (1994a), 'State Organization in Latin America since 1930', in L. Bethell (ed.), *Cambridge History of Latin America*, vi/2: 84–90.

—— (1994b), 'Prospects for a "Transition" from Authoritarian Rule in Mexico', in M. L. Cook, K. J. Middlebrook, and J. M. Horcasitas (eds.), *The Politics of Economic Restructuring: State–Society Relations and Regime Change in Mexico* (San Diego: Center for US–Mexican Studies), 327–46.

'Why Franco is Worried', *The Economist*, 1 February 1969.

Wiarda, H. J. (1982), 'Democracy and Human Rights in Latin America: Toward a New Conceptualization', in H. Wiarda (ed.), *Human Rights and US Human Rights Policy* (Washington DC: American Enterprise Institute), 30–52.

Wickham-Crowley, T. (1992), *Guerrillas and Revolution in Latin America* (Princeton: Princeton University Press).

Wilkie, J., and Ruddle, K. (1992), *Statistical Abstract of Latin America*, 30 (1): 278.

Witker, A. (1984), 'El Movimiento Obrero en Chile', in P. G. Casanova (ed.), *Historia del Movimiento Obrero en América Latina* (México, DF: Siglo Veintiuno Editores).

Wolin, S. (1960), *Politics and Vision* (Boston: Little, Brown and Co.).

Young, I. M. (1987), 'Impartiality and the Civic Public', in S. Benhabib and D. Cornell (eds.), *Feminism As Critique* (Cambridge: Polity Press).

—— (1989), 'Polity and Group Difference: A Critique of the Ideal of Universal Citizenship', *Ethics*, 99: 250–74.

Zac, L. (1989), 'The Politics of Silence: Logical Resources and the Argentine Military Discourse (1976–1980)', University of Essex (unpublished).

Zeller, R., and Carmines, E. (1980), *Measurement in the Social Sciences* (London: Cambridge University Press).

Zermeño, S. (1978), *México, una Democracia Utópica: el Movimiento Estudantil del 68* (México, DF: Siglo Veintiuno Editores).

Index